THE POLITICS OF BELONGING

THE POLITICS OF BELONGING

INTERSECTIONAL CONTESTATIONS

NIRA YUVAL-DAVIS

SAGE

Los Angeles | London | New Delhi
Singapore | Washington DC

SAGE Publications Ltd
1 Oliver's Yard
55 City Road
London EC1Y 1SP

SAGE Publications Inc.
2455 Teller Road
Thousand Oaks, California 91320

SAGE Publications India Pvt Ltd
B 1/I 1 Mohan Cooperative Industrial Area
Mathura Road
New Delhi 110 044

SAGE Publications Asia-Pacific Pte Ltd
3 Church Street
#10-04 Samsung Hub
Singapore 049483

Library of Congress Control Number: 2011921817

British Library Cataloguing in Publication data

A catalogue record for this book is available from the British Library

ISBN 978–1–4129–2129–9
ISBN 978–1–4129–2130–5 (pbk)

Typeset by C&M Digitals (P) Ltd, Chennai, India
Printed in Great Britain by Ashford Colour Press Ltd

Contents

Preface

The project behind this book started shortly after *Gender and Nation* (1997, Sage) was published, although it took quite a few years before it was crystallized into this format. In a way it is both a continuation and a transformation of the project for that book. I have always approached the issues of gender and gender relations intersectionally (e.g. Yuval-Davis, 1980; Anthias & Yuval-Davis, 1983), given my anti-racist, socialist version of feminist political commitment. More recently, however, it became clear to me that the intersectional approach needs to be adopted in much wider circles than those of Women's and Gender Studies alone. In the introduction to this book I quote Lesley McCall's (2005) assertion that to date intersectionality has been feminist theory's most important theoretical contribution to related fields. I recently published an article on intersectionality and stratification (Yuval-Davis, 2011a), arguing that sociological stratification theory should adopt intersectionality as its major theoretical/methodological perspective in the ways that other disciplines, like critical legal theory and social policy, have started to do. In this book, therefore, gendered analysis is only one of the major axes of its intersectional approach (although feminism as a political project is highlighted throughout).[1]

Similarly, nationalisms and nations. Growing up in Israel and coming to oppose the Zionist political project and its (anti-)humanitarian effects, I realized early on how central nationalist thinking is in various local and global social orders. However, I came early on in my development as a social scientist to denaturalize and deconstruct nationalisms and to examine their links with racisms, imperialisms and, more recently, neo-liberal globalization. This was deeply affected by my growing understanding of the nature of the links between the so-called 'Jewish problem' in Europe, which gave the impetus for the Zionist project in the first place, and its global support in the post-Second World War Holocaust. But this chain of events has also brought about,

---

[1]Given the importance I assign to intersectional analysis it is not surprising that I agreed to become a co-editor (with Ange-Marie Hancock) of a Palmgrave (NY) book series on 'the Politics of Intersectionality'

at the same time, the Naqba, the Catastrophe, for the Palestinian people as a result of the establishment of a Jewish settler society, and especially a warfare ethnocratic state. The links between nationalism and religion have also been very explicit in the Zionist project and more and more so in the Palestinian nationalist project as well.

In this book, therefore, the focus widens from an examination of different aspects of nationalist projects to an exploration of different contested contemporary political projects of belonging, with stronger or weaker links with nationalism.

Contemporary political projects of belonging, whether formal state citizenships, memberships in nations and/or religious, ethnic, indigenous and diasporic communities, but also cosmopolitan and transversal ones, are always situated and always multi-layered, which serves to contextualize them both locally and globally, and affect different members of these collectivities and communities differentially. This is where the importance of intersectionality lies.

This situatedness, as illustrated above when discussing what led me to be interested in these topics in the first place, also applies to my own gaze and has obviously affected the many generalizations made in this book. Although I have tried to decentre my perspective and to use illustrative examples from all over the globe, obviously I have been especially informed by debates and developments in Britain, as well as in my various global virtual communities. As Donna Haraway (1988), with her usual wisdom, stated, there is no view from nowhere. So I apologize for the limitations of the perspective of the book and the unevenness of its illustrative examples, but hope that even when it is misguided it will still trigger thoughts on the matter in hand.

I am also very aware that every intellectual product is an outcome of an accumulation of various collective dialogical narratives. In thinking about and writing this book and related papers, I have been very fortunate to be part of local and global networks of friends and colleagues, activists and scholars, who greatly stimulated my thoughts on these issues as well as informing me of developments and debates in other places. I am greatly indebted to them all, while, of course, I take full responsibility for the final product.

Some of these networks are continuous, although new (usually younger) people have joined them in the years since I started to be associated with them. Among my anti-Zionist Israeli Leftist friends I want to thank especially Avishai Ehrlich, Ruchama Marton,

Moshik and Ilana Machover, Haim Bresheeth, Susie Barry and Oren Yiftachel. Women Against Fundamentalism is now celebrating its twentieth anniversary. It was established around the time of the 'Rushdie Affair'. After several years 'on remission' it came back to life when it was greatly needed (the monthly vegetarian soups that helped its resuscitation were a lovely challenge!). As always I'm greatly indebted to them all, but especially to Gita Sahgal, Pragna Patel and Julia Bard, as well as Cass Balchin, Nadje Al-Ali and Sukhwant Dhaliwal (and the honorary member of WAF and WLUML, Chetan Bhatt).

Raya Feldman, another old friend and a WAF member, has been central in establishing the Hackney Migrant Centre where I spend a little time every month (cooking again!). However, the most formative learning experience that I've had in working with refugees in East London has been in the ESRC research project: 'Identity, performance and social action: community theatre among refugees'. I'm greatly indebted to Erene Kaptani who originally approached me with the idea and then became the project's Research Fellow. In addition to proving to be a wonderful communication tool and great fun, the participatory theatre techniques that we used (Playback and Forum) were also found to be a different and complementary sociological data collection tool (Kaptani & Yuval-Davis, 2008a and b) and these greatly helped me in reconfiguring my ideas on identity (e.g. Yuval-Davis & Kaptani, 2009; Yuval-Davis, 2010). They also taught me much about the politics of belonging within the four refugee communities we worked with in East London and their social and political environments. My ideas on spatial security rights have largely developed while working with them. This project was part of the ESRC research programme on 'Identities and Social Action' and I'm grateful to my colleagues there, especially to Margie Whetherell for her inspirational leadership of that programme as well as for her warmth and support.

This research project was taking place in my new academic 'home', the School of Humanities and Social Sciences at the University of East London, which offered me a refuge since 2003 after I (and some other colleagues, especially my long-standing friend and collaborator Floya Anthias) resigned in protest from the University of Greenwich, when they carelessly and short-sightedly destroyed the cutting-edge academic centre within Gender and Ethnic Studies, which we had built up there for more than twenty-five years under difficult 'polytechnic' conditions, under the excuse of 'restructuring'.[2] Gavin Poynter and Haim Bresheeth not only offered me office facilities as a Visiting Professor, they also allowed me to transfer my postgraduate programme in Gender, Sexuality and Ethnic Studies, which worked very well, at least for a few years.

It worked so well because the programme attracted so many wonderful students, both MA and PhD, from all over the world, from Zimbabwe to Australia, from Iran to Bangladesh. I cannot name them all, but some of my students have become such first-rate scholars and activists that I must mention them here, together with my love and gratitude for all that I've learned from them while they've been learning themselves. In no particular order: Amira Ahmed, Bahar Taseli, Cass Balchin, Christian Klesse, Christine Achinger, Diana Yeh, Henriette Gunkel, Hoda Rouhana, Jin Haritaworn, Lejla Somun-Krupalija, Liliana Elena, Manar Hassan, Marcel Stotzler, Mastoureh Fathi, Michaela Told, Nicola Samson, Nicos Trimikliniotis, Niloufar Pourzand, Samia Bano, Rumana Hashem, Tijen Uguris, Ulrike Vieten, Umut Erel.

The inspiration and knowledge that these students have brought to me with their situated gazes have enriched my world, as have many colleagues in the School. Again, I cannot mention them all but (again in no particular order), Abel Ugba, Anat Pick, Corrine Squire, Eva Turner, Haim Bresheeth, Maggie Humm, Mica Nava, Molly Andrews, Phil Cohen, Roshini Kampado and Yosefa Loshitzky have been special friends and colleagues. Special thanks are also due to Phil Marfleet, my co-director of the CMRB, the UEL Research Centre on Migration, Refugees and Belonging, in which we have been able to develop, investigate and organize events which interrogate some of the relationships between new and old forms of racism with migration, religion and citizenship, especially within our East London context. Some of this work has been carried out in common projects with the Runnymede Trust and its director Rob Berkeley and the Migrant Rights Network and its director Don Flynn.

I also want to thank my colleagues in international research networks, especially WICZNET, which focuses on research on women in militarized conflict zones (including Audrey Macklin, Cynthia Cockburn, Cynthia Enloe, Lepa Mladjenovic, Malathi de Alwis,

---

[2] A process which now takes place in many British universities, including UEL, given the barbaric government cuts to higher education and especially Social Sciences and Humanities.

Nadera Kevorkian, Nadje Al-Ali and, of course, Wenona Giles), as well as the ISA Research Committee (RC)05 on Racism, Nationalism and Ethnic Relations, of which I was President during 2002–06 (including Ann Denis, Avishai Ehrlich, Kogila Moodley, Michael Banton, Natividad Guitierez, Peter Radcliffe and Zlatko Skrbis).

The 2001 UN World Conference Against Racism (WCAR), which took place a few days before 9/11, in which ISA RC05 organized an interim conference, was a very important and formative (as well as depressing) experience, as has been my membership of the international women's delegation to the Gujarat in 2002, after the pogroms against the Muslims there. It was in Gujarat that I was exposed to some of the nastiest and most violent aspects of intersectional contemporary politics of belonging. I could not have asked for better guidance and sisterhood than from the local feminist and human rights activists who invited us there as well as from the other members of the delegation, including Anissa Helie, Gaby Mishkovsky, Sunila Abeysekara and the late wonderful Rhonda Kopelon.

There were many other specific forums, places and times which have given me new insights concerning the subjects discussed in this book. These included international feminist and human rights forums, especially Amnesty International, the UNDP and the UN Special Rapporteur on Violence Against Women, and the various academic institutions in which I have spent shorter or longer periods as a Visiting Professor during the time I was thinking about and writing this book. They have all offered me warmth, support and new insights, including Aalborg, Ben-Gurion, Bristol, Roskilde, Tel-Aviv, Wisconsin, my Rockfeller Fellowship on women, human security and globalization in CUNY and NCRW, and my three years part-time visiting professorship at the Centre for Gender Studies in Umea University in Sweden, which offered me sufficient space in which to write much of the final draft of this book. Special thanks for the friendship, warmth and support they have all offered me. Here I can mention just a couple of names, the Centre's Director, Professor Ann Ohman, and its Administrator, Monica Forsell-Allergen.

There is no way I can do justice to all the friends who have inspired me all these years but I want to mention here also Alison Assiter, Avtar Brah, Ann Phoenix, Birte Siim, Gina Vargas, Helma Lutz, Helen Meekosha, Jindi Pettman, Marie deLepervanche, Martha Ackelsberg, Nora Ratzel, Paula Rayman, Peter Waterman, Pnina Werbner, Ronit Lentin, Shula Ramon and Spike Peterson.

Cass Balchin, Avishai Ehrlich, Gita Sahgal, Ann Phoenix and Mastoureh Fathi have, in addition, also read smaller or larger parts of the manuscript and given me invaluable feedback. However, I have learned about belonging and the politics of belonging not just from my friends but also from their families, especially their children, among them Benjo, Kabir, Zum, Pikel, Luz and Aisha.

I also want to thank here Karen Phillips and the other editors from Sage, as well as the anonymous readers of the first draft of the manuscript who gave me such generous and insightful feedback on the draft.

Last but not least, I want to thank my family. Alain, for his continuous support, warmth, knowledge and love, and Gul who, in addition to being my wonderful son, has also taught me more than anyone else in the world about love, pain and what life is actually all about.

And Ora, my sister, who – in her mid-seventies – rediscovered dancing.

I can't end this preface without confessing a certain reluctance to let the manuscript, the project of the book, go. Any ending is artificial, as the subject matter of this book is dynamic, processual and contested while the written word (or any medium of expression) is necessarily static. These are days of major glocal crises and transformation, in which new political projects of belonging are going to emerge, at least in the Middle East, the region I come from, but most probably much more widely. Since continuing to amend/add to/revise the manuscript will never be complete or fully satisfactory, I would ask the reader to see in this book just an interim account and analysis, to be revisited, in one form or another, at a future date.

London, March 2011

1

Introduction: Framing the Questions

In the aftermath of the 7/7 bombings in London during the summer of 2005, one question seems to have bothered many of the journalists who wrote about this – how is it possible that 'British' people were able to carry out such atrocities in Britain? The reasons why these particular people became suicide bombers are no doubt complex and could be found in the particular biographies of these people as well as in some more general micro and macro social and political factors. I shall try and relate to some of these in Chapter 4 which looks at issues concerning religion, fundamentalism and contemporary politics of belonging. However, the theoretical question which is at the heart of the project of this book as a whole concerns the assumptions which led these journalists – and so many others in the general public in Britain and outside it – to feel that carrying a British passport, or even being born and educated in Britain, should have automatically made them belong with other British citizens and 'immune' from taking part in such an attack. In other words, why would people's nationality be more important to them than their religious and political beliefs, and why should they feel more loyal to the British nation than to other political and religious collectivities? Are nationalist politics of belonging still the hegemonic model of belonging at the beginning of the twenty-first century? And if so, what kind of nationalism is this? And if not, what other political projects of belonging are now competing with nationalism? Mohammad Sidique Khan, one of the 7/7 bombers who made a videotape that was shown by *Al Jazeera* (September 1, 2005), does talk about 'my people' in his statement, but he meant Muslims 'all over the world' and definitely not the British people.

The questions of belonging and the politics of belonging constitute some of the most difficult issues that are confronting all of us these days and this book hopes to contribute to the understanding of some of them. In these post 9/11 (and 7/7) times, 'strangers' are seen not only as a threat to the cohesion of the political and cultural community, but also as potential terrorists, especially the younger men among them. The question of who is 'a stranger' and who 'does not belong', however, is also continuously being modified and contested, with growing ethnic, cultural and religious tensions within as well as between societies and states. Politics of belonging have come to occupy the heart of the political agenda almost everywhere in the world, even when reified assumptions about 'the clash of civilizations' (Huntington, 1993) are not necessarily applied. As Francis B. Nyamnjoh points out (2005: 18), 'in Africa, as elsewhere, there is a growing obsession with belonging, along with new questions concerning conventional assumptions about nationality and citizenship'. And Hedetoff and Hjort (2002: x) point out in the introduction to their edited book that 'today belonging constitutes a political and cultural field of global contestation, anywhere between ascriptions of belonging and self-constructed definitions of new spaces of culture, freedom and identity'.

The aim of this chapter is to frame, both theoretically and contextually, the questions which are going to be explored elsewhere in this book. I aim to outline some of the main debates that have emerged both in academia and in the political arena around various major political projects of belonging. Alongside the hegemonic forms of citizenship and nationalism which have tended to dominate the twentieth century, the book also investigates alternative contemporary political projects of belonging that are constructed around the notions of religion, cosmopolitanism and the feminist 'ethics of care'. Constructions and contestations of multiculturalism, multi-faithism, indigenous and diasporic political projects of belonging constitute only some of these debates. The effects of globalization, mass migration, the rise of both fundamentalist and human rights movements on such politics of belonging, as well as some of its racialized and gendered dimensions will also be investigated. A special place will also be given to the various feminist political movements that have been engaged as part of or in resistance to the political projects of belonging discussed in the book.

The analytical perspective which is used is intersectional, deconstructing simplistic notions of national and ethnic collectivities and their boundaries and interrogating some of the differential effects that different political projects of belonging have on different members of these collectivities who are differentially located socially, economically and politically. It is for this reason that the first part of this introductory chapter examines the notion of intersectionality.

Once this theoretical framework has been clarified, the chapter introduces the notions of belonging and the politics of belonging, the subject matter of the book, and the notions of social locations, identifications and values which are central for their understanding. It also illustrates some of the different relationships between different constructions of belonging and different political projects of belonging, using examples from related discourses in the UK.

This introduction then moves on to outline some of the general features of the contemporary globalization context, within which the various intersectional political projects of belonging discussed in this book operate. It discusses globalization, how states have been reconfigured under neo-liberal globalization and the ways in which mass migration and the discourse of securitization can affect and are affected by these processes.

The following chapters, a brief description of which ends this chapter, then explore some of the major contemporary political projects of belonging constructed around citizenship, nationalism, religion, cosmopolitanism and the feminist project of 'ethics of care'. Given the limitations of space in this book, these chapters will mainly focus on various theoretical and political issues relating to these projects and their differential intersectional effects can only be pointed to rather than explored in detail. The final concluding chapter briefly sums up the subjects discussed in the book and highlights their normative, as well as emotional and analytical facets. The book ends with a short meditation on the notion of hope and the role it plays in transversal feminist politics.

Intersectionality

Lesley McCall (2005: 1771) and others would argue that intersectionality is 'the most important theoretical contribution that women's studies, in conjunction with related fields, has made so far'. Indeed, the imprint of intersectional analysis can be easily traced to innovations in equality legislation, human rights and development discourses. Amazingly enough, however, in spite of the term's 'brilliant career' (Lutz, 2002), intersectionality hardly appears in sociological stratification theories (a notable exception is Anthias, 2005; see also Yuval-Davis, 2011a). So what is intersectionality?

Epistemologically, intersectionality can be described as a development of feminist standpoint theory which claims, in somewhat different ways, that it is vital to account for the social positioning of the social agent and challenge 'the god-trick of seeing everything from nowhere' (Haraway, 1991: 189) as a cover for and a legitimization of a hegemonic masculinist 'positivistic' positioning. Situated gaze, situated knowledge and situated imagination (Stoetzler & Yuval-Davis, 2002), construct how we see the world in different ways. However, intersectionality theory was even more interested in how the differential situatedness of different social agents affects the ways they affect and are affected by different social, economic and political projects. In this way it can no doubt be considered as one of the outcomes of the mobilization and proliferation of different identity groups' struggles for recognition (Taylor, 1992; Fraser, 1995).

The history of what is currently called 'intersectional thinking' is long, and many pinpoint the famous speech of the emancipated slave Sojourner Truth (Brah & Phoenix, 2004) during the first wave of feminism as one early illustration of it. Sojourner Truth was speaking at an abolitionist convention and argued that, given her position in society, although she worked hard and carried heavy loads, etc., this did not make her less of a woman and a mother than women of a privileged background who were constructed as weak and in need of constant help and protection as a result of what society considered to be 'feminine' ways.

Indeed, intersectional analysis, before becoming 'mainstreamed', was carried out for many years mainly by black and other racialized women who, from their situated gaze, perceived as absurd, and not just misleading, any attempt by feminists and others, since the start of the second wave of feminism, to homogenize women's situation and especially to find it analogous to that of blacks. As bell hooks, who chose Truth's *crie du coeur* 'Ain't I a Woman' as the title of her first book (hooks, 1981), mockingly remarked in the introduction to that book: 'This implies that all women are White and all Blacks are men'.

As Brah and Phoenix (2004: 80) point out, other black feminists fulfilled significant roles in the development of intersectional analysis, such as the Combahee River Collective, the black lesbian feminist organization from Boston, who as early as 1977 pointed to the need to develop an integrated analysis and practice based upon the fact that the major systems of oppression were interlocking. Angela Davis, who has come to symbolize for many the spirit of revolutionary black feminism, published her book *Women, Race and Class* in 1981. However, the term 'intersectionality' was itself introduced in 1989 by another American black feminist, the legal and critical race theorist

Kimberlé Crenshaw (1989), when she discussed the issues surrounding black women's employment in the USA and the intersection of gender, race and class matters in their exploitation and exclusion.

However, what can be called intersectional analysis was developed roughly at the same time by several European and post-colonial feminists (e.g. Bryan et al., 1985; James, 1986; Essed, 1991; Lutz, 1991) as well. As Sandra Harding claimed, when she examined the parallel development of feminist standpoint theory:

> ...[F]eminist standpoint theory was evidently an idea whose time had come, since most of these authors worked independently and were unaware of each other's work. (Standpoint theory would itself call for such a social history of ideas, would it not?) (Harding, 1997: 389)

This was obviously the case also with the development of intersectionality theory.

My own work in the field of intersectionality (although back then we called it 'social divisions') started in the early 1980s when, in collaboration with Floya Anthias (e.g. Anthias & Yuval-Davis, 1983, 1992), we started to study gender and ethnic divisions in South East London and at the same time became engaged in a debate with British black feminists, organized then as OWAAD[1], on the right way to theorize what would now be called an intersectional approach.

As argued in my (2006b) article, some of the basic debates we had with them then still continue to occupy those who are engaged in intersectional analysis today, after it became 'mainstreamed' and came to be accepted by the United Nations, the European Union and other equality and equity policy organizations in many countries. Part of the differences among those who use intersectionality have resulted from the different disciplines and purposes for which it is being used: others differences have not.

Rather than engage in describing some of the historical debates around intersectionality, whether in Britain or in the UN (as I did in my (2006b) article, but see also Brah & Phoenix, 2004; Nash, 2008), I am going to outline below the main characteristics of the constitutive intersectional approach which is applied throughout this book. While doing so, however, I would also recognize the sense of discomfort that many feminists (including myself) share regarding the term 'intersectionality' itself.

---

[1]Organization of Women of African and Asian Descent

Intersectionality is a metaphorical term, aimed at evoking images of a road intersection, with an indeterminate or contested number of intersecting roads, depending on the various users of the terms and how many social divisions are considered in the particular intersectional analysis. As will be developed a bit further below, this can change considerably from two to infinity. In a lecture in 2008, Kum-Kum Bhavnani used the term 'configurations' as an alternative metaphor, wanting to emphasize the flowing interweaving threads which constitute intersectionality, which she found a much too rigid and fixed metaphor. Davina Cooper (2004: 12) also explains that she used the term 'social dynamics' rather than intersectionality, because she wanted her terminology to trace the shifting ways relations of inequality become attached to various aspects of social life. While agreeing with all these reservations, which are important for the theorization of intersectionality in this book, I do retain the term as being so widespread it evokes an intuitive understanding of the subject matter discussed in spite of all the reservations.

Three main positions in relation to the intersectionality approach used in this book need to be clarified here. The first relates to the division McCall (2005) makes between those approaches to intersectionality which she calls 'inter-categorical' and 'intra-categorical'; the second relates to the relationships which should be understood as existing between the various intersectional categories; and the third relates to the boundaries of the intersectional approach and thus the number of as well as which social categories should be included in intersectional analysis inter- or intra-categories?

According to McCall, studies that have used an intersectional approach differ as to whether they have used an inter- or intra-categorical approach. By an inter-categorical approach she means focusing on the way the intersection of different social categories, such as race, gender, class, etc., affects particular social behaviours or the distribution of resources. Intra-categorical studies, on the other hand, are less occupied with the relationships among various social categories and instead problematize the meaning and boundaries of the categories themselves, such as whether black women were included in the category 'women' or what are the shifting boundaries of who is considered to be 'black' in a particular place and time.

Unlike McCall, I do not see these two approaches as mutually exclusive and instead would ask for an intersectionality approach which combines the sensitivity and dynamism of the intra-categorical approach with the more macro socio-economic perspective of the inter-categorical approach.

As will be elaborated below, I consider as crucial the analytical differentiation between different facets of social analysis – that of people's positionings along socio-economic grids of power; that of people's experiential and identificatory perspectives of where they belong; and that of their normative value systems. These different facets[2] are related to each other but are also irreducible to each other (on the different ontological bases of the different social divisions please see my article – Yuval-Davis, 2006a). Moreover, although I consider intersectional analysis to be a development of feminist standpoint theory, I would also argue that there is no direct causal relationship between the situatedness of people's gaze and their cognitive, emotional and moral perspectives on life. People born into the same families and/or the same time and social environment can have different identifications and political views. For this reason alone it is not enough to construct inter-categorical tabulations in order to predict and, even more so, to understand people's positions and attitudes to life.

The relationship between the social categories

There is another reason for the inadequacy of using an inter-categorical approach on its own. Unless it is complemented with an intra-categorical approach, it can be understood as an additive rather than a mutually constitutive approach to the relationships between social categories.

   Although discourses of race, gender, class, etc. have their own ontological bases which cannot be reduced down to each other, there is no separate concrete meaning of any facet of these social categories, as they are mutually constitutive in any concrete historical moment. To be a woman will be different whether you are middle class or working class, a member of the hegemonic majority or a racialized minority, living in the city or in the country, young or old, gay or straight, etc. Viewing intersectional analysis in this way links the interrogation of concrete meanings of categories and their boundaries to specific historical contexts which are shifting and contested, rather than just abstracting ontological and epistemological enquiries. However, simply assuming

---

[2]In my previous work (e.g. Yuval-Davis, 2006a & 2006b) I related to these different analytical facets as different analytical levels. Cass Balchin drew my attention to the fact that the term 'levels' assumes a hierarchy. And indeed I do believe that the term is a remnant of the old Marxist infra- and super-structural levels. As I do not want to assume a presupposed hierarchy here I'm using the term 'facets'.

that any particular inter-categorical study would result in a full under-standing of the specific constructions of any particular social category in any particular context, as McCall does, is also reductionist.

The boundaries of intersectional analysis and intersectional categories

Kimberlé Crenshaw (1989: 139) define intersectionality as 'the multidimensionality of marginalized subjects' lived experiences'. Other black feminists (e.g. Dill, 1983; Bryan et al., 1985) also remain within the triad boundaries of race, class and gender. Philomena Essed (1991) even limits this to the two dimensions of 'gendered racisms' and 'racist genderisms'. Others have added the specific categories they were interested in, such as age (e.g. Bradley, 1996); disability (e.g. Oliver, 1995; Meekosha & Dowse, 1997); sedentarism (e.g. Lentin, 1999); or sexuality (e.g. Kitzinger, 1987). In other works, however, feminists attempted to develop complete lists and included in them much higher numbers – for example, Helma Lutz (2002) relates this to 14 categories while Charlotte Bunch (2001) has 16. Floya Anthias and I (1983, 1992; see also Yuval-Davis, 2006b; Yuval-Davis, 2011a) would strongly argue that intersectional analysis should not be limited only to those who are on the multiple margins of society, but rather that the boundaries of intersectional analysis should encompass all members of society and thus intersectionality should be seen as the right theoretical framework for analysing social stratification. There is a parallel here with the struggle that many of us witnessed during the 1970s and 1980s to point out (what these days seems much more obvious), that everybody, not just racialized minorities, have 'ethnicities' and that members, especially men in hegemonic majorities, are not just 'human beings' but are also gendered, classed, ethnocized, etc.

In *Gender Trouble* (1990), Judith Butler mocks the 'etc.' which often appears at the end of long (and different) lists of the social divisions mentioned by feminists, and sees it as an embarrassed admission of a 'sign of exhaustion as well as of the illimitable process of signification itself' (1990: 143). As Fraser (1995) and Knapp (1999) make clear, however, such a critique is valid only within the discourse of identity politics where there is a correspondence between social positionings or locations and identifications with particular social groupings. When no such conflation takes place, Knapp rightly finds that Butler's talk 'of an illimitable process of signification' can be reductionist if it is generalized in an unspecified way ... [and] runs the risk of levelling historically constituted 'factual' differences and thereby suppressing 'differences' on its own terms. (Knapp, 1999: 130)

Knapp's critique of Butler once again clarifies the crucial importance of the separation of the different analytical dimensions in which social divisions need to be examined as discussed above. Nevertheless, the question remains of whether there are, or are not, in any particular historical condition, specific and limited numbers of social divisions that will construct the grid of power relations within which the different members of the society are located.

As I mentioned elsewhere (Yuval-Davis, 2006b), I have two different answers to this question which are not mutually exclusive. The first one is that while in specific historical situations and in relation to the daily lives of specific people there are some social divisions which are more important than others in constructing their specific positionings relative to others around them, there are some social divisions, such as gender, stage in the life cycle, ethnicity and class which will tend to shape most people's lives in most social locations, while other social divisions such as those relating to disability, membership in particular castes or status as indigenous or refugee people will tend to affect less people globally in this way. At the same time, for those people who are affected by these and other social divisions not mentioned here in particular historical contexts, such social divisions are crucial and thus rendering them visible needs to be fought for. This is a case where recognition – of the social power axes, not of social identities – is of vital political importance.

My second answer relates to what Castoriadis called the 'creative imagination' (1987; see also Stoetzler & Yuval-Davis, 2002) that underlies any linguistic and other social categories of signification. Although certain social conditions may facilitate this, the construction of categories of signification is, in the last instance, a product of human creative freedom and autonomy. Without specific social agents who will construct and point to certain analytical and political features, the rest of us would not be able to distinguish between them. Rainbows include the whole spectrum of different colours, but how many of these colours we distinguish will depend on our specific social and linguistic milieu. It is for this reason that struggles for recognition will always also include an element of construction and it is for this reason that studying the relationships between positionings, identities and political values which, as can be seen below, I view as central to the study of belonging, is so important (and impossible if these are all reduced to the same ontological level). So what are belonging and the politics of belonging?

Belonging and the politics of belonging

It is important to differentiate between belonging and the politics of belonging. Belonging is about an emotional (or even ontological) attachment, about feeling 'at home'. As Hage (1997: 103) points out, however, 'home is an on-going project entailing a sense of hope for the future' (see also Taylor, 2009). Part of this feeling of hope relates to home as a 'safe' space (Ignatieff, 2001). In the daily reality of the early twenty-first century, in so many places on the globe, this emphasis on safety acquires a new poignancy. At the same time, it is important to emphasize that feeling 'at home' does not necessarily only generate positive and warm feelings. It also allowes the safety as well as the emotional engagement to be, at times, angry, resentful, ashamed, indignant (Hessel, 2010).

Belonging tends to be naturalized and to be part of everyday practices (Fenster, 2004a and b). It becomes articulated, formally structured and politicized only when it is threatened in some way. The politics of belonging comprise specific political projects aimed at constructing belonging to particular collectivity/ies which are themselves being constructed in these projects in very specific ways and in very specific boundaries (i.e. whether or not, according to specific political projects of belonging, Jews can be considered to be German, for example, or abortion advocates can be considered Catholic). As Antonsich (2010) points out, however, these boundaries are often spatial and relate to a specific locality/territoriality and not just to constructions of social collectivities. Of course, according to Doreen Massey (2005), space in itself is but an embodiment of social networks. However, as Carrillo Rowe (2005: 21) points out: 'belongings are conditioned by our bodies and where they are placed on the globe'. Nevertheless, as will be discussed in Chapter 3, diasporic and transnational belongings, especially those which use the virtual realities of the internet can, at least partially, transcend these limits of physical geography. Also bell hooks (1990) talks about 'home-space' as something which transcends the domestic. As Ulf Hannerz (2002) claims, home is essentially a contrastive concept, linked to some notion of what it means to be away from home. It can involve a sense of rootedness in a socio-geographic site or be constructed as an intensely imagined affiliation with a distant locale where self-realization can occur.

Belonging and the politics of belonging have been some of the major themes around which both classic psychology and sociology emerged. Countless psychological, and even more psychoanalytical, works have been dedicated to writings about the fears of separation of babies and children from the womb, from the mother, from the familiar, as well as the devastating – often pathological – effects on them when they cannot take belonging for granted (for more elaborate accounts of this, see, for example, Rank, 1973 [1929]; Bowlby, 1969, 1973). Similarly, much of social psychology literature has been dedicated to people's need to conform to the groups they belong to for fear of exclusion and inferiorization and the ways people's interpersonal relationships are deeply affected by their membership or lack of membership of particular groups – as well as their positions in these groups (e.g. Lewin, 1948; Billig, 1976; Tajfel, 1982).

In sociological theory as well, since its establishment, many writings have been focused on the differential ways people belong to collectivities and states – as well as the social, economic, and political effects of instances of displacement of such belonging/s as a result of industrialization and/or migration. Some basic classical examples are Tonnies' distinction between *Gemeinschaft* and *Gesellschaft* (1940 [1935]), Durkheim's division of mechanical and organic solidarity (1893) or Marx's notion of alienation (1975 [1844]). Anthony Giddens (1991) has argued that during modernity people's sense of belonging becomes reflexive and Manuel Castells (1996–98) has claimed that contemporary society has become the 'network society' in which effective belonging has moved away from civil societies of nations and states into reconstructed defensive identity communities.

This introduction – as well as the rest of the book – does not attempt to sum up this vast literature in any way. Instead, it attempts to differentiate between and identify some of the major building blocks that a comprehensive analytical framework for belonging and the politics of belonging would require. To do so, the chapter first explores the notion of 'belonging' and the different analytical facets in which it needs to be studied, and then focuses on the politics of belonging and how these relate to the participatory politics of citizenship as well as entitlement and status. It then illustrates, using examples from Britain, some of the ways in which different political projects of belonging relate to the different analytical facets of belonging. While the rest of the book uses illustrative examples from all over the world, I thought that remaining within the boundaries of one state and society might better clarify how different political projects of belonging can construct the same collectivity in different ways and with different boundaries.

Belonging

People can 'belong' in many different ways and to many different objects of attachment. These can vary from a particular person to the whole of humanity, in a concrete or abstract way, by self or other identification, in a stable, contested or transient way. Even in its most stable 'primordial' forms, however, belonging is always a dynamic process, not a reified fixity – the latter is only a naturalized construction of a particular hegemonic form of power relations. Belonging is usually multi-layered and – to use geographical jargon – multi-scale (Antonsich, 2010) or multi-territorial (Hannerz, 2002).

To clarify our understanding of the notion of social and political belonging, it would be useful to differentiate between three major analytical facets in which belonging is constructed.[3] The first facet concerns social locations; the second relates to people's identifications and emotional attachments to various collectivities and groupings; and the third relates to ethical and political value systems with which people judge their own and others' belonging. These different facets are interrelated, but cannot be reduced to each other.

Social locations

When it is said that people belong to a particular sex, race, class or nation, that they belong to a particular age group, kinship group or a certain profession, we are talking about people's social and economic

---

[3]As will become clearer further on in the chapter, these facets can be reconstructed and reconfigured in many different ways by different political projects of belonging.

locations, which at each historical moment would tend to carry with them particular weights in the grids of power relations operating in their society. Being a man or a woman, black or white, working class or middle class, a member of a European or an African nation, people are not just different categories of social location, with different contextual meanings, they also tend to have certain positionalities along axes of power that are higher or lower than other such categories. Such positionalities, however, would tend to be different in different historical contexts and are also often fluid and contested. Sometimes, however, as Sandra Harding (1991) and Nancy Fraser (in Fraser & Honneth, 1998) have commented, certain differences would not necessarily have differential power positionings but are only the markers for different locations. This, again, can only be related to specific differences in particular historical moments and contexts.

Social locations, however, even in their most stable format, are virtually never constructed along one power vector of difference, although official statistics – as well as identity politics – would often tend to construct them in this way. This is why the intersectional approach to social locations is so vitally important.

Marxists and other sociologists have traditionally tended to prioritize class, even when recognizing other axes of social location, while feminists have tended to prioritize gender and those who are focused on issues of race and ethnicity have tended to prioritize people's locations according to these categories. Indeed, in different historical moments, different systems of stratification tend to give differential weight to different intersectional categories of location and axes of power and they might operate in many different ways – hence the need for case studies using an intra-categorical research approach to complement more macro inter-categorical ones. Much depends on people's ability to move up those grids of power and the extent to which locations ascribed at birth can be transcended, either by moving from one category of location to another, such as becoming 'middle class' while being originally 'working class', or – even more dramatically – being trans-gendered or becoming assimilated into a different national, ethnic or even racial collectivity. Different locations along social and economic axes are often marked by different embodied signifiers, such as colour of skin, accent, clothing and mode of behaviour. However, these should not be collapsed and automatically equated with subjective identifications and social attachments.

Identifications and emotional attachments

Identities are narratives, stories people tell themselves and others about who they are (and who they are not) (Martin, 1995; see also Kaptani & Yuval-Davis, 2008b; Yuval-Davis, 2010). Not all of these stories are about belonging to particular groupings and collectivities – they can be, for instance, about individual attributes, body images, vocational aspirations or sexual prowess. However, even these stories will often relate, directly or indirectly, to self and/or others' perceptions of what being a member of such a grouping or collectivity (ethnic, racial, national, cultural, religious) might mean. Identity narratives can be individual or they can be collective, with the latter often acting as a resource for the former. Although they can be reproduced from gen-eration to generation, it is always in a selective way: they can shift and change, be contested and multiple. These identity narratives can relate to the past, to a myth of origin; they can be aimed to explain the present and probably; above all, they function as a projection of future trajectory.

Margaret Wetherell (2006) argues that identity narratives pro-vide people with a sense of 'personal order'. As will be discussed in greater detail elsewhere, I would argue that identities are not just personal – and in some way these are never just personal – and that collective identity narratives provide a collective sense of order and meaning. At the same time, as Cavarero emphasizes (1997: 3), 'nar-ration reveals the meaning without committing the error of defining it'. This is particularly important because, as Hall (1996) argues, the production of identities is always 'in process', is never complete, con-tingent and multiplex. In this sense, 'order' should not be seen as the equivalent of 'coherence', but rather as pointing towards the sense of agency and continuity that encompasses changes, contestations, even raptures within the identity boundaries of the individual and/or col-lective subject. At Gayatri Spivak (1994) pointed out, in her seminal essay 'Can the subaltern speak?', a narrative of identity is a necessary condition for any notion of agency and subjectivity to exist.

Identity narratives can be verbal, but can also be constructed as spe-cific forms of practices (Fortier, 2000). While MacIntyre (1981: 140) conceives identity practices as 'embodied narration in a single life', I would argue that such 'embodied narrations' are even more crucial in the construction and reproduction of collective identities. Narratives of identities can be more or less stable in different social contexts, more or less coherent, more or less authorized and/or contested by the self and others, depending on specific situational factors, and can reflect routinized constructions of everyday life or those of significant moments of crisis and transformation. They include both cognitive and emotional dimensions with varying degrees of attachment:

> individuals and groups are caught within wanting to belong, wanting to become, a process that is fuelled by yearning rather than positing of identity as a stable state. (Probyn, 1996: 19)

In her Deleuzian analysis, Probyn (1996; see also Fortier, 2000) constructs identity as transition, always producing itself through the combined processes of being and becoming, belonging and longing to belong.

Of course not every belonging is important to people in the same way and to the same extent, and emotions, as perceptions, shift in different times and situations and are more or less reflective. As a rule, the emotional components of people's constructions of themselves and their identities become more central the more threatened and less secure they become. In the more extreme cases people would be willing to sacrifice their lives – and the lives of others – in order for the narrative of their identities and the objects of their identifications and attachments to continue to exist. After a terrorist attack, or after a declaration of war, people will often seek to return to a place of less 'objective' safety, as long as it means they can be close to their nearest and dearest, and share their fate.

The narrative approach to the understanding of identities is considered in the literature (e.g. Williams, 2000; Lawler, 2008) to be just one specific approach to the theorization of identities. As I elaborate elsewhere, however (Yuval-Davis, 2010), the narrative approach encompasses, as well as being implied in, other major approaches to the study of identity, such as the performative and the dialogical, which are, at the same time, also very different from each other in their understanding of the identity question.

As Bell (1999) and Fortier (2000) comment, following Butler (1990), constructions of belonging have a performative dimension. Specific repetitive practices, relating to specific social and cultural spaces, which link individual and collective behaviour, are crucial for the construction and reproduction of identity narratives and constructions of attachment. It is in this way, as Sara Ahmed (2004) points out, that free-floating emotions 'stick' to particular social objects. However, as Butler clarifies in her later work (1993; see also Lovell, 2003), in the performative approach to identity theorization, identity narratives can be constructed within, counter and outside pre-determined social discourses, through subversive performances, such as drags. What is hardly discussed in performative theorizations of identity, however, is from where and how – except for repetition and an assumption of social power and authority – these discourses themselves become constructed. This has been the focus of a very different theoretical approach of identity theorizations which follows on from Bakhtin's work (1981, 1984) as well as the Chicago School of Cooley (1912) and Mead (1934). It emphasizes another aspect of theatre practice, i.e. dialogue, as the constitutive element of identity construction. To use Bakhtin's words:

> to be, means to be for the other and through him, for one-self. Man has no internal sovereign territory, he is always on the boundary; looking within himself he looks in the eyes of the other or through the eyes of the other. I cannot do without the other; I cannot become myself without the other; I must find myself in the other; finding the other in me in mutual reflection and perception. (1984: 311–12; see also Williams, 2000: 90)

The dialogical construction of identity, then, is both reflective and constitutive. It is not individual or collective, but involves both, in an in-between perpetual state of 'becoming', in which processes of identity construction, authorization and contestation take place. It is important to emphasize, however, that dialogical processes, by themselves, are not an alternative to viewing identity constructions as informed by power relations – just the opposite: analyzing the processes by which identity narratives are constructed in the communal context is vital in order to understand the ways intersectional power relations operate within the group. Otherwise one can easily fall into the trap of an identity politics which assumes the same positioning and identifications for all members of the grouping, and thus each member can, in principle, be a 'representative' of the grouping and an equal contributor to the collective narrative – which, of course, is virtually never the case. It is for this reason that dialogical understandings of identity constructions often lead to studies of identity constructions via conversation or narrative analysis in which the actions and interactions of ordinary people become the primary focus of direct enquiry (see, for example, Boden & Zimmerman, 1991; Silverman, 1998; Kaptani & Yuval-Davis, 2008a).

The issue, however, is not just the manner in which identity narratives are being produced, but also whether their production implies any particular relationship between self and non-self. Judith Butler (1993) argues that the construction of identities depends on excess – there is always something left outside, once the boundaries of specific identities have been constructed. In this sense all identities are exclusive, as well as inclusive.

One might argue that such a statement amounts to no more than a linguistic truism. However, an important counter-argument to that of Butler would be Jessica Benjamin's (1998) claim that by incorporating identifications into the notion of the subjective self, psychoanalysis has put in doubt the clear separation of self and non-self. It can be argued that similar reservations to the total separation between self and non-self are implied in the theorizations of the in-between 'becoming' of the dialogical approach. Charles Cooley (1912: 92) argues that 'Self and other do not exist as mutually exclusive social facts'. The way in which identities are perceived to be constructed within pre-determined discourses in the performative approach also throws doubt on the clear separation of self and non-self in the construction of the subject.

Identity theories often emphasize that identities are relational, the necessary 'excess' mentioned by Butler above. However, highlighting the fact that this relationality is not homogeneous and can be very different in nature is of vital importance for any theorization of identity, belonging and their constructions of boundaries. While a lot of the literature talks about the relationship between 'self' and 'other/s', there are many ways in which these relationships can be constructed. In my (2010) work, I've discussed four generic relations of the self and non-self in which recognition has very different implications: 'me' and 'us'; 'me'/'us' and 'them'; 'me'/'us' and 'others'; 'me' and the transversal 'us/them' (for a more detailed discussion of these issues see Chapters 5 and 6 in this volume). However, whatever kinds of boundaries are constructed between the 'me' and the 'not me', it is necessary to emphasize that not only are those boundaries shifting and contested, but also that they do not have to be symmetrical. In other words, inclusion or exclusion is often not mutual, depending on the power positionality and normative values of the social actors as well as, and in relation to, their cognitive and emotional identifications. Constructions of self and identity can, in certain historical contexts, be forced on people. In such cases, identities and belonging/s become important dimensions of people's social locations and positionings, and the relationships between locations and identifications can also become more closely intertwined empirically. This still does not cancel out the importance of the differentiation between these analytical facets of analyzing belonging. On the contrary, without this differentiation, there could be no leverage and possibility of struggle and resistance. Biology – or belonging – would become destiny when there would not be any space for alternative imaginings. As Fanon (1967) crucially argued, politics of resistance need to be directed not only towards oppressed people's social and economic locations, but also against their internalizations of forced constructions of self and identity.

Ethical and political values

Belonging, therefore, is not just about social locations and constructions of individual and collective identities and attachments, it is also concerned with the ways these are assessed and valued by the self and others, and this can be done in many different ways by people with similar social locations who might identify themselves as belonging to the same community or grouping. These can vary not only in how important these locations and collectivities seem to be in one's life and that of others, but also in whether they consider this to be a good or a bad thing. Closely related to this are specific attitudes and ideologies concerning where and how identity and categorical boundaries are being/should be drawn, in more or less permeable ways, as different ideological perspectives and discourses construct them as more or less inclusive. It is in the arena of the contestations around these issues where we move from the realm of belonging into that of the politics of belonging.

The politics of belonging

The politics of belonging involves not only constructions of boundaries but also the inclusion or exclusion of particular people, social categories and groupings within these boundaries by those who have the power to do this. But what are these kind/s of power?

Politics involves the exercise of power and different hegemonic political projects of belonging represent different symbolic power orders. In recent years, the sociological understanding of power has been enriched by the theoretical contributions of Foucault (e.g. 1979, 1991a) and Bourdieu (e.g. 1984, 1990). Traditionally, power was understood and measured by the effects those with power had on others. However, feminists and other grass-roots activists, following Freire's *Pedagogy of the Oppressed* (1970), promoted a notion of 'empowerment' in which people would gain 'power of' rather than 'power on'. While this approach has been used too often to cover intra-communal power relations and the feminist 'tyranny of structurelesness' with which Jo Freeman (1970) described the dynamics of feminist politics, the notion of empowerment does fit with alternative theoretical approaches to power which focus on symbolic power.

Max Weber's (1968) classical theory of power, which differentiated between physical and charismatic powers – those dependent on individual resources and those emanating out of legitimate authority – has been supplemented, if not supplanted by, other theoretical frameworks which have sought to explain what is happening in the contemporary world where social, political and economic powers have become more diffused, decentred and desubjectified. The most popular of these new approaches have been those by Foucault (1979, 1986 [1969], 1991a) and Bourdieu (1984, 1990; see also Bourdieu & Nice, 1977). Foucault constructed a notion of a 'disciplinary society' in which power increasingly operates through impersonal mechanisms of bodily discipline and a governmentality which escapes the consciousness and will of individual and collective social agents. Under such conditions, power, as was formerly known, starts to operate only when resistance occurs.

However, as Cronin (1996: 56) points out, while Foucault's genealogical perspective of power is of crucial importance in understanding contemporary politics, it is too radical and monolithic, and therefore 'it is impossible to identify any social location of the exercise of power or of resistance to power'. This is where Bourdieu's theory of symbolic power, while sharing some of Foucault's insights, such as the role of body practices as mediating relations of domination, can serve us better. For Bourdieu the subject is both embodied and socially constituted. His theory of practice (in which there is a constant interaction between the individual symbolically structured and socially inculcated dispositions of individual agents which he calls '*habitus*' and the 'social field' which is structured by symbolically mediated relations of domination) offers a more empirically sensitive analytical framework for decoding impersonal relations of power.

Symbolic powers are of crucial importance when we deal with political projects of belonging, although more often than not, they are the focus for contestations and resistance. Adrian Favell (1999) defined the politics of belonging as 'the dirty work of boundary maintenance'. The boundaries the politics of belonging are concerned with are the boundaries of the political community of belonging, the boundaries which, sometimes physically, but always symbolically, separate the world population into 'us' and 'them'. The question of the boundaries of belonging, the boundaries of the Andersonian (1991 [1983]) 'imagined communities' (see the discussion in Chapter 3), is central in all the political projects of belonging examined in the following chapters. The politics of belonging involve not only the maintenance and reproduction of the boundaries of the community of belonging by the hegemonic political powers (within and outside the community), but also their contestation, challenge and resistance by other political agents. It is important to recognize, however, that such political agents would struggle both for the promotion of their specific position on the construction of collectivities and their boundaries as well as using these ideologies and positions in order to promote their own power positions within and outside the collectivities.

The politics of belonging also include struggles around the determination of what is involved in belonging, in being a member of such a community. As such, it is dialogical (Yuval-Davis & Werbner, 1999) and encompasses contestations both in relation to the participatory dimension of citizenship as well as in relation to issues related to the status and entitlements such membership entails. This is discussed in detail in Chapter 2 on the state citizenship question, although it also arises in all the other chapters which discuss citizenship, i.e. membership of political communities, as constructed by other political projects of belonging than the so-called 'nation-state'.

In order to understand some of the contestations involved in different constructions of belonging promoted by different political projects of belonging, we need to look at what is required from a specific person in order for her/him to be entitled to belong, to be considered as belonging, to the collectivity. Common descent (or rather the myth of common descent) might be demanded in some cases, while in others it might be a common culture, religion and/or language.

Loyalty and solidarity, based on common values and a projected myth of common destiny, tend to become requisites for belonging in pluralist societies. In other words, in different projects of the politics of belonging, the different facets of belonging – social locations, identities and ethical and political values – can become the requisites of belonging and the delineation of boundaries.

Requisites of belonging that relate to 'ascriptive' social locations – origin, 'race', place of birth – would be the most racialized and the least permeable. Language, culture and sometimes religion are more open to a voluntary, often assimilatory, identification with particular collectivities. Using a common set of values, such as 'democracy' or 'human rights', as the signifiers of belonging can be seen as having the most permeable boundaries of all.

However, these different discourses of belonging can be collapsed together or reduced down to each other in specific historical cases. Moreover, some political projects of belonging can present themselves as promoting more open boundaries than they actually do. In the next section I shall illustrate this by briefly outlining three different political projects of belonging in the United Kingdom that have utilized discourses relating to different facets of belonging. However, such contesting political projects exist virtually everywhere, whether it is the contestation in India between its being a pluralist secular society in which belonging is defined by being born in the country or a Hindutva nation; or whether it is if aboriginals can be part of an Australian nation or need their own self-determination as a 'first nation'; or whether it is if Afrikaners can be considered 'indigenous' people in the South African context rather than 'settlers'.

Three British political projects of belonging

The first British political project of belonging to be discussed here was articulated by Enoch Powell, a major Conservative political figure in post-Second World War Britain. He can be seen as the first 'public intellectual' who tried to establish boundaries to British or, rather, English belonging in the post-imperial era. He understood early on that the empire was a lost cause and called for a return to and a strengthening of the homeland itself: 'Englishman, go home!' (Barker, 1981). Although, as a minister in the Conservative government of the day, he was responsible for the importing of black British citizens from the Caribbean islands to work in England, he excluded them by definition from any possibility of belonging to the English national collectivity. He argued that 'the West Indian does not by being born in England, become an Englishman' (Powell, 1968).

For Powell, descent was the ultimate criterion for belonging. Moreover, he collapsed descent and cultural and political identification. He was eventually expelled from the Conservative Party when he argued that, unless those who did not belong were returned to their 'proper' countries, there would be 'rivers of blood' in England, as people who originated in different countries and cultures could not, by definition, become part of the same integrated society.

About ten years after Powell was expelled, another Conservative minister, this time in Margaret Thatcher's government, Norman Tebbit, promoted in 1990 another British political project of belonging that is popularly known today as the 'Cricket Test'. One of the Conservative election posters under Thatcher presented a picture of a young black man with the subtitle 'Labour claims he is Black, we claim he is British'. In this way, the Thatcherite political project of belonging distinguished itself from Labour's political project of belonging which was built around the notion of multiculturalism, as well as tackling skin-colour, descent-based racism, and the focus of the political project of belonging of the extreme right. This was in spite of the fact that during her original election campaign Mrs Thatcher did speak about her worry that newcomers would 'swamp' the local people and their culture. However, as the Thatcherite neo-liberal project crystallized, its discourse opened the door, at least rhetorically, to black middle-class assimilationism (see the discussion on the citizen as consumer in Chapter 2).

Norman Tebbit's contribution to the Thatcherite project was to establish the boundary of belonging not only in terms of assimilation and economic contribution, but also in terms of identification and emotional attachment. He claimed that if people watched a cricket match between Britain and a team from the country from which they or their family had originated and cheered that latter team, this meant that those people did not really 'belong' to the British collectivity, even if they had formal British citizenship, and had been born and reared in it.

Another political project of belonging was developed by New Labour, although some of its characteristics were partially overlapping the Thatcherite one, and continues to be developed by Cameron's Conservative–Lib Dem coalition governnment. David Blunkett, for

instance, as Home Secretary in Tony Blair's New Labour government a decade later, was careful not to use the cricket metaphor, but
football matches were often mentioned in his various papers which
emphasized the importance of social cohesion and social solidarity.
New Labour also wanted to distance itself from the multiculturalism
that had become the official policy of the Labour Party since the
1960s.[4] The multiculturalist political project of belonging was basically aimed at post-imperial Britain and the non-assimilatory integration of coloured British citizens who had come to live and work in
post-war Britain from its previous colonies, but over the years there
has been a growing critique of multicultural policies not only from
the right but also from the left, as essentialist, homogenizing, reifying boundaries and inherently linked to Britain's empiric past (see
e.g. Cohen & Bains, 1988; Anthias & Yuval-Davis, 1992; May, 1999;
and the discussion on multicutural citizenship in Chapter 2). New
Labour attempted to tackle multiculturalism after the 2001 riots
in the north of England when Cantle's Report basically claimed in
the same year that multiculturalist policies had gone too far and had
effectively caused, at least in northern England, social segregation
between the English and the ethnic minority communities, made
up mostly of Muslim South Asians. Multiculturalism was declared
'dead' and social and community integration became the new goals of
the British politics of belonging. The British people, in this political
project, which was so often articulated by David Blunkett, are not
constructed out of a common descent or culture, but their solidarity
and loyalty have to be to the British state and society. In his 2002
White Paper, *Secure Borders, Safe Haven*, Blunkett even encouraged
people from South Asian communities to find marriage partners for
their children from other families living in Britain rather than in
their countries of origin, so that such cultural and social cohesion
would be easier to achieve. Learning English became a requirement
for attaining formal citizenship under the new legislation, again in
order for such social cohesion to be facilitated. However, while this
political project of belonging is primarily based on the identificatory
and emotional facet of belonging, it also assumes an adherence to the
specific political and ethical values that are seen as inherent to good
democratic citizenship (Crick, 1998). The emphasis on democracy

---

[4]See, for example, his 2002 White Paper on *Secure Borders Safe Haven*, http://www.privacyinternational.
org/issues/terrorism/library/uksecureborderssafehavens.pdf and the articles on this in the special issue of *Ethnic and Racial Studies* edited by G. Lewis and S. Neale (2005).

and human rights became much stronger with British involvement in the wars in Kosovo, Afghanistan and Iraq, and came to be presented as a signifier not only of British belonging for its citizens but also of its mission in the world. This political project had been promoted mostly by Gordon Brown when he was the Chancellor of the Exchequer. Shortly before he became Prime Minister, he suggested the establishment of a 'Patriotism Day' to cement British political loyalty and, significantly, proposed 'Liberty, Responsibility, Fairness' as the British equivalent to the French political values of '*Liberté, Egalité, Fraternité*'. Although many in the media saw in this politics of belonging project a way for the Scottish Brown to strengthen overall British identity at a time when the devolution of Scotland, Wales and Northern Ireland had weakened it, and thus legitimize his claim to becoming the next Prime Minister of Britain, this political project was linked much more centrally to the overall political project of New Labour.

In several speeches Brown emphasized values rather than origins or social and political institutions, as what he saw as constituting 'the sense of shared purpose, an idea of what your destiny as a nation is'. For Brown, the 'common qualities and common values that have made Britain the country ... [are] our belief in tolerance and liberty which shines through British history. Our commitment to fairness, fair play and civic duty' (Brown, 2005a).[5] This view of Britishness and British history has led him to declare, on other occasions (Brown, 2005b), that 'the days of Britain having to apologize for its colonial history are over' and that 'we should be proud ... of the Empire' (Brown, 2004). In New Labour's politics of belonging, human rights and democratic civic values were part of what Britain had to offer not only to its citizens but also to the world at large. The re-elevation of the British Empire to becoming an occasion for British national pride, in spite of all the terrible chapters in its history (see Milne, 2005), goes hand in hand with the contemporary 'civilizing mission' of the humanitarian militarism in which Britain, alongside the United States, is playing a central role (see Chandler,

---

[5]This emphasis on shared liberal values as the basis for national cohesion and culture also continues under the Conservative-Lib-Dem government. In his speech on 'muscular liberalism' (5/2/20-11) Cameron declared that the values of 'Freedom of speech; freedom of worship; democracy; the rule of law; equal rights regardless of race, sex or sexuality' are 'what defines us as a society; to belong here is to believe in these things' (http://www.number10.gov.uk/news/speeches-and-transcripts/2011/02/pms-speech-at-munich-security-conference-60293).

2002; and the discussion in Chapter 5), and which has often had terrible consequences for the people it is supposed to liberate. This is an issue that all human rights activists, as well as all those who promote, unproblematically, a cosmopolitan world government in which the moral values of human rights are dictated from the top down, have to confront these days (see Held, 1995; Kaldor, 2003; and the discussion in Chapter 5). Emancipatory ethical and political values can be transformed, under certain conditions, into the inherent personal attributes of members of particular national and regional collectivities (Britain, the West) and, thus, in practice, become exclusionary rather than permeable signifiers of boundaries.

These different British political projects of belonging mentioned above – which are, of course, far from representing the full range of British political projects of belonging – construct differential boundaries as well as a different 'essence' of Britishness. Each of them is anchored in a different facet of belonging – the Powellian one of social location, Tebbit's emotional identification, and Brown's normative values – although each of them at the same time also utilizes discourses that have been borrowed from the others. In this they illustrate how various political projects of belonging can target the same collectivity but construct it in different ways so as to promote their legitimate representativeness and thus leadership of the collectivity. As such, these political projects of belonging represent different symbolic power orders and locate, in least potentially, the same people in different positionings along the intersectional social and political axes in the society at each particular moment.

It is vitally important, therefore, to remember, that in order to understand these political projects of belonging, it is not enough to discuss the hegemonic political discourses such as in government documentation or the popular media. The ways different members of the collectivity experience the implications of these discourses as well as interpret them can differ vastly, according to their intersected situated locations, identifications and normative value systems.

The political projects of belonging discussed above, and the others mentioned briefly earlier on in the chapter, are nevertheless small examples of the contested ways in which different states and societies are trying to grapple with what Stuart Hall has called 'the multicultural question':

> What are the terms for groups of people from different cultural, religious, linguistic, historical backgrounds, who have applied

to occupy the same social space, whether that is a city or a nation or a region, to live with one another without either one group (the less powerful group) having to become the imitative version of the dominant one – i.e. an assimilationism – or, on the other hand, the two groups hating one another, or projecting images of degradation? In other words, how can people live together in difference? (Hall with Yuval-Davis, 2004)

According to Hall, the multicultural question is 'the question that globalization has unconsciously produced' (Hall with Yuval-Davis, 2004). I would argue that it is not only the multicultural that needs to be seen in this perspective, but also the contemporary politics of belonging as a whole – hence the focus on globalization in the next contextual section of the chapter.

Globalization and glocalization

Globalization and – as discussed below – glocalization, need to be seen as the context within which contemporary contesting political projects of belonging are taking place. However, they are in themselves ongoing contesting and shifting processes which are continuously being modified by various internal and external factors in which political projects of belonging play significant roles. The tendency, therefore, to see globalization – and the growing inequalities attached to it – as a 'natural' development, an unshifting reality which has been so hegemonic even among many who are on the left, especially before the start of the major economic crisis in 2009 (Peterson, 2010), needs to be resisted. Any generalization as a result would need to be assessed as contingent at best. This, however, does not diminish the crucial import of globalization and glocalization for understanding contemporary politics of belonging, the subject matter of this book.

Globalization, especially in its neo-liberal format, has become increasingly visible in the post-Cold War period, with the fall of the Soviet Union and the rule of Ronald Reagan in the USA and Margaret Thatcher in the UK. As Scholte (2005) claims, however, harbingers of globality can be traced back hundreds, if not thousands, of years. Colombus was definitely not the first 'foreigner' to 'discover' America, even if we do not accept Gavin Menzies' controversial (2002) thesis that a huge Chinese fleet had visited America already in 1421. Raiders, and before them traders, have continuously advanced routes of (often unequal) exchange and communication across different parts of the globe.

Notable transworld connectedness existed from the middle of the nineteenth century. However, the greatest expansion of transplanetary relations has transpired since the middle of the twentieth century and the 'Bretton Wood' agreements that established the World Bank and the International Monetary Fund (IMF). Saskia Sassen (2006: 17) points out that internal transformations in nation-states, which enabled globalization 'proper', started in the late 1970s. She sees globalization as 'an epochal transformation, one as yet young but already showing its muscle' (2006: 1).

There is only loose agreement about what actually constitutes globalization. Part of the confusion relates to different theories defining or emphasizing different elements as characterizing globalization as well as its connections with neo-liberalism. Wallerstein (1976, 1980, 1989), who first put forward the model of the 'world system', described it basically in terms of the development of a world economy in which unequal relationships existed between the centre and periphery. Other models of globalization (e.g. Meyer, 1980; Robertson, 1992; and Beyer, 1994), have added to this model aspects of a global polity, global culture and global society.

Scholte (2005), however, claims that most of the characteristics that are usually counted to typify globalization – i.e. internalization; liberalization; universalization and westernization – have existed previously. Only the 'respatialization with the spread of transplanetary social connections' (Scholte, 2005: 3) is distinctive and key to contemporary historical development (although, no doubt, the sense of respatialization occurred in each age in which major new transport and communication technologies have been introduced). This time/space compression, the specific respatialization of the present globalization, has been possible as a result of the micro-chip revolution, revolutionary changes in speed and the cost of global transport (Dicken, 2003; Rodrigue, 2006), and even more so in global communication, especially the internet (Block, 2004), creating what Castells calls 'information societies': 'social organization in which information generation, processing and transmission become fundamental sources of production and power because of new technological conditions emerging in this historical period' (Castells, 2000 [1998]: 21). These developments – and the differential access to them by different populations and segments of a population[6] – have been crucial in shaping and structuring some of the central characteristics of contemporary politics of belonging.

The contemporary rise of transplanetary and supraterritorial connectivity has by no means brought an end to territorial geography and associated economies, governments and identities. Global and territorial spaces coexist and interrelate in complex fashions. I would also argue that to strip the description of the specificity of contemporary globalization from its neo-liberal political and economic context is a gross misrepresentation, although this political and economic homogenization in itself, as I shall detail more below, is misleading, and in recent years – especially since the global economic crisis of 2007 – major shifts have started to gain momentum.

It is not only descriptions but also explanations of the phenomenon that vary. In some ways there is collusion between Marxist and liberal economic theories which see in globalization a natural continuation of the development of the logic of capitalism and the market economy since the nineteenth century. The Soviet Union, the Cold War and the resultant welfare social democratic states are seen, from this perspective, as a temporary aberration that camouflaged, interrupted and distorted this development until the global political

---

[6] The internet, which originally was invented in the USA as a mode of national defence against Soviet nuclear attack during the Cold War, created a global space which is infinitely extensible, adaptable and, at least in principle, non-hierarchical when, in 1992, the World Wide Web was released for general use. The role of the internet in nationalist, diasporic and cosmopolitan projects of belonging is explored later on in the book. Here, however, it is important to point out that unlike predictions during early days of the internet that it would promote the English language as a universal language, the reality, like that of globalization in general, has proven to be more nuanced. Although 80% of the interactions over the internet are carried out in English, it has also provided a virtual space not only for other major languages, such as Spanish, Arabic or Chinese, but also for specific local dialects like Catalan, and the preservation/reproduction of dying languages, like Yiddish.

At the same time, it is also important to remember that the democratic, decentralized face of the internet is, to a large extent, misleading. The UNDP in 1999 pointed out that while 26% of Americans were using the web, only 3% of Russians, 0.4% of the population in South Asia and 0.2% of African states were doing so. Since then the percentages of use among the latter have grown significantly, as 25.6% of the world population had been using the internet in 2009. However, the unequal distribution of resources and power continue to exist. While in North America 74.2% of the population are using it, only 6.8% are doing so in Africa and in Asia 19.4%. In Europe as a whole, 52% of the population are now using the internet (*Internet World Stats*, 2009). Moreover, there is evidence of more and more states trying to block internet use, admittedly with varying amounts of success, from China and Iran to the USA (and the Wikileaks).

balance of power shifted towards the time of the fall of the Soviet Union. For others, the post-Second World War period prepared the grounds for globalization with the development of various regulatory[7] apparatuses which were provided through a host of state, suprastate and private governance mechanisms that have since brought about these new epochal changes, enhanced by the changing political context and the scientific and technological developments which changed basic relations and the mode of production.

As Sassen (2006) argues, the capabilities required for globalization developed within the context of (western) nation-states and reached tipping points in which they were transformed by and became part of the new assemblage of the global economic and political order. Globalization reshaped and expanded capitalism, i.e. the economy, which is centred on surplus accumulation. The growth of transworld spaces has encouraged major extensions of capitalist production, including in the areas of information, communications and finance biotechnology. Notable shifts occurred in the ways that processes of surplus accumulation operate – e.g. offshore arrangements and transworld corporate alliances – towards what Sassen calls 'hypercapitalism'.

'Hypercapitalism', or 'neo-liberalism', however, is driven by the same impulses that drove nineteenth-century imperial capitalism, and it has found new fields for the 'primitive accumulation of capital' with the appropriation of capital and goods from the public sector – spectacularly, in the 'post-communist' countries but also in the spreading control of neo-liberal market norms in more and more sectors of the state, both in the so-called 'developing world' as well as in the West.

The notion of the 'global' is usually constructed as opposite to that of the 'local'. Local communities can have different relationships with the globalization process. They can, to a certain extent at least, still exist outside the globalization processes; they can coexist with the global environment/influence; and they can also be constituted as a reaction to the processes of globalization and become a site of resistance to it. As Swyngedouw (1997) argues, glocalization relates to

---

[7] These regulatory apparatuses and mechanisms, while enabling the progressive growth of neo-liberal globalization, were not strong enough to contain and prevent the systemic crisis within the global economic system. The extent to which they would be able, in the long term, to facilitate overcoming that crisis has still to be seen, as is the differential effects this crisis would have on different localities, different states and societies and people who are differentially located, socially, economically and politically.

transformations in the international political economy and urban geography – the parallel shifts towards global and local scales of political relationships, such as the rising influence of the EU and G8 on the one hand, and the proliferation of local economic partnerships and initiatives on the other. There is an important role here for metropolises in connecting the local, the national and the international.

However, we should not necessarily assume that naturalized and harmonized relationships always exist between the local and the global. The complex connection/relation between them does not necessarily imply mirroring but can also produce conflict and resistance. Silva and Schwartzman (2006), for instance, discuss the different and contradictory ways in which affirmative action policies were received in Brazil. Rather than being perceived as anti-discrimination policies based on human rights, they were seen by many as the cultural imperialism of the USA, which threatened, under the different conditions in which affirmative action policies were carried in Brazil, certain constructions of 'local essence'.

It is for this reason that Robertson (1995), who developed the notion of 'glocalization', argued that successful glocalization does not simply produce or reproduce random forms of cultural heterogeneity. It also registers the 'standardization of locality' so that various localities may possess very similar structures, reference points and symbolic textures or contents. The local becomes globally institutionalized. This will be crucial when we examine the glocal nature of various contemporary political projects of belonging.

Nevertheless, this does not mean that globalization equals homogenization. Jan Pieterse (1995) points out that globalization is instead developed more by the fluid and critical engagement of local social actors and results more in the processes of creolization and hybridization. Talal Asad (1986) has introduced within that context the important notion of 'translation', which is much wider than the linguistic one. Even McDonald's, which has been used by Barber (1995) and others to illustrate the impact of the commodification and standardization of globalization, in spite of the universal golden M, conducts local market surveys and adapts its menus to local demands. Moreover, the local meaning of McDonald's can vary hugely, given its specific historical context. While in Moscow the arrival of McDonald's in 1990 was hailed as a welcome signifier of the opening of the Soviet Union to the big wide world, there was for quite some years a fierce local resistance to establishing a McDonald's in Paris.

Resistance to (as well as incorporation into) western-dominated, neo-liberal globalization has been conducted on different levels, both by states, e.g. the Chinese state-controlled economic globalization or the Latin American globalizing economic anti-imperialism led by leaders such as Chavez and Morales, and by non-statist movements, networks and organizations, such as the World Social Forum (which started as an anti-Davos event) and the anti-globalization movement as a whole (discussed in Chapter 5). Other movements of resistance have been the fundamentalist Islamist groups and organizations loosely coordinated by the Al-Quaeda network. (These will be discussed along with fundamentalist movements and organizations from other religions in Chapter 4.)

States and neo-liberal globalization

The transformation of state apparatuses under neo-liberal globalization is usually constructed as their 'modernization' – a discourse which was aggressively promoted, for instance, by Tony Blair and others under British New Labour (but see also, for instance, the [2007] paper on governance, written for the EU by Petr Vymtal of the University of Economics in Prague).

States, in various forms and scales, from cities to empires, have existed since ancient times in different parts of the world. Since the French revolution, although empires have continued to exist and grow (including, at certain times, the French empire), states have come to be seen as 'nation-states' in which, to use Max Weber's classical definition (1948 [1947]: 78), 'a human community (successfully) claims the monopoly of the legitimate use of physical force within a given territory'. This definition assumes a particular 'human community', the nation, with particular boundaries, that is living in a particular territory, the 'homeland', with particular borders, that is governed by a state which assumes a monopoly of the legitimate use of physical force to police that state within and fight its enemies without. The 1648 Treaty of Westphalia assumed this to be the basic legitimate form of geopolitical organization and it was hegemonic in international relations, at least in Europe itself, until the late twentieth century (Brenner et al., 2003: introduction).

This 'holy trinity' of people, territory and state was always more fiction than fact, as both collectivity boundaries and territorial borders have been continuously contested by both state and non-state agencies, and there have been more often than not blurred edges to what passed as the monopoly of legitimate use of physical force by the state.

In Chapter 3 these questions will be explored in relation to the various constructions of nations and homelands. Here I would like to examine some of the issues relating to states' governability and how these have been affected by processes of globalization that are dominated by the spread of the neo-liberal market.

With the growing hegemony of neo-liberal ideologies and policies and the strengthening of neo-liberal global market forces, more and more agencies and apparatus of the state, in more and more countries, have been privatized partially or fully (e.g. Panitch, 1994; Jessop, 2002; McBride, 2005). This raises the same old question of what constitutes the specific sphere of 'the state' to differentiate it from the sphere of 'civil society' (which itself needs to be subdivided into economic, social and domestic spheres) (see my discussion of these issues in Yuval-Davis, 1997a: 12–15). In one pole of the debate we have the classical Weberian definition in which the state has a monopoly on the legitimate use of physical power (1948 [1947]), and on the other we have the Foucauldian perspective (e.g. Foucault, 1979, 1991b), according to which no such specific powers can be seen universally as the exclusive property of the state.

Part of the difference between these two perspectives stems from their different theorizations of the meaning of power. However, part of the difference between the two, is also, I believe, a result of the different historical times in which Weber and Foucault wrote their theorizations of the state. As Foucault pointed out (1991b), late modernity brought with it new technologies of governance, a 'governmentality' in which much of the work was done within the subjectivities of the citizens, rather than by the state exercising the external powers in its disposal. Given the number of civil wars throughout the globe, in which the military and other power sources of the state are used against particular sections of the population, such a Foucauldian portrayal of contemporary states seems however, though partial at best, to lean much too heavily on the liberal fiction of the individual relationship between an abstract non-embodied citizen and the state – as will be discussed more in the next chapter.

A related question is whether, under globalization, the state as the 'container of power' (Giddens, 1985; Taylor, 2003), is 'withering away' – becoming weaker and less able to impose its power on the other social, economic and political carriers of power. This is an important question, whether or not we believe in the Weberian definition of the power of the state (1948 [1947]), a diluted version of it (as when Floya Anthias and I, for example, argued that the state has the intentionality of having the monopoly of legitimate power: Yuval-Davis & Anthias, 1989), or the Foucauldian or Bourdieuvian ones (Foucault 1991b; Bourdieu and Nice, 1977).

Saskia Sassen (2007) argues that rather than weakening overall the state has changed internally and that the executive powers have strengthened on account of the legislative branches of the state. With the privatization of the state, a lot of the regulative tasks of the legislative have been lost, and at the same time, it is virtually exclusively the executive branch which negotiates with other national and supranational governance executives (such as the EU, the UN, the World Bank, the World Trade Organization [WTO]) as well as with private, national and especially transnational corporations.

This is an important observation which can explain some of the growing alienation of individuals from the state (discussed in Chapter 2). This disenchantment is particularly important in countries where voting in elections is only in order to elect members of parliament, rather than also the head of the executive. At the same time, as in parliamentary democracies, the formal endorsement of particular parties to have the right to rule the state is what gives that state legitimacy, hence the growing worry by governments about the lack of involvement by the electorate in these processes. (This worry about legitimacy also often drives ruling powers in non-democratic states to force citizens to vote, in order to get a formal endorsement – often in percentages close to 100%.[8])

I would argue, however, that Sassen's position is somewhat over-optimistic, and that states have not only shifted their internal balance of powers overall, but are also suffering a certain depletion of their power overall. As the recent economic crisis has shown, with the growing entanglement and dependency not only of local and global markets but also of the local private and public institutions, various states have been forced to bail out banks[9] and large corporations for fear of a total

---

[8]For quite a comprehensive picture regarding the rates of votes in different countries as well as where voting is compulsory or not, see http://en.wikipedia.org/wiki/Voter_turnout#Compulsory_voting

[9]For example, http://news.bbc.co.uk/1/hi/business/7666570.stm; and http://www.voxeu.org/index.php?q=node/4634

economic collapse while at the same time the governability of state agencies to reinforce regulations on that same private sector is highly limited. It is not that such regulations are impossible – and indeed, some of these regulations, such as the reintroduction of the separation between retail and investment banking, might well be introduced as well as further bank levies. It is more because of the basic legal relationships between corporations and states in which companies have the status of fictional citizens which enable the people who run these companies to escape responsibility for the results of their corporations' action – the famous 'LTD' affix.[10] In a time of globalization, companies' ability – and that of the people who run them – to change locations and thus escape having to bear the social, economic, environmental and other consequences of their actions is becoming clear in the North and not just in the South, as was the case in the past, the prosecution of BP for the oil leak in Florida in 2010 notwithstanding.[11] Moreover, while states were forced to bail out banks to avoid major economic collapses, states themselves – such as Ireland, Greece and others – found themselves forced to cut their state budgets severely, against the interests of their citizens, because they had become dependent on their credit assessment by the global financial market.[12] However, as Bichler and Nitzan (2010) point out, one can also detect major systemic fears among the most successful, contemporary, global neo-liberal corporations. Part of the explanation for this, probably, is that the two largest commodities traded globally – i.e., oil and arms – have an inherent instability as well as complex relationships with states in both the North and the South and might prove to be unsustainable in the long term under the present globalized political and economic system.

---

[10]See http://www.britannica.com/EBchecked/topic/86277/business-organization/21818/History-of-the-limited-liability-company. Interestingly, although in medieval Europe limited liability was given to members of monasteries and trade guilds, the first capitalist companies that enjoyed the protection of limited liabilities were those like the East India Company which worked as an unofficial arm of the state or empire. Gradually, however, since the mid-nineteenth century, the 'ltd' expanded to all shareholders, and more recently also to managers of capitalist companies in order to encourage investments in an expanding market.

[11]On the other hand, it is important also to realize that ecological concerns have not just been the focus for political and policy concerns but also one of the major new lucrative (or potentioally lucrative) areas into which the global neo-liberal market has been expanding – whether it is the manufacture of cars using environmentally friendly fuels or handling and recycling refuse.

[12]See, for example, the global Financial Stability Report at http://www.imf.org/external/pubs/ft/gfsr/2010/02/pdf/summary.pdf

A sense of belonging, as was argued above, is about feeling 'at home', feeling 'safe', and if not necessarily feeling in control, at least feeling able enough generally to predict expectations and rules of behaviour. It is not surprising, therefore, that under such conditions, many people feel that their entitlements as citizens who belong are under threat, or are even already being taken away from them. The discourses in which these frustrations are being expressed can follow very different directions. We shall explore in the next chapter how various constructions of contemporary citizenship have grown as a result of and in resistance to these developments. Here, however, I want to expand on another facet of contemporary globalization – mass international migration – which, in addition to the growing pressure on citizens as a result of the reconfiguration of the state and citizens' social rights, has affected and changed people's politics of belonging, whether they choose to migrate or stay in their countries of origin.

International migration

The relationship between citizens and their states is constructed as a permanent if not a static one. However, such an image is currently being challenged and technologies of governance have to be reinvented when in various states large numbers of people move in or out for a variety of economic, political, social and ecological reasons. In their by now classic book, *The Age of Migration* (2003), Castles and Miller claim that the contemporary era is the 'age of migration'. They argue that as a result of the transport and communication revolutions, the deregulation of the neo-liberal global market as well as the growing numbers of local wars and natural disasters, there are unprecedented numbers of people who are searching for a better future for themselves and their children, both as economic migrants and as asylum seekers. Some would be settling in other countries, some would be returning to their homes and/or their countries of origin after several years, and many would be developing transnational identities and lifestyles by carrying on travelling between the different locations. On the other hand, there are those, like Hein De Haas (2005), who would argue that the above picture is a myth – that these days, the percentage of international migrants in the total world population is almost on the same level as it was a century ago (about 2.5–3%).

This statistical picture, however, covers over a much more complex reality. First, given the huge growth of the global population during the last century, the actual number of people moving these days is much larger – about 150 million[13] – even if the percentage has remained more or less the same. Secondly, and even more importantly, while the percentage of migrants has largely remained static, the direction of migration has largely changed. A century ago, most of the migration was directed towards 'the New World': colonies and settler societies and countries dominated by the West in America, Australia, Africa, and to a lesser extent Asia, in which a growing economy, as well as other social, political and military factors, depended on more immigration. 'Populate or perish' was a popular slogan in the Australia of these days. However, this slogan was also accompanied at the same time by what is known as White Australia immigration legislation, guided by the principle that the immigrant population had to be of 'the right kind'. For example, the 'yellow peril' from the Pacific rim countries was kept away by force for many years until both the economic demands and a lack of alternative migrant power, as well as the rise of international anti-discrimination human rights legislation, have now changed the formal rules dominating Australian as well as other western racialized immigration legislation into these becoming a bit more open, at least on the surface (deLepervanche, 1980).

Today, most of the migration is not from Northern to Southern countries but the other way around (with the exception of 'tiger economies' like India or the Gulf oil countries), unless it is to the 'near abroad' countries, as is the case with most of those who are fleeing war and famine (UN, 2008[14]; Athukorala & Manning, 2009).

In western countries like Britain and France, although the popular slogan among anti-immigration restriction campaigners is that 'we are here because you were there' is much too over-simplistic, the interdependencies that have developed between European powers and their ex-colonies have played important parts in the development of new ethnic communities in western countries. Similar phenomena also happened in other European and industrial countries in which migrant workers were brought in to fulfil specific economic needs in post-Second World War Europe and were never envisaged to become permanent parts of the society. Many arrived under visas which constructed them as 'guest workers', which entitled them to

---

[13]See http://news.bbc.co.uk/1/hi/world/europe/1003324.stm

[14]UN Trends in Total Migrant Stock: the 2008 revision, http://esa.un.org/migration

work for a specific time in specific places and then go back to their countries of origin. However, the reality has been that many of these people have remained, 'permanently temporary' – some getting local citizenships, many bringing in other family members and many establishing a transnational lifestyle of movement between countries, as long as the political and economic situation has allowed it.

Many others arrived under refugee and asylum-seeking legislation. While in many countries there has been a long tradition of giving sanctuary and refuge to persecuted minorities (Marfleet, 2011), the formal international protection of refugees was produced in the post-Second World War period but was heavily constructed in the West, and especially in Germany, towards accepting refugees from the Eastern Bloc. With the growing number of asylum seekers from the South, especially in the post-Cold War period, we can see paradoxically that, on the one hand, the Refugees and Asylum Act becomes part of domestic legislation in Europe in the 1990s, but on the other hand, more and more regulations were passed that were making applications for refugee status increasingly difficult. In the post-9/11 era, when often anyone resisting their government was constructed as a potential terrorist, the legal status of a refugee has become more and more difficult to achieve (Fekete, 2009).

It is important to point out, however, that the legal dichotomy which is so often made in the literature and official statistics between economic and asylum types of migration is based on a falsehood. The drive for migration, which is never taken lightheartedly, is most often spurred on by a generic aspiration to have a better chance of the good life, especially for children. To a great extent this upward mobility of aspirations works, especially relative to those in the South who have not migrated, even when, in terms of local class structure in the North, these migrants and refugees remain at the bottom of the scale, given the average income gap between North and South. Moreover, in order to be able to migrate to the West, rather than just to camps in the 'near abroad', there is usually a need for migrants to have extra personal – or familial – economic resources which would enable them to arrange transportation to the West – often in indirect and illicit ways, and involving a lot of personal hardship. Therefore, rather than a bi-polar typology, voluntary and forced migration need to be seen as two extremes of the one long continuum.

Similarly, it is difficult to draw a clear line between legal and illegal migration. With the tightening up of both asylum legislation as well as that of work permits, it has become much more difficult to immigrate by legal means. On the other hand, in the deregulated neo-liberal economic markets, a lot of the leisure industry, from waiters to sex workers, as well as other unskilled branches of the economy, have come to depend on illegal migrants who are prepared to work for under the minimum wage and in extremely exploitative conditions (EWCO, 2007).

One also cannot often differentiate easily between countries of immigration and countries of emigration. In all European countries, for example, there is, on the one hand the immigration of both unskilled workers as well as professionals, especially in the high-tech and service and care industries for Europe's aging population. On the other hand, there is emigration of 'ex-pat' experts, the retired and other people who are attracted by the chance to live in other warmer and cheaper countries in Europe and outside it (Knoweles & Harper, 2010). The BBC quotes a 2006 study which started that more than 5.5 million Brits were living abroad,[15] 4 million Americans[16] and 2 million French.[17]

One of the characteristics of 'the age of migration' that Castles and Miller (2003) talk about is 'the feminization of migration'. The International Organization for Migration website says 'Women account for 49.6 per cent of global migrants', quoting the United Nations' *Trends in Total Migrant Stock, the 2005 Revision*.[18] This includes women who migrated as family dependents – either with their husbands or following them – as well as the growing number of women who migrated on their own, whether they were leaving behind them families of their own in their countries of origin or not. Again, the dichotomy between women workers and family dependents which has existed in official statistics is fictitious, as so many of the women who migrate as family dependents both want and need to work. The situation is similar concerning women asylum seekers and refugees. Often both husband and wife have been politically active, but only the husband receives the status of refugee. As a result there have been many cases in Britain, for instance, when the husband had died and the legal protection of the refugee status has been

---

[15]http://news.bbc.co.uk/1/hi/uk/6210358.stm

[16]http://www.shelteroffshore.com/index.php/living/more/americans_living_abroad/

[17]http://www.french-property.com/news/french_life/french_living_abroad

[18]http://esa.un.org/migration

taken away from the family whose immigration status then becomes precarious (Bhabha & Shutter, 1994). The whole question of the rights of family members to immigrate when one of them is granted such a right has been central in many debates concerning migration and reflects contesting ideologies about the importance of the family, whether it is always the duty of the wife to follow the husband or also the other way around, and probably most importantly, what is the family and what are its boundaries? This also covers whether elderly parents could be allowed to accompany their adult children, whether extended family are also family for the sake of migration, whether common-law families have such rights and, of course, whether partners of the same sex can be constructed as a family in migration legislation. All these questions have been paradoxically affected by, on the one hand, the tightening rules and regulations of migration and, on the other hand, the growing hegemony of formal anti-discrimination legislation.

With the growing trend of 'people on the move' and the economic and social interdependencies on migration, there is an increasing blurring of the line for 'insiders – outsiders', those who are considered 'indigenous' citizens, those who are naturalized, those who are on work permits, those who are applying for asylum, those who receive 'exceptional leave to remain', those who are on temporary contracts of work, which may or may not be open for extension, as well as the many who enter a country on a tourist visa and do not leave afterwards, remaining in the country after their asylum application has been rejected, etc. Probably one of the most confusing and problematic ways of dealing with migrants who want to stay permanently has been the recent British proposal of 'earned citizenship' (discussed in the next chapter). As Gordon Brown, as British Prime Minister, stated in his speech, when announcing a further tightening of immigration controls in the UK, the case for managed and controlled migration is not 'an issue for fringe parties nor a taboo subject' but about 'what it means to be British' (Mulholland, 2009).

'Earned citizenship' is but one extreme technology among many others which have developed in recent years in numerous countries in order to maintain some stability and control of the citizenship boundaries of belonging. Part of the reason for this – especially in the case of welfare states – is the state duty to provide various public services to migrants, from housing to health to education, as well as to monitor their incomes for tax purposes. Part of the reason for this development, however, has been as a result of a nationalist and racist autochthonic anti-immigration discourse (discussed in Chapters 2 and 3). In Israel, for example, the extreme right has co-opted the discourse of some on the left who have been calling for a one-state solution in which both Jews and Palestinians would have equal rights, but are also demanding that the Palestinians would not only swear allegiance to the state but would have to wait for up to twenty years to prove their loyalty and good citizenship.[19]

Moreover, with the growing number of migrants, the changing nature of economy and society, and especially after 9/11, technologies for regulating migration have become part of the growing discourse of 'securitization', in which (some) people's belonging to their state of residence and even citizenship has become more and more contingent (Bigo, 2002; Huysmans, 2002).

The 'securitization' discourse

During the late 1980s and 1990s, the privatization of many branches of states started to take place. This happened as a result of conservative governments' decisions, the conditions of the structural adjustment policies imposed by the World Bank and the IMF, and the dismantling of the post-communist states after the fall of the Soviet Union. During that period, as part of the 'dividends of peace', military budgets were reduced all over the globe.

Various military and policing agencies in western states tried during that period to find themselves a new *raison d'être*. This was the time when the securitization of international borders against undocumented migrants started to intensify and the notion of environmental security was also born.

'Terrorism' is a strategy for radical groupings all over the world and of various persuasions, from extreme right to extreme left, secular and religious. It has been used throughout the world, including in the West, well before 9/11 (even if we discard its popularity in Russia in the nineteenth century), during anti-colonial struggles and by Irish and Palestinian resistance movements, as well as various others, including Al Qaeda. It was also used by extreme right organizations, like those behind the 1995 Oklahoma bombing in the USA or the Tokyo subway train attack by a member of the

---

[19]See http://www.mideastweb.org/log/archives/00000783.htm, July 19, 2010.

Aum Shinri Kyo (Supreme Truth Sect) in the same year. However, the scale of the hit and the targeting of the US Pentagon and the twin towers of the World Trade Center in 9/11, and especially the timing, given the political needs of the US administration and other western governments at the time, have legitimized the rise of securitization as a primary political discourse both locally and globally and pushed some alternative official political discourses which developed in the post-Cold War political reality (including that of 'human security', discussed in Chapter 5 on the cosmopolitan question) aside. The military–industrial complex has found a much more lucrative outlet. While no doubt Bichler and Nitzan (2004) are right in claiming that much, if not most, of the profits during this era have been the result of an indirect manipulation of the market, the domination of the White House by the extreme neo-cons has opened up the arena to a whole new field of privatization, one which touches – and threatens – the heart of contemporary politics of belonging in the West, as well as in the rest of the world.

Naomi Klein (2007) and others have drawn attention to the growth in private militias and 'armed security contractors' at an unprecedented scale during the conflicts in Iraq and Afghanistan, although their role had expanded in importance even before that in other conflict areas such as in Africa.

Mercenaries are nothing new in inter- as well as intra-military conflicts. In some ways, since the end of the citizen–soldier in many western countries in the post-Vietnam war period, most of the soldiers in regular armies are not there because of their national citizenship duty but because of the pay and other 'career opportunities'. The main difference between state-controlled professional armies on the one hand and individual mercenaries who volunteer to fight for a particular state (as in the case of the Foreign Legion in France) or for particular leadership contenders (such as the failed coup which involved Mark Thatcher, the son of the ex-British Prime Minister in Equatorial Guinea in Africa) on the other hand, is that today mercenaries mostly work for companies which are run along the lines of other corporations, with shareholders and annual profits. As with many other new corporations that appeared as a result of states 'outsourcing' their services in particular areas, states (especially the USA in the case of Blackwater USA, for instance) have helped the extreme profitability of such companies not only by buying their services in bulk but also by subsidizing the building of their infrastructure.

This applies not only to military conflicts. Blackwater USA, for instance, was also centrally involved with the emergency and security services after hurricane Katrina in New Orleans.[20]

However, much of the profitability of this sector is not necessarily in providing privatized human power but in the mass development of security devices. As Naomi Klein (2007) pointed out, the securitization discourse has created a massive new market for various surveillance devices. She highlights the leadership role Israel has had in this industry and how the Palestinian occupied territories have become a global laboratory for technological innovations of this kind, especially in various surveillance technologies, which are also used more widely in civic areas of our lives, from border checks to public transport to poor housing estates.

Obama's entry into the White House and the global economic crisis which has saddled western governments with unprecedented levels of debt might curtail somewhat the continuation of the mass expansion of this market (as has been hinted at by Obama's decision to cut the 'Star Wars' programme). Nevertheless, it seems that in other areas of militarization, relating to the war in Afghanistan and NATO's expansion in the south of Europe towards Iran and the Middle East, Obama's rule in the White House has perhaps intensified this expansion rather than reduced it (Chomsky, 2009).

Overall, however, if globalization has been characterized by huge movements of goods, capital and people across the globe, it is the movement of people which has been constructed as one of the major security risks for which so many new technological devices have been produced and marketed. The effects of international migration on states' *modus operandi* and contemporary constructions of citizenship go far beyond the securitization of borders and affect the constructions of citizenship and belonging of all residents of the state, especially its racialized minorities, who might or might not have legal citizenship.

The technology for profiling the population, from school age upwards, for instance in terms of 'potential home grown terrorists', cannot but affect the differential sense of belonging of citizens.

---

[20]See http://blog.mises.org/archives/004852.asp.9. However, with the growing complexity and risk of the operations in Iraq and Afghanistan, Blackwater changed its name to Xe, and shifted its business focus to training facilities (see http://www.washingtonpost.com/wp-dyn/content/article/2009/02/13/AR2009021303149_pf.html).

At the same time, as will be discussed in the next chapter, there are also growing sentiments of anxiety and resentment among members of the hegemonic majority, especially among the relatively less well off, that they 'don't count' any more. This leads to them feeling more alien and less attached to the state and other sections of civil society.

While part of the explanation of this growing disenchantment with the state and political parties relates to the centrality in these societies of 'the multicultural question' (Hall with Yuval-Davis, 2004) and the growing ethnocization of states (which will be discussed in Chapters 2 and 3), part of this change can also be seen as a result of internal shifts within the state apparatus and the relative power of various branches of the state which affects the relationship between citizens and the state and their sense of accessibility and claim on it, as well as the contestations which arise out of the presence of contesting political projects of belonging among various members of the same society.

There are many contemporary political projects of belonging, and this book is not even trying to be exhaustive. I believe, however, that the clusters of such projects that focus (often in a non-mutually exhaustive fashion) around notions of citizenship, nationalism, religion and cosmopolitanism, constitute the heart of the political projects of belonging agendas in the contemporary world. I leave the task of discussing others – such as, for example, political projects of belonging constructed around issues of youth, sexuality, ecology, work and consuming cultures – to others. However, as a feminist, I am interested in particular in feminist political projects of belonging, and therefore will discuss briefly, at the end of each chapter, specific feminist projects that are linked to these. In addition, the penultimate chapter of the book will be dedicated to the ethics of care, which many would argue is the feminist political project of belonging.

Outline of the book

After the contextual introduction in Chapter 1, Chapter 2, on the *Citizenship Question*, explores the notion of state citizenship as well as the major kinds of rights which have been commonly associated with it – civil, political, social, cultural, and what I call spatial security rights. The chapter examines some contemporary constructions of citizenships which denote various political projects of belonging, some inspired by the state and some more demotic, emerging from the grassroots. The main ones to be discussed in this context are active/ivist citizenship, 'intimate' citizenship, consumerism as citizenship, multicultural citizenship, and multi-layered citizenship. The chapter then turns to discuss some of the main technologies that states have been using in order to define who belongs and who does not in their citizenship body, including official statistics, the registering of births and deaths as well as the use of the passport.

Modern states are usually constructed as 'nation-states', although the boundaries of both are virtually always not completely overlapping. Chapter 3, on the *National Question*, examines the ways in which constructions of nations and nationalist rhetoric have changed in the growing processes of separating national and citizenship belonging. Discourses of autochthony, indigeneity and diasporism as alternative nationalist discourses will also be explored.

Modern theorists of nationalism have often tended to see nationalist ideologies as replacing religious ones. This has never been completely the case, but in recent years, religion has been becoming more explicitly a major principle around which both national and transnational political projects of belonging are being organized. This is going to be discussed in Chapter 4, on the *Religious Question*, which explores the role of religion in contemporary politics of belonging and how this relates both to globalization and neo-liberalism. Notions of secularism, fundamentalism and multi-faithism are examined, as are the roles that religious organizations play in civil societies as well as in state legislations and policies, particularly in relation to women, sexual and ethnic minorities. The relationships between religion and culture and both of these to constructions of collective boundaries which affect people in differential ways will be highlighted.

However, Chapter 5, on the *Cosmopolitanism Question*, focuses on what seems to many to be *the* political project of belonging under globalization, i.e. cosmopolitanism. The chapter focuses on the relationships between various discourses of cosmopolitanism and their 'others', and explores notions of situated cosmopolitanism, vernacular, visceral and 'rooted'. It then examines the notions of 'human rights' and 'human security' as specific technologies of cosmopolitan governance as well as discourses of resistance to inequalities of recognition and distribution.

While each chapter briefly discusses specific feminist political movements which have been constructed in association with or in resistance to the specific political projects of belonging discussed there, Chapter 6, on the *Caring Question*, focuses on what can be seen as *the* feminist political project of belonging, i.e. 'the ethics of care'. 'Ethics of care' aim at constructing an alternative model of social and political relationship to the neo-liberal discourse of self-interest. Unlike other political projects of belonging, the ethics of care do not focus on if/where the boundaries of belonging should exist, but rather on the ways people should relate to each other. However, the chapter argues that while this question has been central to feminist, especially transversal feminist politics, it is a general question which concerns the relationships between the political, the normative and the emotional.

The *concluding* chapter of the book sums up some of its main arguments, returning to the question of the relationship between the political, the emotional and the normative, and ending with some thoughts relating to the role of hope in emancipatory feminist and non-feminist politics.

2

The Citizenship Question: of the State and Beyond

The notion of citizenship can be seen as the participatory dimension of belonging to a political community. Not all citizenships involve the same kinds of participation and not all of them relate to citizenships in a state. Indeed, one of the interesting debates in relation to particular kinds of citizenships is to what extent they differ from the status of the subject, which, unlike the citizen, is ruled but has no part in the ruling (to use Aristotle's famous definition of citizenship (see Allen & Macey, 1990). Some – and probably Hannah Arendt (1986 [1951]) would be the most extreme among them – would argue that no political system which is based on parliamentary democracy can be really democratic and produce 'proper' citizens. She thus interrelates such system of governance to the origins of totalitarianism (ibid.). Such debates have their own importance, not only generally but also in terms of highlighting the differential access to political and other powers, rights and responsibilities that different individual and groupings of people have. Being a subject or a citizen, therefore, needs to be seen as a continuum rather than a dichotomy and to be analyzed intersectionally.

Notwithstanding these differences and differentiations, however, it is the formal identification of people as having a particular nationality, or state citizenship, which constructs them as belonging to a particular collectivity, probably (still?) more than any other form of belonging, at least formally. While in some languages (e.g. Russian, Hebrew, Urdu), there are different terms to signify belonging to a national collectivity and being a citizen in a particular state, there is no such separation in English and other west European languages (such as French and Swedish) (Shanin, 1986; Yuval-Davis, 1997a: 72). And while regional, ethnic, racial and religious differences might be crucial signifiers of citizenship and belonging – and growing to be more so – when people travel to other countries they are usually identified formally, and most often informally as well, by their nationality/state citizenship – or, at least, this tended to be the situation until 'the global war on terrorism' when many, especially those of Muslim background, started to be identified everywhere by their presumed religious affiliation. Racialized black skin (or Roma origin in other cases) has also tended to have that influence, although since the 1970s informally rather than formally.

In the first section of the chapter, the notion of citizenship will be discussed as it has been debated in the literature. The notion of 'the citizen', unlike that of 'the subject', is usually marked by at least a certain sense of entitlement (C. Squire, 2007), an important public emotion which is crucial in various political projects of belonging. I discuss, therefore, the major kinds of rights which have been commonly associated with citizenship – civil, political, social, cultural, and what I call spatial security rights.

Following this, the chapter explores some contemporary constructions of citizenship which denote various political projects of belonging, some inspired by the state and some more demotic, emerging from the grassroots. The main ones to be discussed in this context will be active *vs* activist citizenship; intimate citizenship; consumerism as citizenship; multicultural citizenship; and multi-layered citizenship.

The chapter then turns to describe some of the main technologies states have been using in order to define who belongs and who does not to their citizenship body, technologies such as official statistics and the registering of birth and death, the use of the passport as a major boundary signifier of belonging, as well as more temporary forms of inclusion and exclusion.

As will be the case in the following chapters, the last section of the chapter, before its conclusion, briefly describes feminist political projects which have arisen in relation to the political projects of belonging described in this chapter.

What is citizenship?

The notion of citizenship has been contested and debated both in political and sociological theory and has come to occupy the centre-stage also in feminist debates during the last fifteen or twenty years (e.g. Hall & Held, 1989; Turner, 1990; Evans, 1993; Lister, 1997; Yuval-Davis & Werbner, 1999). One focus of the debate has been the extent to which citizenship needs to be seen as an individual contractual relationship between the person and the state, as liberal theory has tended to see it, or whether that relationship has to be seen as mediated by the (national) community within which the citizen has grown up and been shaped by, as republican and communal theorists have claimed in their different ways (e.g. Sandel, 1982; Oldfield, 1990; Avineri & Shalit, 1992). Related to that debate is the extent to which citizenship needs to be seen as an abstract category of 'the citizen' or as an embodied category, involving concrete people who are differentially situated in terms of gender, class, ethnicity, sexuality, ability, stage in the life cycle, etc. Feminists and anti-racists who have worked on the question of citizenship have tended to emphasize the latter and thus de-homogenized the notion of citizenship (e.g. Pateman, 1988; Kymlicka, 1995; Lister, 1997).

Another related debate has been the extent to which citizenship needs to be seen as a relationship between people and nation-states at all. As Jean Cohen (1999) has argued, the notion of citizenship was originally conceived in a different political context – in the Greek *polis*, the city-state. There (as mentioned above) citizenship meant the reciprocal relationship of 'rule and being ruled'. In contrast to this participatory model of citizenship, another polity, the Roman Empire, developed citizenship to be a form of legal status, with specific rights and responsibilities. Jean Cohen argues that in the nation-state these two different meanings of citizenship have come together. However, this has been a specific historical development within a specific historical moment. Many would argue that in these days of globalization, citizenship has, once again, diverged from the liberal model of citizenship in a nation-state. Yasmin Soysal (1994), for instance, has examined the notion of a regional European citizenship; David Held (1995) has examined citizenship of a world government; and Mary Kaldor (2003) has talked about citizenship in a global civil society.

More controversially, Seyla Benhabib (1999) has argued that the whole notion of state citizenship is based on the obsolete and misleading notion of the 'closed society', and Sylvia Walby (2003) states in even stronger terms that in the global era to say that society corresponds to the nation-state is more mythical than real. She discusses citizenship as membership in different kinds of polities, and of course I basically share this view of citizenship. However, I would also accept much of Bruce and Voas's (2004) critique of Walby's position (Walby, 2003), which corresponds to what I have argued in the previous chapter and also highlights the resilience of the nation-state as the major tool of governance, in spite of the many changes and limitations to its power under globalization. Hence is the continuous crucial importance of state citizenship as a political project of belonging.

The primary importance of state citizenship for the politics of belonging stems from the fact that, in spite of globalization and the rapid growth in the importance and hegemony of human rights discourse (to be discussed in Chapter 5), states are still, in most of the world, the primary source of different kinds of entitlements and rights. Engin Isin (2009), however, makes the important distinction between different components of citizenship which can be very helpful in analyzing concrete case studies of multi-layered citizenships. He differentiates between actors, sites, scales and acts of citizenship. However, as I've argued in a public seminar on the subject, it is vital for any intersectional understanding of citizenship to also add to this the component of accessible resources.[1]

T. H. Marshall, the best known communitarian theorist of citizenship in Britain (e.g. 1950, 1981), developed an evolutionary model of different kinds of citizenship rights – civil mainly in the eighteenth century, political during the nineteenth century, and social rights with the development of the welfare state in the twentieth century. Many (e.g. Turner, 1990; Walby, 1994) criticized this model as being wrong historically and as being too much based on the specific history of Britain. Indeed, Brubaker (1992) has shown in his comparative study of Germany and France how different national traditions have constructed different state citizenships and their associated rights. Moreover, rights, even if they are anchored in particular states' constitutions or protected by various UN agreements, are never fixed and secure and can never be taken for granted, as the reconfigurations of states under globalization discussed in the previous chapter are able to show. Also, different sections of the population will have easier or more difficult access to these rights as a resource.

Political rights

Liberalism has been associated with a particular type of state regime, parliamentary democracy. Parliamentary democracy is but one variant

---

[1]This debate took place at the workshop on 'Globalization, Migration and Citizenship: Shifting Boundaries, Changing Lives', organized by Elain Ho at the Royal Holloway, University of London, in January 2008.

of democracy which has been defined by Socrates as simultaneous 'ruling and being ruled' (in Allen & Macey, 1990) and by Lincoln, in his famous Gettysburg address, as government 'by the people for the people'.[2] Different western nation-states developed somewhat different models of parliamentary democracy, varying these especially with regard to the kind of relationships they constructed between the executive, legislative and judicial facets of the state. These also differed in the extent to which local government has had autonomous powers from that of central government, the space citizens have had for direct decision powers via referendums, etc. During the twentieth century, however, the two main alternative political regimes which labelled themselves as democratic have been the western multi-party parliamentary democracies and the Soviet-style 'people's democracies' in which one party ruled in the name of 'the people'. The development of welfare states in the West has been considered as a way of preventing people from supporting the Soviet-style regimes in which civil and political rights might have been curtailed but the state provided material and economic support and services. Aid policies to 'Third World' countries served a similar purpose. Indeed, after the fall of the Soviet Union, Fukuyama wrote his famous *End of History* (1992), in which he celebrated the victory of liberal democracy over its historical regime competitor. It is not surprising, therefore, that in the post-Soviet era, while in the West citizens have been reconstructed into consumers, and the welfare state has been privatized if not eroded, part of the conditions of much of international governmental, non-governmental and supra-governmental aid, has been conditioned not just on economic 'structural adjustments' but also – when the former usually failed – with establishing 'good governance' which would in principle respect citizenship and human rights.[3] Of course, when elections in such democratic regimes produced the 'wrong' kinds of government (as with the reaction of the US and other western governments to the Palestinian elections when Hamas won or the French government using the Islamic Justice and Development Party (AKP) victory in the elections in Turkey as a valid reason to prevent it from entering the EU), the emphasis on formal democratic procedures seems to have disappeared in the

---

[2]See http://showcase.netins.net/web/creative/lincoln/speeches/gettysburg.htm

[3]See, for example, http://www.law.harvard.edu/programs/about/pifs/education/sp31.pdf and http://www.g8.utoronto.ca/governance/santiso2002-gov7.pdf

international relations 'human rights and democracy' discourse. (See the further discussion on international human rights discourse and its relations to political and military interventions in Chapter 5.) The rate and quality of voting in the 2009 Afghani elections has become yet another illustration of token civil participation as gesture politics covering the real politics of military conflict between the West and the Taliban and Al Qaeda there.

And yet one should not underestimate the sense of empowerment, entitlement and belonging that this participation in elections can give to people (which, however, tends to erode to a large extent when people feel its limitations, as discussed above), as has been so clear in the first elections in post-apartheid South Africa, post-Saddam Iraq and post-conflict Sierra Leone. It is a signifying ritual where, together with the voting paper cast in the ballot box, people will reaffirm being part of, belonging to, a collective self and playing a part in determining its future direction, something which was not possible for them to do before their country gained independence or the previous dictator was removed. Most of the 'orange'/'velvet'/'rose' revolutions in Central and Eastern Europe followed a collective sense of injustice and frustration when the voting was manipulated and corrupted, and similar public emotions have had also profound effects in countries such as Zimbabwe and Iran, where the ruling groupings were better equipped to resist, at least partially, the popular challenge to the outcomes of the voting, but not to suppress them completely.

This sense of empowerment and belonging can be very misleading, however. As mentioned above, Hannah Arendt (1986 [1951]) has argued that this is where the 'origins of totalitarianism' lie, as there is no real participatory power-sharing in parliamentary democracies in which the people give up their sense of political power, the ability to affect political decisions, to a detached grouping of supposed representatives. In this sense there is a continuum rather than a binary opposition between parliamentary democracies and totalitarian regimes.

Moreover, the reconfiguration of states under neo-liberal globalization has brought about a growing apathy and alienation among the citizens of many, and especially western, states. As discussed in the last chapter, under globalization we can see the relative strengthening of the Executive branch in the state, rather than the parliamentary legislative, as it works directly with dominant capitalist agents in civil society, locally and globally, as well as with other Executives from other governments (and in the EU also the Executive in Brussels). Under most parliamentary democracies, citizens have no direct influence on the Executive, which is selected either by the head of government or by the leaders of the political parties. They vote for who will have legislative power in the parliament which, with the privatization of many of the agencies of the state, has much reduced decision-making and regulatory power (although in some parliamentary systems, such as in the UK, the voters have no influence even on who will become members of one of the two parliamentary Houses, the House of Lords). However, in a parliamentary democracy, as in a 'people's democracy', the Executive needs at minimum the nominal legitimation of the backing of the citizens in whose name they formally act. It is for this very reason that in some countries there has been a practice of compulsory voting under threats of fine and/or imprisonment. Although, depending on the type of regime in these countries, this has not always secured very high rates of voting,[4] nevertheless when, in countries like Venezuela and the Netherlands, compulsory voting was removed, the rate of voting largely declined. Western parliamentary democracies do not aspire to – and would even regard with the suspicion of corruption – too high rates of endorsement. However, when voting rates start to drop to a third or less of the population which is entitled to vote, any sense of a popular mandate is eroded, and the political project of belonging within state citizenship is endangered.

Civil rights

Civil rights are those which protect citizens' freedom, their safety, their right to own property, earn a legal income, and to be protected by the law, etc. Unlike Marshall's evolutionary model, full civil rights were far from being fully achieved for all citizens (let alone denizens and residents) at that time. Indeed, especially for women, many civil rights, such as equality before the law, freedom of expression, the right of privacy, the right to buy or right to travel without her family's permission, have not yet been fully achieved even now in many countries in the world. In the West, sex equality legislation was passed only during the last quarter of the twentieth century, although

---

[4] See http://timesofindia.indiatimes.com/voter-turnout/Compulsory-voting-may-not-be-answer-to-low-turnout/articleshow/658282.cms

in practice the gender gap persists in a variety of ways (from persisting differential rates of average salaries and glass ceilings to persisting gaps in rates of participation in domestic and reproductive labour). Outside the West, the situation is often worse and is usually linked to specific constructions of 'culture and tradition' (as will be discussed in more detail in Chapters 3 and 4). Indeed, there is also clear evidence that in many places gender as well as other forms of social inequality grew under globalization (see, for example, regarding Africa, Baliamoune-Lutz, 2007; Britwum & Martens, 2008). In many countries the state obliges women to get their husbands' permission in order to be able to work and travel, their rights of inheritance and ownership are only partial and they do not constitute full autonomous adults in courts and in contractual relationships.[5]

Globalization, however, has helped women in many cases to achieve more civil rights. Given the changing industrial production patterns, the development of trade free zones, or just the 'farming out' of industrial productions to cheaper global zones, many women all over the globe were able for the first time to have direct access to the money economy and paid labour, their highly exploitative conditions of work notwithstanding, often just when men of their socio-economic strata have found it much more difficult to find work (Mitter, 1994). At the same time, more women than ever have gained the right not only to travel but also to migrate to other countries on their own. As discussed in the previous chapter, however, the civil and human rights of migrants often fall into a grey zone in which any entitlement for civil rights is, at best, precarious.

Generally, 'the global war on terrorism' discourse has been used in many cases as a justification for curtailing people's civil rights, including freedom of movement and the right to proper judicial processes. There is a growing focus on both the curtailment of rights as well as the resistance struggles regarding the freedom of expression and information on the internet and other media, where an increasing number of states are attempting to block channels of information

---

[5]For example, in Saudi Arabia women cannot leave the country without permission from a male guardian (http://www.cnn.com/2009/WORLD/meast/07/10/women.saudi/); in the Philippines' Family Code Article 96 [a Christian-based law], in the event that the spouses have a community of property agreement but disagree on how to manage the property, 'the husband's decision shall prevail' and the wife has to go to court to seek remedy (http://www.chanrobles.com/executive orderno209.htm).

that the government of the state does not approve of[6] at the same time as information sites, such as Wikileaks,[7] are breaking the conventional boundaries for information that is openly available to the media and the citizenship public, locally and globally. This is just one example of the difficulties of attempting to construct citizenship within the boundaries of the 'nation-state' as a closed society in a reality which does not fully correspond to this.

Social and economic rights

Liberal discourse largely confines itself to the realm of civil and political rights and responsibilities. The support and protection of those members of the society who could not support and protect themselves was largely left to civil society, the family and charitable and philanthropic organizations, many of which were embedded within particular religious traditions and institutions. State governance was about defending the population from enemies outside and lawbreakers within, with the exception of some 'deserving poor'. It has taken the local as well as global rise of socialist and workers' movements, the fear of communist revolutions and the political strength of social democratic parties to establish different styles of welfare states in most of at least the western countries, in which people acquired rights to care for the needy and the elderly, education and health, according to different systems of entitlements (Esping-Andersen, 1990).

As discussed in the last chapter, with the rise of neo-liberal globalization, the structures of many welfare states started to change and there is a growing process of privatization for many welfare agencies which were previously controlled by the state. The primary relationship of citizenship between individuals and the state (as liberal political theorists have it, or mediated by the community, as communitarians and republicans have it, e.g. Sandel, 1982; Oldfield, 1990; Avineri & Shalit, 1992) has been replaced, to a large extent, by a relationship between them and private corporations or, alternatively, unelected quangos, which behave in a similar way to private corporations. However, the transformation has been even more radical. Part of the

---

[6]See http://www.telegraph.co.uk/news/worldnews/8166547/WikiLeaks-US-cables-focus-on-Iran.html (Iran) http://www.telegraph.co.uk/news/worldnews/asia/northkorea/8169468/WikiLeaks-China-would-back-one-Korea-run-by-South.htmlandhttp://www.guardian.co.uk/commentisfree/2010/nov/30/wikileaks-china-north-korea (China).

[7]See http://wikileaks.org.uk/

governmentality of neo-liberal globalization has been the discourse of self-responsibility and self care. The denial of the existence of 'public interest' has also entailed a severe curtailment of 'public responsibility' which has been the moral foundation for the establishment and evolvement of the welfare state (Offe, 1996; Timmins, 2001; Titmus, 2002). (However, as will be discussed in Chapter 4, the moralization of the 'public interest' is reconfigured in yet another way under religious fundamentalist regimes and movements.)

The classical division of the subjects of care into the 'deserving' and 'undeserving' has reinstituted itself to the extent that there are moves afoot to remove public health care from sick people who are suffering from illnesses which are partly caused by their lifestyle – such as drug abuse, alcoholism and obesity. And, of course, there is the reinforcement of the monitoring of ID papers in health and education institutions so that undocumented migrants would not be entitled to have free state services is a different manifestation of the same dichotomy.

Of course, not all welfare states have developed in the same way. Esping-Andersen (1990) has famously distinguished between three models of western welfare states, depending on the overall balance they maintain between their state and private sector services. In the developing world, many states could develop only partial, if at all, universal welfare provisions. However, as discussed in the previous chapter, under pressures of neo-liberal globalization, and mediated by supranational regulatory bodies such as the World Bank and the IMF, the demands for 'structural adjustments' in order to bring the fiscal state of these states in order conditioned further support, with drastic cuts to state expenditure that usually resulted not in more efficient state machinery or smaller military machines, but in the total or partial removal of state agencies aimed at the social, educational and caring needs of the population. The privatization of state utilities meant that in some places, such as in South Africa (where, it is reported, up to ten million people are cut off from regular drinking water supplies),[8] even the supply of drinking water, let alone electricity and gas, became in some places available only to those who could afford to pay for them.[9]

---

[8] See http://projects.publicintegrity.org/water/report.aspx?aid=49

[9] For example, see http://www.freewebs.com/lodevandendriessche/deregulationvsprivati.htm; http://energysolutionsforum.energia.org/refs/day4_summary.pdf

Cultural rights

The importance of cultural rights and how they relate to other kinds of entitlements which are part of full citizenship and belonging have arisen during the 1980s and 1990s with the growing hegemony of multiculturalist policies in more and more countries (Alund & Schierup, 1991; Parekh, 2000b). Below I discuss constructions of 'multicultural citizenship'. Here I just want to point out some of the issues involved in defining what cultural rights are and who these rest with.

As is discussed in more detail in Chapter 4, culture and tradition' are not essential, fixed, homogeneous or uncontested. However, the notion of cultural rights arises out of a paradoxical contradiction. On the one hand, it arises out of the denaturalization of culture, when the various practices of daily life, life passage ceremonies and ways of viewing the world cease to have the hegemonic discursive performative authority and the possibility of diversity is publicly accepted. On the other hand, for any definition of cultural rights which include multiplicity of cultures, there is a need to define what cultures are, or at least what are the cultures of the non-hegemonic majority. This involves a construction of homogeneous communities with fixed boundaries which, more often as not,are defined by particular cultural agents which have been picked by the state as 'authentic' representatives or the leadership of the minority or 'other' cultural collectivities. Very often, the mere act of the state sponsoring particular cultural agents as defining what is the 'culture and tradition' of the 'other' invests them with additional powers which in turn help them to dominate within their own communities contesting agents with contesting versions of those cultures.

A third, related issue is the dilemma regarding cultural rights that Jayasuriya raised in 1990. He argued that protecting cultural rights involves more than the state just making sure that particular people do not suffer discrimination as a result of their different cultures in terms of access to employment or welfare provisions. It also involves collective rights in terms of issues such as education and the law. Jayasuriya, writing in the context of Australian multiculturalism at its height, ponders where the boundaries of cultural rights should pass, distinguishing in principle between cultural needs that should be provided by the state and cultural wants that should be provided by civil society organizations and/or the realm of the family.

Under the growing privatization of the state, one would assume that the realm of cultural rights would be one of the first to be transferred to the private and civil domain. However, as will be discussed more in Chapter 4, the growing privatization of the state has been accompanied in many countries, paradoxically, with increasing state involvement as well as with the funding of separate faith schools and the growing practices of legal pluralism. At the same time, as will be discussed more below, the notion of multicultural citizenship itself has become at least partially delegitimized.

Spatial security rights

The term 'spatial security rights' is not regularly used, not in political theory literature, nor in the human rights declaration, which mentions civil, political, social, economic and cultural rights. And yet, many would argue that the most basic task of states is to keep their citizens safe and secure from both internal and external enemies.

Spatial security rights can be seen as an important bridge between those who are citizens and those who are not but are under the control of a particular state. Spatial security rights include the right to enter the territory of a state, to remain there, to work and/or study there – in short, to plan a future in a more or less secure manner.

The right for this spatial security is threatened these days not only among documented or undocumented 'people on the move' (to use the words of Kofi Annan, the previous Secretary-General of the UN). Part of neo-liberal governmentality is to remove from most people their expectations, let alone guarantees, of long-term employment in the same place, or even in the same kind of work, having regular holidays and sufficient funds in their pension to live on when they retire. Other elements of the 'risk society' (Beck, 1992) follow on, including housing and place of residence, networks of friends and even membership of a family unit. All of these push people into memberships of what Castells (1997) has called 'defensive identity movements', either ethnic or religious, which will be discussed in the following chapters. These anxieties by majoritarian members of the society are also important for policy makers, who are using the deprivation of migrants' and refugees' rights as an easy way to appease these anxieties (Fekete, 2009; V. Squire, 2009) and to reinforce a weakening sense of national 'cohesion'. The basic underlying political issues here, however, concern what the boundaries of belonging are and to what extent the construction of 'us' *vs* 'them' in this debate continues to be naturalized. This is the context in which the rise of the extreme right autochthonic movements discussed in the next chapter need to be analyzed.

Citizenship duties and responsibilities

Until now we have discussed different kinds of citizenship rights. However, the most common definitions of citizenship – theoretical and political, liberal, republican and communitarian – involve not just rights but also duties and responsibilities. One of the most controversial political issues that has arisen, since the reconfiguration of the welfare state started under the pressures of neo-liberal globalization, has been the extent to which these rights and responsibilities are autonomous of each other or whether rights are conditioned by responsibilities. The 'welfare to work' programmes, initiated in the USA under Bill Clinton, for example, and closely followed by New Labour in the UK as well as on a much more radical scale by the following Conservative/Lib-Dem government, are examples for the conditional approach. Originally, however, for example under the Beveridge Report (1942)[10] that many see as the foundation document for the British welfare state, citizenship rights, especially social rights, were perceived as being autonomously important. These were aimed at improving the public good, as the improved education and health of the nation and its worker citizens were seen as preconditions for the capacity of the nation-state to compete successfully with others.

From a different stance, those who have been active in the disability movement, for instance Mike Oliver (1996), have argued that such conditionality transforms citizenship entitlements into acts of charity, depending on the precarious availability of public or private providers. By definition, this makes social rights impossible or available only on an extremely exclusive basis, which would contradict any notion of universal human rights. This is indeed the case, as the rights of the disabled, the old, the young and other vulnerable people are by definition non-reciprocal (see the discussion in Chapter 6 on the caring question).

Which duties/responsibilities are considered important for state citizenship? These depend, at least in part, on the various political projects of belonging. Obeying the law of the land is probably seen as the most preliminary and generic citizenship duty. Payment of taxes by property owners and later on by most citizen workers is another. The duty to sacrifice one's life for the nation(-state) has mostly been highly gendered (Yuval-Davis, 1997a), and the incorporation of women into combative roles in the military has often been accompanied by the professionalization of the military and the end of national service.

---

[10]See http://www.sochealth.co.uk/history/beveridge.htm

Other duties, while often implied, are differentially important in various constructions of citizenship political projects of belonging. I would therefore like briefly to describe several such constructions – not mutually exclusive – of contemporary citizenships which have emerged both from hegemonic interests as well as from those demotic social movements that have arisen in resistance to them.[11]

Different constructions of contemporary citizenship

Active *vs* activist citizenship

In *Gender and Nation* (Yuval-Davis, 1997a: 84–5), I discussed the Thatcherite notion of the 'active citizen', which was defined by one of her ministers, Douglas Hurd (quoted in Lister, 1990: 14), as a necessary complement to the enterprise culture: 'Public service may once have been the duty of an elite, but today it is the responsibility of all who have time or money to spare'. This construction of the 'active citizen' as a voluntaristic act of philanthropy indeed does go back to the pre-welfare state period (as well as the US model of civil society which probably inspired it) and corresponds closely with the model of the 'Big Society' introduced by David Cameron in the UK with the return of the Conservative party to power in 2010 and the minimization/privatization of the state. Under New Labour, however, this construction of 'active citizenship' received a further twist when they introduced the notion of 'earned citizenship', according to which anyone applying for naturalization and the acquisition of British citizenship would have to prove that, during a period that could amount to 12 years, not only would they be obeying the law and supporting themselves and the members of their family economically without any dependency on the welfare state, but also that they would be engaged in 'voluntary' public activities in community or charitable organizations, no matter whether or not they would have the necessary time or money to spare!

In contrast, Engin Isin (2009) describes the emergence of what he and others call 'activist citizens', who are involved in new acts of citizenship, both organized and spontaneous, which can be

---

[11]However, I do not discuss here constructions of citizenship which are primarily concerned with identity politics, nationalism, indigineity, diasporism and religion, which are going to be discussed in the following chapters.

situationist, carnivalesque or focused around international courts, the social media and other forms of social networking. These 'active citizens' campaign for various citizenship rights which often transform the boundaries between human and civil rights, political and social rights, and also campaign for new additional kinds of rights such as ecological, indigenous and sexual. Importantly, activist citizens do not campaign for their rights alone or just for their grouping or collectivity: their focus of campaigning can be anything from the local neighbourhood, national, regional or global,[12] putting citizenship 'in flux' and blurring the boundaries and articulations of rights – and responsibilities – between the state and beyond the state. A similar construction of citizenship, applied mostly to Latino migrants in the USA, has been called 'cultural citizenship' (e.g. Ong, 1996; Rosaldo, 1997). However, as Isin rightly describes, the range of issues activist citizenship campaigns have covered has been much wider than that of the cultural or even identity politics arena. The recent series of popular uprisings in various Middle Eastern countries is a good example of such activist citizenship which has been focusing on generic issues of freedom and democracy. Their heavy reliance on new communication technologies such as mobile phones, the web and social networks has also been typical.

Intimate citizenship

Isin (2009) counts campaigning for sexual rights among the new acts of citizenship. Ken Plummer (2003, 2005), Sasha Roseneil et al. (2011) and others who discuss intimate citizenship focus on sexual, reproductive and other related rights concerning people's bodies and intimate relationships, and the arena of 'the personal is political' relationship, which the second wave of feminism highlighted, as a particular construction of contemporary citizenship.

Roseneil et al. (2011) explore the ways the women's movement in different countries has campaigned to help bring about changes in the law and policies concerning a wide range of issues covering, among others, marriage and divorce, both heterosexual and same sex, the recognition of same-sex relationships in immigration legislation, as well as in adoption rights, policies relating to contraception and abortion, pornography, prostitution and trafficking.

---

[12]Please see more discussion on these social movements in Chapter 5 on the cosmopolitan question.

Plummer (2003, 2005), however, covers a much wider area for what he calls the 'moral chaos' resulting from the rapid advances of technology, creating a need for new legislation on a whole range of issues, from using genetic research to create 'designer' babies' and cloning to 'redesigning' adult bodies as a result of new radical techniques for cosmetic surgery, sex changes and the transplantation of body parts.

The access to, as well as the political importance of these issues and campaigns for change would vary extremely, as Plummer (2005) points out, according to the intersectional location of people who are concerned in their societies as well as the overall political, economic and social location of their societies globally. However, as we shall discuss more in Chapter 4, many of these issues are not only hotly contested but also have come to signify important political boundaries locally and globally. As can be clearly seen in *Warning Signs of Fundamentalisms* (ed. Imam et al., 2004), active campaigns against abortion rights and gays' rights (which can be easily differentiated from more traditional conservative attitudes to these issues) can be seen as a 'litmus test' and as a warning sign of the rise of fundamentalist movements in countries in both the global North and South.[13] The political struggle for who controls the hegemonic discourse on issues relating to intimate citizenship has been fierce in recent UN conferences on the position of women, especially in the Beijing +5 and +10 conferences,[14] but also has strong local ramifications for people's lives everywhere.

The citizen as consumer

While moral, religious and political contestations around issues relating to the arena of intimate citizenship are highly prescriptive, they also need to be seen in the context – and contest – of another construction of citizenship which closely adheres to the 'free market' model of neo-liberal globalization, that of the 'citizen consumer'.

One of the first to articulate this development was Evans in his book *Sexual Citizenship* (1993), in which he discusses, among other

---

[13]See, for example, Baird-Windle (2001) on the situation in the USA; Oaks (2003), on Ireland, and Gunkel (2010) on South Africa.

[14]See http://www.un.org/womenwatch/daw/followup/beijing+5.htm; http://www.unescap.org/esid/gad/issues/Beijing+10/index.asp

issues, the ways gays and lesbians have enjoyed new inclusionary locations in British society largely as a result of their roles – and economic resources – as consumers of particular leisure, housing and other services. As I commented in *Gender and Nation* (Yuval-Davis, 1997a), the transformation of the citizen into a consumer has meant that while citizens had no power to prevent the privatization of the British rail industry, they have acquired a right, as consumers, to complain and get [symbolic] compensation if the train was late. Or, to take a somewhat different example, although they have the right to unlimited choice in seeing an NHS dentist, in reality there is such an acute national shortage in the number of dentists who are prepared to have a contract with the NHS that finding any NHS dentist in many areas of Britain is a very difficult, if not impossible, task.

While this tendency continued to develop in the UK under New Labour and more radically under the swingeing cuts to state services by the Conservative/Lib-Dem coalition government, similar developments have taken place all over the world.

Since the early 1990s various international covenants[15] as well as aid conditionality demands by the World Bank and the IMF have put pressure on most states to 'restructure', which has often meant shrinking the state apparatus, its support of needy citizens, and the abolition of state protectionism against the global market. This has become much more noticeable in the 'North' rather than just in the global 'South' after the beginning of the global economic crisis of the late 'noughties' and the crisis in the Euro, especially in Southern Europe and Ireland.

The conditionality of aid to developing countries and to others undergoing economic hardship has been reflected in the tighter connection between the 'rights' and 'duties' of the citizen and the development of the 'workfare' regime, which has been enhanced with the growing erosion and privatization of the welfare state to different degress worldwide.

An entire discourse which intrinsically connects market relations to claims of rights developed in many international and global forums. The language of 'supply' and 'demand' or 'service providers' and 'service users'

---

[15]The major ones being the United Nations Declaration on Human Rights, the International Covenant on Civil and Political Rights (ICCPR), the *International Covenant* on Economic, Social and Cultural Rights (ICESCR), and the Convention on the Elimination of All Forms of Discrimination Against Women (CEDAW).

is often used when speaking of justice.[16] Similarly, the promotion of the market economy dominates the report of the Commission on Legal Empowerment of the Poor (2008). Whereas the 'moral unacceptability' of inequality and unfairness is mentioned only in passing, the economic growth aspects are discussed at length: 'The current situation ... stunts economic development and can readily undermine stability and security.' The latter two are needed, as the report states, to enable people to enter national and global markets. The report also sees a two-way relationship between the market and human rights: 'The market not only reflects basic freedoms such as association and movement, but also generates resources to provide, uphold, and enforce the full array of human rights' (Commission on Legal Empowerment of the Poor, 2008: 3).[17] This market-based vision is further emphasized by the three 'pillars' of legal empowerment that the report highlights in addition to access to justice and the rule of law: property rights, labour rights, and 'business rights'. The protection of the market from the anarchy of a people's-led lawlessness clearly lies beneath the Commission's concern with legal empowerment. Immediately following a paragraph highlighting the benefits of the market, the report warns: 'If law is a barrier to the poor who wish to better their condition, if it is seen as an obstacle to dignity and security, then the idea of law as a legitimate institution will soon be renounced'.

The privatization of state services – and the transformation of those who have not been privatized into a quasi-corporation model – has created a new discourse of belonging. Part of the popularity of Margaret Thatcher in Britain has been the fact that for the first time all citizens/consumers were encouraged to apply for shares in the newly privatized utilities or to buy their council flats. This offered, at least formally, new arenas of ownership and control, but they were illusionary and brought about new financial burdens and a lack of control as many of them proved ultimately to be both to the people involved and to the global financial system as a whole. In the new politics of belonging of the citizen as consumer, the 'users' have contractual rights and the 'providers' formal targets for their expected performance.

At the same time, as was mentioned in the report above, the other side of the depoliticization of citizenship into consumerism is a

---

[16]See, for example, *Indonesia Framework for Access To Justice* (Byrne et al., 2007: 10–11).

[17]Thanks to Cass Balchin who brought this source and the previous one to my attention.

language of legal empowerment and the development of the discourse of the 'activist citizen' (Isin, 2009) as discussed above. As in the arena of 'sexual citizenship', this combination of consumerism and depoliticization has also had a paradoxical effect on the inclusion and exclusion of Blacks and Minority Ethnics (BME) and their 'cultural rights' in their constructions as 'multicultural citizens'.

Multicultural citizenship

In recent years we have seen the decline of multiculturalist ideologies which have come to dominate western (especially Anglo-Saxon) societies in the second half of the twentieth century. It is important to investigate the reasons for both their rise and decline and link them to constructions of citizenship and belonging.[18]

Carl-Ulrik Schierup (1995) claimed that multiculturalism was an ideological base for a transatlantic alignment whose project was the transformation of the welfare state in late or post modernity into a pluralist state in which cultural diversity rights would be incorporated into the more traditional welfare social rights. John Rex described multiculturalism as an enhanced form of the welfare state in which 'the recognition of cultural diversity actually enriches and strengthens democracy' (Rex, 1995: 31). As discussed above, however, the inclusion of 'cultural rights' as part of the legitimate provisions of the welfare state raised some fundamental issues concerning who defines cultures as well as cultural rights and how they would do so. At the same time, it is also important to realize that in many European countries and elsewhere, a recognition of pluralism and diversity has been originally linked to issues of a recognizing national minorities of long duration and only later, and in many places, in a much more partial way, included the 'new ethnicities' in their diversity policies.

The manner of devising and delivering multiculturalist policies has also been different in different states. In some, like Germany, for instance, multicultural policies were imposed top-down, while in the UK, for instance, there was much more space for initiatives within various community organizations of the same ethnic minorities. European states in general contributed more towards specific services for

---

[18]A rich resource for discussion of various aspects of multiculturalism, in Australia and globally, is Andrew Jakubowicz' website on the subject at http://andrewjakubowicz.com/

various minorities than the USA, where the focus was more on offering African Americans and other racialized minorities a greater number of opportunities in education and employment. The construction of the 'cultural' minorities also varied in the various states, differentially emphasizing issues of race, religion, language and nationality.

With all their differences, after the Second World War multicul-turalist policy makers mostly aimed to accommodate labour migra-tion from former colonies and other Southern countries, which did not seem to follow the assimilatory trajectory assumed in previous generations (Glazer & Moynihan, 1970 [1963]). This was due to many demographic and social factors, but also, to a large extent, was a result of the changes in transport and communication technologies which facilitated continuous closer contacts between immigrants and their countries of origin (see the discussion on diasporas in the next chapter). It was also an outcome of the rise in identity politics (or the 'politics of recognition', to use Charles Taylor' terminology (Taylor, 1992), in which keeping one's identity of origin and being proud of its culture and tradition were seen as the valid basis for successful maturation (see, for example, the UK 'Rampton Report' of 1981 and the Swann Report of 1985). This was the time that witnessed the rise of 'multi-cultural citizenship' (Kymlicka, 1995).

With all their relative success in normalizing plural societies in metropolitan societies, multicultural policies also faced cer-tain common difficulties. Although multiculturalism was gener-ally hailed by its promoters as a major anti-racist strategy and has been constructed by the Right as a threat to the survival of the 'national culture', if not 'the nation' itself, it has also been a target for criticisms from the Left as well. Multiculturalist policies, aimed at the betterment of the situation of minorities, still naturalize the western hegemonic culture. At the same time minority cultures became reified and differentiated from normative human behav-iour (Parekh, 2000b). They usually also ignored questions of power relations, of accepting as representative of minorities people in class and power positions very different from those of the majority of members of that community, and of being divisive by emphasiz-ing the differential cultures of members of the ethnic minorities rather than what united them with other Blacks who share with them similar predicaments of racism, subordination and economic exploitation (Bourne & Sivanandan, 1980; Mullard, 1984; Anthias & Yuval-Davis, 1992). Other critiques from the Left have been directed against both the 'multiculturalist' and 'anti-racist' positions (Rattansi, 1992; Sahgal & Yuval-Davis, 2001 [1992]). These critiques have pointed out that both approaches were based on the inherent assumption that all members of a specific cultural collectivity are equally committed to that culture. They tended to construct the members of minority collectivities as basically homogeneous, speaking with a unified cultural or racial voice which was constructed to be as distinct as possible (within the boundaries of multiculturalism) from the majority culture in order to be able to be 'authentically different'.

Such constructions did not allow any space for internal power conflicts and interest differences within the minority collectivity and tended to assume fixed, static, a-historical and essentialist collectivity boundaries. At the same time they did allow legitimate space in the public sphere for non hegemonic ethnicities as part of civil society and, contingently, the nation (as with the debate on whether 'there is Black in the Union Jack' (Gilroy, 1987) which can illustrate the case in the UK).

Towards the end of the millennium, various scholarly as well as policy attempts to construct 'critical multiculturalism' took place,[19] in which culture was theorized as a dynamic, contested resource (e.g. Bottomley, 1992; Bhabha, 1994; Yuval-Davis, 1997a: Chapter 3). However, with the growing hegemony of neo-liberal globalization, and especially after 9/11, multiculturalism as a guiding principle for diversity management policy (as well as 'aversion' management, to use Wendy Brown's [2006] terminology) has lost its hegemonic position in many countries and has even been used as a 'strawman' for explaining various social, political, security and economic crises (Vidmar Horvat, 2010). If multiculturalism has been a project for the reform of the welfare state, it should not be surprising that with the growing privatization of the state under neo-liberal globalization (as well as its securitization, especially after 9/11), its provisions should also be cut severely. After the fall of the Soviet Union and with continuous militarized conflicts in various parts of the South, especially Africa, the nature of the immigrant population has also changed to what Vertovec (2007) called 'Super-diversity'.

As Carl Schierup stated in what he calls *The European Dilemma* (Schierup et al., 2006), under such conditions, policy makers are

---

[19]For example, Werbner & Modood, 1996; May, 1999; Hesse, 2000; *The Stephen Lawrence Inquiry* (Macpherson, 1999), as well as the 2000 government report by the Working Group on Forced Marriage: *A Choice By Right*, http://www.fco.gov.uk/resources/en/pdf/pdf14/fco_choicebyright2000

caught between promoting national and European solidarities on the one hand and universal social justice in their welfare state allocations on the other hand. In the UK, Trevor Phillips, while fulfilling the role of Chairman of the British Commission for Racial Equality has declared 'the death of multiculturalism' and throughout Europe, under the guise of 'mainstreaming', new pressures have been applied to minority members to prioritize their integration into the hegemonic national collectivity in the name of 'social cohesion' (Skjeie & Squires, forthcoming; see also the special issue of *Ethnicities*, 2010).). Moreover, where multiculturalism has not disappeared as a policy (e.g. Australia), it has often been transformed into multi-faithism (see the discussion in Chapter 4).

Given the constraints on the governability of contemporary states, including well-established western states, the scale of migration and the nature of contemporary transport and especially communication technologies, such a social and political agenda as 'social cohesion' on a national scale is doomed to failure, except in those states which are in a war situation. Even there, as surveys in Israel on the growing alienation of certain sections of the youth[20] and in-fighting among the Palestinians (especially between the Fatah and Hamas) can show, such an agenda is often more a case of wishful thinking. The close connections between the 'social cohesion' agenda and the 'global war on terrorism', with their common exclusionary rhetorics (and often policies) regarding 'the different Other' (often the different Muslim Other), are therefore not incidental. At the same time, consumerist constructions of citizenship have helped to transform some of the politics of multiculturalism into issues of lifestyle and choice and enabled sections of the entrepreneurial classes among BME to occupy positions of wealth and power which were not open to them in earlier times. Hence the presence of unprecedented numbers of BMEs in Bush's right-wing government – let alone the election of Obama for presidency. Similarly, we have seen the entrance of BME women into governments in countries like France and the UK.

It is important to emphasize, however, that it is not only western societies that are continuously grappling with issues of pluralism and heterogeneity, but that this is also very much at the heart of the social and political agenda of many societies in the global South (Nyamnjoh, 2005). This is so, not only because of the ways in which the borders

---

[20]For example, http://www.haaretz.com/hasen/spages/935829.html

and boundaries of their states and nations were originally constructed when they gained independence (see the discussion in the next chapter), but also because of the effects of more recent events, partly located in the South, such as natural disasters and wars, and partly as a result of the growing restrictions on migration to the North as well as the global economic and ecological crises. In some cases, like with many African states, the debate is less, however, about multiculturalism and consumerism and more about post-conflict restructuring, tribalism and the problem of the ethnocization of the state. In the Southern states this has often been manifested as a national debate over secularity, so national belonging is framed as religious belonging, as has been happening, for instance, in countries like Algeria, India, Pakistan and post-Soviet Uzbekistan. This will be discussed in greater detail in the next chapter.

Multicultural citizenship is often just one, often contested, layer of what might be called constructions of multi-layered citizenships.

Multiple and multi-layered citizenship

Before turning to discuss multi-layered citizenship in its wider meaning, it is vital to examine the extent to which states will claim or not claim exclusive rights to people's citizenships.

States differ on the extent to which they are prepared to grant citizenship to people who also carry passports for other countries. The UK and Israel, for example, have always been very liberal in endowing dual or multiple formal citizenships, while many others, including many post-colonial countries, have refused to do so. Many people in the UK, for example, who failed to register for British citizenship when their Caribbean island became independent, lost their British citizenship because these new states refused to allow people dual citizenship. As a result, once they left Britain to visit their families in their countries of origin for a few months, they lost their right to British residency as well.

In Germany the situation was very different. Until 1991 its citizenship law was based on origin and even today it does not recognize dual citizenship. Migrant workers from Turkey who did not want to lose their rights as Turkish citizens (e.g. before 2003 foreigners were not allowed to buy immovable property in Turkey), spent their lives in Germany as 'denizens', with rights of residency but no formal political citizenship rights (Cohen, 2006; Gülalp, 2006). While originally their children, born in Germany, had no right of becoming German citizens in 2000 the legislation changed and now such children can choose, when they are 18–23, which citizenship they would prefer.

In the USA, naturalizing citizens are required to undertake an oath renouncing any previous allegiances, although this was not always obligatory (for example, Albert Einstein was not required to abolish his Swiss citzenship, although the matter had to go before the Supreme Court). For many years dual citizenship in the USA hardly existed in practice, but then more and more cases took place of American Jews who migrated to Israel and then of Americans in Canada. After that, as long as there was no perceived conflict of loyalty or a security risk, the practice became more widespread.

While some states consider multiple citizenship undesirable and legally forbid it, which results in an automatic loss of a citizenship if another citizenship is acquired voluntarily (for example, in Malaysia, China, Denmark, Japan, Singapore) or even criminal charges for carrying a foreign passport (as in Saudi Arabia), other states will allow a citizen to have any number of nationalities and may even see this as desirable as it increases the opportunities for their citizens to compete and build contacts globally, which has resulted in some states depending on the remittances of migrant workers to liberalize their nationality laws and accept dual nationalities in recent years (like the change in the Phillipines in 2003) or because they are depending on immigration (Israel).

When we talk about multiple, or, rather, multi-layered citizenships (Yuval-Davis, 1999) it is important to remember that people's citizenship is not only of a state, to which most of the discussion in this chapter has been dedicated. People's citizenship, as a full membership of a political community with its rights and obligations, is usually multi-layered, composed of local, regional, national, cross and supranational political communities, as well as often more than one national community. In the next chapter some of these communities, especially diasporic and indigenous people's communities, will be discussed and in Chapter 4, religious political communities.

It is necessary to recognize, however, that accepting dual or multiple state citizenship or incorporating plural legal systems does not mean equality for all citizens, even before the law, let alone for policy makers. One of the unintended outcomes of formal multiple citizenships is that some states, such as the UK and Israel, have passed laws which allow the state to remove the status of citizenship from people they consider undesirable, as long as this removal does not make them stateless, so as not to contradict agreed international treaties. This is clearly discriminatory towards these individuals. A blatant example in which dual citizenship has adversely affected the treatment of the state towards these citizens was the evacuation of western citizens from Beirut when Israel launched the war on Lebanon in the summer of 2006. Daiva Stasiulis (2006) described how Canadian evacuation forces picked up Canadian citizens but not those who also had Lebanese citizenship as a secondary one. This racialized approach (often the decision of the evacuation forces was made on 'visible' grounds – picking up and evacuating those who did not seem to be of Middle Eastern origin) is but a single manifestation of the ways in which belonging will construct and affect formal citizenships (see also Macklin, 2007).

In some cases, however, the has opposite has also happened. In recent years, various women's organizations in Britain and in Bangladesh, India and Pakistan have worked closely to bring about a sea change in British government policy towards dual nationals who were forced into marriage in their non-British country and to recognize their responsibility to protect these dual nationals as they would mono-British citizens.[21]

People's citizenships in their different layers of citizenship affect and are affected by their citizenships in other layers, of state and non-state polities, as collectively they have differential political powers and often differential hegemonic political projects. However, it is also worthwhile noting that people's citizenships are also affected by their locations within each polity, as these are constructed (often in unstable and contested ways) by other intersecting social divisions, such as gender, class, stage in the life cycle, sexuality, ability, etc. In this sense, the notion of multi-layered citizenship is firmly attached to those who would view citizenship as embodied. Similarly, while multi-layered citizenship does not give a monopoly to citizenship in nation-states, it recognizes that while states' roles might be changing in today's globalized world, they are definitely not withering away as some wishful thinking by certain cosmopolitan theorists would like us to believe. With the growing securitization of today's borders and

---

[21]This recognition of responsibility ironically came with its own racist baggage – that the civilized British nationals should not be dragged down by their barbaric other nationality ... This is the reason why originally the unit working on the issue of forced marriages was annexed to the British Foreign Office, rather than the Home Office.

boundaries (Bigo, 2002; Yuval-Davis, 2005a), and with the growing impossibility of gaining refugee status in any straightforward legal way and with the threat that in the future, even if it is gained, it would not be constructed as a permanent status and could be withdrawn at any time the state sees fit – such a view would be dangerously naïve.

The commonality as well as the impossibility by the 'nation-state' to contain and/or abolish multi-layered citizenship draws our attention to the different technologies which various states have been using to determine as well as control state citizenship belonging.

Official statistics and other delineating technologies of state citizenship belonging

Modern bureaucracies thrive on what is known under the umbrella terms of 'official statistics'. Regulatory mechanisms of states relate to people in terms of their statistical attributes which determine to a large extent the differential rights and responsibilities that they have as workers, voters, tax payers, soldiers and benefit receivers. Benedict Anderson (1991 [1983]), Ashish Nandy (1983) and others have commented on the profound effects the introduction of the census and official statistics have had on the construction of societies in colonial countries. For instance, instead of belonging to ambiguous and multiple ethnicities and religions, they became categorized as members of one sub-community or another, a fact that many people related to the 'divide and rule' governance technology of western colonialism.

However, many of these attributes of official statistics are not static and can change according to shifting hegemonic discourses (e.g. the incorporation of the 'ethnic question' in the 1991 British census and the 'religious question' in the 2001 one). At the 2001 UN World Conference Against Racism, for instance, Mary Robinson, who was then the United Nations High Commissioner for Human Rights, emphasized an urgent need to desegregate official statistics in order to be able to find out more accurately the position of women in many aspects of society. Kimberlé Crenshaw, who developed a socio-legal theory of intersectionality (Crenshaw, 1989), pointed out in her presentation to this session of the 2001 conference that unless such statistics were desegregated not just according to gender or race, for example, the discrimination and exclusion of particular categories of people, such as that of Black women, cannot be visible. Official statistics, therefore, and the categories according to which they are organized can have crucial effects on the ways both the boundaries of belonging and differential social locations of those who belong, are constructed in particular states in particular historical moments. It is probably not incidental that as part of their project to minimize the state and fit it more closely with neo-liberal globalized social order, the new British Conservative Prime Minister, David Cameron (*Daily Telegraph*, 9/7/2010),[22] suggested abolishing the national census in the UK after 200 years and letting the state rely on private market research data, as a more efficient and cheaper way to access the data on population that the state requires. However, given the tightening securitization discourse of the state as well as new information technologies, it is more the availability of official statistics data to the public which might be at risk rather than the centralization of all available data under this kind of new arrangement. However, as has been admitted more than once by public officers, as a result of the multiple ways and purposes by which people travel internationally these days, the ability of states to register who resides in their territory (to differentiate from who 'belongs' to it) is becoming more and more problematic with or without a national census.

Birth registration and other official statistics

It is debatable whether or not babies constitute full citizens of a particular nation-state. They are definitely not expected to fulfil any citizenship duties at that stage of development, but being registered at birth does entitle them to some rights of belonging, either directly or via their parents, such as the entitlement to an abode and the entitlement for welfare (in states where social welfare rights exist). In struggles around abortion rights in various states, the discourse of 'the rights of the unborn child' can occupy a central role in pro-life movements, such as those in Ireland or Nicaragua.

In different states and in different historical moments, babies could automatically become citizens of the state in whichever territory they were born in and/or of the state in which their legitimate father and/or mother were citizens (the *jus soli* or the *jus sangui*

---

[22]See http://www.telegraph.co.uk/news/newstopics/politics/7882774/National-census-to-be-axed-after-200-years.html

principles). Paradoxically, it was during the same historical moment in the 1980s that equality legislation was granted for the first time in many European countries, as a result of which mothers, and not just fathers, became entitled to endow citizenship on their children even when living outside their countries and/or being married to 'aliens', that other new legislation increasingly limited or made it more difficult for 'aliens' settling in these countries to gain citizenship. In Thatcherite Britain it was also the time in which the previously existing right for babies born in the country to automatically gain British citizenship was removed (WING, 1985). This was just one facet of the beginning of deterritorialization and the ethnocization of nation-states in the global era (another one, the rise of dual and triple citizenships, was discussed above).

Registration of a birth, as with marriage and death, started in the West in relation to membership of the local community, or the local parish, and it was the priest or vicar who was responsible for that registration. At a certain historic moment, usually taken as the mid-nineteenth century,[23] this registration was duplicated and then moved to a national bureau, but it was not until the computer age that a rapidly accessible list of all citizens was established and the status of each of these (or, rather, the validity of their documents) could be checked at border controls and other relevant locations.

It is important to note that already at the point of birth, registration of babies' records is more than just the fact that they belong and are member citizens of the nation. Their sex is always recorded, and thus, they are constructed already at the point of birth as one of two possible genders (something which, as many feminists engaged in the sex/gender debate have pointed out, flies in the face of biological realities, as was widely publicized in the case of the South African

---

[23]For example, in the UK, registration of births began on 1 July 1837 in England and Wales (parishes had been mandated to keep records in 1538 but many parishes ignored the order), and from then on the records were held centrally (but also duplicated by parishes) with the Registrar General of the General Register Office, who was based at Somerset House (http://www.genuki. org.uk/big/eng/civreg/).

In Italy, civil authorities began registering births, marriages and deaths in 1809 in many areas. By 1866 civil registration had became the law (https://wiki.familysearch.org/en/ Italy_Civil_Registration-_Vital_Records).

In Germany, the civil registration of births, marriages and deaths began following the French Revolution in 1792. Beginning with regions of Germany under French control, most German states eventually developed their own individual systems of civil registration between 1792 and 1876 (http://genealogy.about.com/od/vital_records/p/germany.htm).

runner Caster Semenya[24]). As their date of birth is registered, their age affects their citizenship rights and duties in issues such as the right to education, the right to vote, the right to get married and even the right to drink alcohol in some states. Moreover, in duties such as military service, their age usually intersects with their sex and ethnicity categories in terms of being called for national service in states where this exists.

Similarly, their place of birth is registered and this, in states structured in some kind of federal framework, might give them certain rights and obligations which are due only to people who are associated with particular locations, especially those identified as underdeveloped, whether it is via tax subsidies to start a business or privileged access to local universities.

Last, but not least, birth certificates will usually register the occupations of a baby's parents and immediately locate her/him within the national class structure.

Passports

States will differ on whether or not they require their citizens to carry national IDs with them. Often the requirement to carry these has been part of internal policing in states with large ethnic minorities or a multi-ethnic communal structure (e.g. Israel, the former Soviet Union and Pakistan), but also in states like France where the duty/right to carry a national ID has been associated with a strong Republican sentiment of belonging. With improving micro-chip technology and the introduction of a driving licence with a photo in countries where most of the adult population drive (e.g. the USA), the need for IDs has become more questionable, as can be seen in the recent debates in the UK on the possible introduction of national ID cards.[25] (It is important to note, however, that the debate is about the efficiency and price of such a technology of citizens' [and especially other residents'] identification, not about the need for surveillance.)

Unlike the case of IDs, carrying a passport when outside one's country has become more and more important, except for specific regional arrangements (such as in the Schengen countries of the

---

[24]See http://news.bbc.co.uk/sport1/hi/athletics/8219937.stm

[25]For example, see http://www.epractice.eu/en/news/283705

EU[26]). Carrying the passport of a specific state normally identifies people as 'belonging' to a specific nation-state when they travel outside it. Specific passports – and specific visas attached to them – will entitle or not entitle people to enter, stay, reside or work in other states. Indeed, one of the signals of the attempt to build a super-state 'Europe' has been the issue of a European passport for all EU members. While the formal intention has been to establish a 'borderless Europe', the transfer of responsibility for illegal immigration to the air and shipping companies has resulted in many cases in an even more scrupulous checking of passports than before, while the 'borderzones' have expanded to include all public arenas, from train stations to workplaces, where the border police would raid and check people's passports and legal right to be in the country.[27] An international system of stratification has been created, at the top of which can be found western passports, which can almost always guarantee their carriers the right of free international movements (including, as we have seen in the 2006 Lebanon war, the right of evacuation during emergency times), and at the bottom of which are those who have no right to carry any passport at all. In parallel, as will be discussed in more detail towards the end of the chapter, there has been a growth in the number of people who will carry two, three or even more passports of different states but whose freedom of movement and other rights have not always correspondingly grown.

Interestingly, the practice of issuing passports was internationally standardized only in 1920, although most states introduced these around the time of the First World War.[28] (The first to issue passports was the Russian Tsar, Peter the Great, in 1719. He used passports to control taxes and military service among his subjects.) Given that the association between carrying (or having the right to carry) passports

---

[26]See http://europa.eu/abc/travel/doc/index_en.htm

[27]For example, on trafficked women in UK, see http://www.guardian.co.uk/uk/2004/apr/18/immigration.ukcrime2; on the US police's raid in Iowa for illegal migrants http://www.desmoines-register.com/apps/pbcs.dll/article?AID=/20080512/NEWS/80512012/1001 (at a kosher slaughter-house!); on Malaysian-Indonesian–Australian raids regarding Sri Lankans, see http://www.sbs.com.au/news/article/1087812/Malaysia-detains-illegal-migrants;and on Germany's 'Labour Police', see http://www.nytimes.com/1993/04/02/world/german-labor-police-round-up-illegal-workers.html

[28]See, for example, Torpey (2000) and Mongia (1999).It is interesting to note, that, anticipating the Schengen agreement, France temporarily abolished passports during the era of the first European globalization – with the introduction of European cross rails in 1861.

and state citizenship is less than a hundred years old, it is interesting how thoroughly 'naturalized' that practice is.

When studying contemporary politics of belonging, it is necessary to problematize the formal as well as informal ways in which people are classified as belonging or not belonging to particular states and societies. It is important to explore the history of passports, where they and the visas linked to them were first issued, how they came to be used for immigration controls (some of which, like the British Aliens Act of 1905, preceded mandatory passports) and how they and other modes of identification documents have been used to control and regulate various other facets of citizenship. An interrelated question is what are the reasons and conditions under which certain 'foreigners' can become 'naturalized' while others – including permanent residents and sometimes even people born in certain countries – cannot.[29]

It is in these ways that the boundaries of membership in the national citizenship bodies are constructed, and these citizens need to be differentiated from all other members of the civil society under the authority of particular states on the one hand, and all members of the national/ethnic collectivities in and outside the state on the other hand. It is also vital to note the differential intersectional effects on the citizenship of people who are differentially located socially, economically and politically, let alone spatially. This will be discussed further in the next chapter on the national question.

Feminist politics of citizenship

Inclusion in the citizenship body and becoming entitled to the different kinds of citizenship rights is what much of feminism has been about, especially in the early stages of the feminist movement. Although feminists have tended to have internationalist tendencies since their inception, the history of the feminist movement has often focused on the right not only to belong, but also to participate as

---

[29]For example, Palestinians who fled from their homes during the 1948 war and thus were not there during the census were denied Israeli citizenship even if they did not move further than a few hundred yards from their home (Jiryis, 1973). Another very different example is that in 2008 France's highest administrative body, the *Conseil d'Etat*, denied citizenship to a Muslim woman from Morocco (whose husband and three French-born children are all nationals), ruling that her practice of 'radical' Islam was not compatible with French values (http://news.bbc.co.uk/2/hi/europe/7503757.stm)

equal adults in their political communities (see, for example, Lloyd, 1971; Rowbotham, 1973; Routledge *International Encyclopedia of Women*, ed. Kramarae & Spender, 2000). The first wave of feminist politics focused, at least in the West, on suffrage – the right to vote. This political right was won in many western countries at the beginning of the twentieth century (beginning with New Zealand in 1893), although in Switzerland, for instance, it was not won until 1971. In Qatar and the United Arab Emirates the right to vote was granted in 2005–06 and exercised for the first time in national elections in 2010. In the Vatican and Saudi Arabia women are still not allowed to vote.[30]

This lag in women voting after men has been explained by Carol Pateman (1988) and Ursula Vogel (1989), who argued that the right to vote was originally given to men as representatives of their familial household in the fraternal contract that replaced the pre-French revolution patriarchal one, rather than on their own.

While the right to be elected, as well as to elect, followed the suffrage, the ratios of women as elected representatives of governments and parliaments have tended to remain very low. In the case of elected positions, the global average women's participation rate has increased approximately 3% over the past ten years, and while in Nordic countries 40% of the political representatives are women it is much lower everywhere else, including the rest of Europe.[31]

Surprisingly (but much less so if one has followed the recent history of the country and the role of women in the peace process), the highest representation of women in parliament has been in Rwanda, where in 2008 56% of those elected were women.[32]

It is not incidental that citizenship – especially in its activist construction – has become a rallying cry for women in many post-colonial and Southern countries (Kabir, 2005), in which women, in rural as well as urban locations, have been struggling in a great number of ways for full participation in their political communities. The notion of citizenship has been most articulated in the Latin American women's movement, during and after the time of

---

[30]See http://en.wikipedia.org/wiki/Timeline_of_women's_suffrage#1990s

[31]See IPU, http://www.ipu.org/wmn-e/classif.htm, Women in National Parliaments: World Classification (October 2005, IPU (Inter-Parliamentary Union).

[32]See http://www.unifem.org/news_events/story_detail.php?StoryID=736

their countries' transition to democracy during the 1990s (Vargas &
Yuval-Davis, 1999).

Wishing nothing less than the right to participate in the political system, feminists historically struggled to establish the full legal
rights of women as adults, in order enable them, among other civil
and social rights, to independently own property, handle their affairs
and work, and when they worked to receive a level of pay equal to
that of men. It was not until 1981 that CEDAW (the international
convention on the elimination of all forms of discrimination against
women) was recognized by the United Nations. While in most states
legislation affirming these rights now exists, the reality is still far
from corresponding to the law in most countries and is often hotly
contested in the name of 'culture and tradition', as will be discussed
in the following two chapters.

Conclusion

When examining the politics of belonging of contemporary citizenships several issues seem to be of general importance here transcending the differentiated locations, socially and spatially, of citizens.
Paradoxically, three of these seem to contradict each other, although
mostly they are directed towards various segments of the population.
On the one hand, there seems to be a distancing between many citizens and their states, while at the same time there is an unprecedented
penetration of state surveillance into the intimate lives of the people
under their control – citizens and non-citizens. In addition, there is
also a rise in activist citizenship, which protests against the reconfiguration of the state and its associated diminishing and depolicization
of citizenship rights. This, in turn, helps to blur and transcend state
citizenship boundaries. It affects the sense – and politics – of belonging of the citizens and directs them to be active not just, or even not
primarily, in response to state policies, but also within other political
communities which transcend the state, as well as in other modes of
identity politics, both legal and illegal (which will be discussed in the
following chapters). This, together with the growing porosity of territorial borders as a result of technological as well as social, economic
and political changes under neo-liberal globalization, has created a
growing need for vigilance by the state towards growing segments of
its population. The 'minimalist state' model promoted by neo-liberals
is focused on the maintenance of law and order, although to a certain

extent, under the global economic crisis, it is also being forced to adopt some minimal re-regulation in the economic financial sector. The state has always constructed 'the private sphere', and its penetration and vigilance has always been much more intense regarding those marginal elements it has considered as potentially threatening its stability. This penetration intensified in the welfare state and the policing of the poor has been done by internalizing certain sets of values rather than just by threatening the power of the state. At the same time, the technology of surveillance has largely developed, facilitating external rather than the internal imposition of law and order.

The contradictory intensifying shifts in the construction of multi-layered citizenship under neo-liberal globalization reflect changes in both the governmentality and the governability of the state. Another dimension of these shifts reflects what Stuart Hall calls the multicultural condition of contemporary society (Hall with Yuval-Davis, 2004). This relates to what Paul Gilroy (2004) terms the conviviality of difference, in which people in metropolitan societies live today which has changed but by no mean eradicated racialization, and which Ali Rattansi (2011) calls interculturalism. It also relates to the ways in which states construct borders and boundaries that differentiate between those who belong and those who do not. Much of the literature on globalization refers to the 'deterritorialization' that comes with it (Basch et al., 1994). As we have already seen, some of the new technologies of determining belonging have been deterritorialized in the sense that these days 'borders are everywhere'. Passports and visas are checked in the workplace, in train stations and in airports when exiting, rather than when we reach our destinations.

This, however, has not affected the construction of belonging to particular states and territories. As discussed above, there is a growing phenomenon of dual and multiple state citizenships on the one hand, but also a growing of statelessness on the other, which threaten the governability of states as these blur the linear boundaries of belonging.

Dual and multiple citizenships – a reflection of growing transnational migration in the post-Second World War era, and especially in the post-Cold War era – are legally and politically complex, but possible in principle to regulate using various intergovernmental agreements. Statelessness is much more problematic, not only because of the unregulated – often criminal – ways in which the migration of such people takes place, and their lack of papers, which can be a result of either the ways they had to leave their home or because they got rid of them so as not to be able to be sent back there. This is also problematic because it challenges the fundamental logic of a twentieth-century politics of belonging, which were based on state citizenship.

The citizenship politics of belonging, therefore, in spite of their continuous primary importance, in some ways have come to play a secondary role, or rather have become imprinted with, other political projects of belonging. As in the UK with 'Norman Tebbit's Cricket Test', mentioned in the introductory chapter, people can be born in a particular state, be educated there, be its formal citizens, and yet not be constructed as 'really' belonging. For that to occur, they would have to be not just citizens but also members of 'the nation'.

We shall now turn, therefore, to examining the national question and its corresponding contemporary politics of belonging.

3

The National Question: from the Indigenous to the Diasporic

Introduction: nationalism and belonging

In the previous chapter we discussed the ways contemporary forms of state citizenship affect and are affected by contemporary politics of belonging. It was stated that often citizenship and nationality – especially in western societies – are being equated as a result of what Shanin (1986) has described as the 'missing term' in many western languages, where the 'nationality' of a person does not differentiate between citizenship of the state and membership of a national collectivity. Indeed, the term 'nation-state' points to a political project that aims to obliterate the difference between the two, as Gellner's famous definition of nationalism states: '[Nationalism is a] theory of political legitimacy which requires that ethnic boundaries should not cut across political ones' (1983: 1). And yet, throughout history, many states have not been national (from city states to religious empires) (Cohen, 1999) and it is also argued by many – indeed by most nationalists – that the existence of the nation often preceded the establishment of the nation-state (see below for some of the main theoretical positions in this debate). National membership is more ephemeral than that of citizenship. It is not (or, at least not always) constructed by written (state or non-state) law. At the same time, in twentieth- and early twenty-first-century discourse, it has been both wider and more naturalized than state citizenship (when it was not equated with it). Indeed, the Roma, who do not have a nation-state of their own, have claimed the right to be called a nation in order to obtain collective rights in the governing of Europe and the UN:

> Acknowledging the transnational character of the Roma identity and its common roots from India, we strongly support the right of Roma to be recognized by the UN, by the regional inter-governmental bodies and organizations, by States and by the whole world, as a non-territorial nation.[1]

So what is 'a nation' and how does one belong to it? This is the first question discussed in this chapter, which goes on to examine the relationship between such 'nations' and 'nation-states' as well as 'homelands' and the spatial locations of these nations.

The chapter then turns to investigate the different hegemonic and alternative discourses of belonging to nations. In particular, it examines the discourse of indigenousness within both hegemonic and racialized minorities and relates these to the notions of autochthonic belonging/s. It then explores the notions of diasporism as another common contemporary political project of belonging, which is differentially experienced by various members of the same national and ethnic collectivities. Towards the end of the chapter there will also be a brief discussion of feminism and nationalism.

We shall turn now to examine the notion of the nation and how this relates to questions of ethnic and cultural heterogeneity and belonging.

What is 'a nation'?

Some scholars and experts on nationalism have composed a kind of 'shopping list' of national characteristics so as to enable those who are confused by these to determine whether a particular collectivity constitutes a nation or not. One such popular list, composed by Stalin (who, before becoming the ruler of the Soviet Union was considered the expert on the national question in the Bolshevik party), has played a major role in the politics of Eastern and Central Europe during most of the twentieth century. His list, composed of five items, was very strict. Any collectivity that did not incorporate all the items on his list, would not be considered a 'proper' nation (1976 [1929]: 13):

> A nation is a historically evolved, stable community of language, territory, economic life and psychological make-up manifested in a community of culture.

---

[1] See http://academic.udayton.edu/race/06hrights/WCAR2001/NGOFORUM/Roma.htm par. 177

Because of this definition, for instance, the Jews in Tsarist Russia were not considered by the Bolsheviks to be a nation, as they did not have their own territory. Although Stalin later attempted halfheartedly to 'correct' this by formally establishing Birobijan as the 'Jewish homeland' in Soviet Russia, Jews continued to bear the results of not being recognized as a 'proper' nation in the Soviet Union throughout its existence and as a result suffered from certain disadvantages *vis-à-vis* members of other 'proletarian' nationalities in the USSR.

Unlike the strictness of Stalin's definition, others, like Craig Calhoun (1997: 4) and, following him, Umut Ozkirimli (2005), have produced much longer lists, but are much more inclusionary in their approach. Calhoun applies the principle of 'family resemblance' and considers that 'the rhetoric of nation' includes at least some of the following features: boundaries of territory or people or both; indivisibility of the national unit; sovereignty, or at least the aspiration of it; government legitimacy by 'the people'; popular participation in collective affairs; direct membership of individuals; culture – including some combination of language, shared beliefs and values, habitual practice; temporal depth, including past and future generations; common descent or racial characteristics; special historical or even sacred relations to a certain territory.

The difference between Calhoun's and Stalin's definitions, however, is not just in terms of the length of their 'shopping lists' and their inclusivity, but also in the much more important ontological difference between an attempt to define the 'essential' nation and a list of observed types of 'national rhetoric'. This difference cuts to the heart of the debate on what a nation is.

This debate is closely related to others concerning the time of nations' first historical appearance. 'Primordialists' (such as Van den Bergh, 1979; Geertz, 1993 [1973]) claim that nations have always existed and are simply a natural extension of family and kinship units. The boundaries of the nation are therefore determined by its genealogical continuity from generation to generation and the role of nationalist intellectuals and activists has been to liberate the nation that has always been there, even though it was never free and independent before modernity. 'Ethno-symbolists' (such as Armstrong, 1982; Smith, 1986) have made a weaker argument, claiming that although the nation as such is a product of modernity it is not completely new, but rather a continuation of its pre-modern ethnic origins. 'Modernists' (such as Gellner, 1983;

Hobsbawm, 1990; and Anderson, 1991 [1983]) have seen nations as an invention of historically specific times, as a result of industrialization, the need for national markets and, above all, as will be discussed below, the needs of the modern state. This last tendency has been especially strong among Marxist scholars, although Stalin's shopping list of a definition is closer in some ways to the primordialist approaches.

Whether primordialists or modernists, all these approaches view nations as a concrete objective reality that can be identified. However, Sami Zubaida, another 'modernist', who demonstrated the central role of strong states in 'producing' nations in the Middle East as well as in the West (Zubaida, 1989), has argued nevertheless, that historically there is no common origin or characteristics of nations which have emerged in different historical contexts, involving various processes of migration, conquests and settlements, carried by different classes – or even by the same class but with a very different sociological character – in different parts of the world (Zubaida, 1978; 1989). He argued that although different nationalists share the same ideological field, nationalist ideologies themselves have been very different, from crypto fascist to socialist to liberal.

The analytical shift from nations to nationalist ideologies has been vastly aided by the ground-breaking work of Benedict Anderson (1991 [1983]), who defined the nation as an 'imagined community'. We shall discuss Anderson's work further when we examine nations and their boundaries below. Here it is important to emphasize that by defining the nation as an imagined community, its ontological basis is no more in the world 'out there', and instead resides in the minds of the people who view themselves or specified others as belonging or not belonging to that nation. Homi Bhabha (1990a, 1994) continued to develop this theoretical approach and wrote about 'the nation as narration', as does Calhoun (1997) when he discusses 'the rhetorics of nations' rather than nations. Calhoun (1997: 6) distinguishes, however, between nationalism as a discourse (which produces the idea of the nation), nationalism as a project (pursued by specific social movements), and nationalism as an evaluation (political and cultural ideologies that claim superiority to particular nations). Floya Anthias and I (1992; Yuval-Davis & Anthias, 1989) have also written in this tradition when we argued that there is no inherent difference between ethnic, racial and national collectivities, they are all constructed around boundaries that divide the world between 'us' and 'them', usually around myths of a common origin and/or common destiny. The same people can be labelled at a specific historical moment and/or location as an ethnic community (such as, for example, the Jews in the USA), as a race (because they were constructed in Nazi Germany) and as a nation (because they are in Israel). We differentiated between the specific projects around which these collectivities are constructed. While ethnic collectivities are about the recognition of difference and the specificity of culture and tradition, racial collectivities are about fixating and reifying the boundaries of difference so as to exclude and inferioritize the Other. The national collectivities' project is about some form of political self-determination, often, but definitely not always, in the form of a separate state. This political discourse can use certain ethnic and racial signifiers as a tool to justify its claim for the unification of certain people, territory and state.

It is important to examine the notion of 'national self-determination' in this context. This is one which has been widely accepted by both 'Right' and 'Left' throughout the twentieth century. Interestingly, however, the UN has never defined what is meant by either 'national' or 'self-determination', while incorporating the principle of 'national self-determination' as part of its constitution (Yiftachel, 2003).

This is probably not only because the notion has been very controversial, but also because different nations have been constructed in different ways and continue to evolve and be reconfigured in contested ways. This has created a vague context (conveniently left open to accomodate shifting political circumstances) for a variety of political struggles in different parts of the globe. And yet, as Delanty (1995) has commented, the principle of national self-determination has created a 'moralization of geography'. This morality can take on a fundamentalist bent when the holy unity of the trinity of people, state and territory is sanctified in a religious, as well as nationalist, discourse. This happens often, but not exclusively, in settler societies, when the claim for self-determination is reinforced by narratives about the 'promised land', 'the chosen people' and a 'New Jerusalem'. However, the same 'promised land' can be 'promised' to and definitely claimed by more than one nationalist project – either wholly, as in the case of Palestine/Israel and other settler societies, or in relation to specific locations, such as Alsace or Gdansk, or particular regions for which particular nationalist movements claim the right of cessation, such as in the Basque country or Eritrea (see the further discussion on the relationships between nationalist and religious political projects of belonging in Chapter 4).

In our book, *Unsettling Settler Societies* (1995), Daiva Stasiulis and I claimed that the differentiation between 'nation-states' and 'settler societies' cannot be seen as mutually exclusive, as

> the cleavages and conflicts that characterize 'settler societies' can be found in virtually all contemporary societies which involved encounters between indigenous and migrant groups and successive waves of free and coerced migration corresponding to different phases of capitalist development and political upheavals. (Stasiulis & Yuval-Davis, 1995: 2)

The indigenous population of the Saamis who can be found in different North European countries are but one contemporary example of the ethnically fragmented societies out of which homogeneously constructed 'nation-states' were constructed even in Europe. The growing saliency of separatist regional nationalist struggles in various Southern European countries is another example of these processes of national formation.

Nations and 'nation-states'

Michael Hechter (2000: 323–4) argues that nationalism arises when there is non-congruence, i.e. a lack of fit between governance unit (e.g. empire) and nation. This is a bit of tautological reasoning because it assumes the nation as a pre-given, while historically the nations themselves were often constructed during the struggles to establish the nation-state.

A common approach in the literature on nationalism (e.g. Snyder, 1968; Smith, 1971; Ignatieff, 1993) is to create a typology that distinguishes between civic nationalisms which rely on state citizenship to signify membership of the nation and ethnic nationalisms which rely upon ethnic origin of my own work (1997a), I have argued that rather than dichotomize these types of nationalisms, which often correlates to a binary distinction between the good (civic) and bad (ethnic) nationalisms, we need to look upon these as different facets of specific historical constructions of nationalisms which are often contested, and must also differentiate between the genealogical facet of ethnic nationalist projects that rely on 'blood' and the cultural ones which rely on a common language and/or 'tradition'.

Liah Greenfeld (1992) outlines 'five roads' to the establishment of modern nations: of England, France, Russia, Germany and the

USA. She sees these nation-states as the earliest and most important ones in the construction of the contemporary world. She differentiates between the individualistic civic nationalism, which she
claims developed first in England and was inherited by its colonies and later by the USA, and the collectivist ethnic nationalist
ideologies of Russia and Germany. France, she claims (1992: 14),
represents an ambivalent case, as its nationalist project was both
collectivist and yet civic.

It is not clear whether Greenfeld sees her 'five roads' as not only
the earliest ones but also as the archetypical models which were followed by later nationalist movements elsewhere. Benedict Anderson
(1991 [1983]) is clearer on this point. Anderson also sees in nationalism the product of modernity. While defining nations as 'imagined
communities', he emphasizes the fundamental socio-economic and
communication media changes that enabled new ways of understanding the world to be possible. The emergence of national
consciousness was possible because print languages created unified
fields of exchange and communication and also created new fixities
in languages of power.

Unlike Greenfeld's 'five roads', Anderson differentiates between
three distinct historical models of nationalism: of the American
'creole nationalism'; the European 'linguistic nationalism'; and
Imperial Russia's 'official nationalism'. Third World nationalisms, in
the works of Anderson as well as those of other 'modernists' (e.g.
Gellner, 1983; Hobsbawm, 1990), have tended to be seen as a product of specific groupingss of elites and *intelligentia* in emerging national
movements, choosing and 'buying' one of these available western
historical models – or sometimes choosing and picking some combination of elements of more than one model. Partha Chatterjee (1993
[1986]), however, challenged this 'modular' approach and claimed
that the process was more complex than this and includes imagined
differences from, as well as similarities to, western nationalist models. While defining nationalism in the Third World as a derivative
discourse, he points out the ambivalence in political, and especially
cultural, national discourses, as they have had to signify at the same
time modernization and national independence. As such, the process of mimicry of the colonial powers in nationalist projects in the
colonial world was limited. Igor Cusack (2003) talks of the constructions of African 'national cuisines' used by various African national
leaders as signifiers of the cultural essence of African nations, which

makes them at the same time similar to and different from western nations. Chatterjee (1990) argued that this ambiguity is the reason the position of women and the ways they behave and dress has been so central in nationalist discourses – it has been a reflective response to the centrality of discourses on women as signifying the culture of 'the other' in the racialized colonial gaze. The unveiling (or reveiling) of women, their education and participation in the military, have all been perceived as crucial moments of change in the nation as a whole (see also, Yuval-Davis, 1997a: Chapter 3).

Similarly, Chatterjee points to the crucial roles that non-state national movements played in the production of the nation, especially in what he calls its spiritual domain. He argues that anti-colonial nationalism creates its own domain of sovereignty, of the 'authentic' national culture, within colonial society well before the political battle with the imperial power begins. The crystallization and legitimation of this are crucial for any chance of political change and the emergence of the new post-colonial state.

The post-colonial 'nation', then, has been constructed before it had a state. As Monserrat Guibernau (1999) and others point out, there is also a growing number of nations today that have been constructed with little or no reference to a state at all, as will be discussed later in the chapter. Questions of national boundaries and belonging, however, exist in all nations and citizenship in a state is virtually never the one exhaustive way of national belonging, even in nations with the most civic construction.

Ethnic, cultural and religious differences have been endemic to most societies, although, as Michael Mann (2005) and in a somewhat different way Ghassan Hage (1997, 2002) have argued persuasively, the drive for homogenization has been central to all nation-building movements and under certain circumstances a tolerance of ethnic differences can be transformed into violent, and not just cultural, ethnic cleansings. This drive for homogenization has existed throughout nationalist histories, but it has gained strength under globalization. Arjun Appadura (2006) described this phenomenon, somewhat poetically, as the transformation of identities under these conditions into 'predatory identities', which reject a pluralist co-existence with other identities. As Yiftachel (2003) points out, in states controlling divided ethnic/national communities, the dominant community attempts to construct an ethnocracy, i.e. a state which systematically privileges it in terms of access to power, resources and symbolic belonging. As we have seen in the example of the Roma above (as well as in more general diasporic politics which will be discussed below), ethnocization of the state and deterritorialization of the nation can go hand in hand.

Diverse societies, as Michael Walzer (2004) has argued, have developed highly successfully under empires. In a similar vein to Mann, Walzer claims that democratic regimes are much less able to tolerate ethnic diversity than empires. This is the reason why, after the fall of empires, so many ethnic conflicts and wars take place. Moreover, the borders of nation-states in post-empires, especially in the post-colonial world, have often been agreed upon in international agreements by super- and imperial-powers in which very little consideration has been given to the wishes and sentiments of the local populations. This can be seen in the history of border delineations of states as different from each other as Zambia, Thailand and Finland. The fall of the Soviet empire, therefore, has been one of the reasons for the proliferation of ethnic conflicts and wars during the 1990s throughout Eastern Europe/Central Asia as well as the Balkans.

However, the change in political regimes, or even more generally, the specific sense of insecurity which comes as a result of political or economic crises and/or living in 'failing states', needs to be seen as only one of the factors that have affected the ethnocization of national politics of belonging in the contemporary world. This is a reflection of a much wider shift, a shift towards the hegemony of identity politics in the world of the late modernity 'risk society' (Giddens, 1991; Beck, 1992). Prescribed identities seem to become almost the only stable thing in one's shifting world in which place of abode, employment or even family, let alone friends, are not stable, long-term fixtures of one's life anymore. Under such conditions, there is a growing attraction to political projects of belonging which will mobilize these prescribed identities into what Manuel Castells (1997) has called 'defensive identity communities'.

Nations and their boundaries

Liah Greenfeld (1992: 7) argues that 'different nationalisms share little' except that all members of all nations, no matter what their class positions are, will think that as a result of their membership of that specific nation, they can 'partake in its superior, elite quality'. And thus, in some ways, all peoples are the 'chosen people'.

But who is a member of the nation, and how does one become this?

As mentioned in Chapter 1, this depends on particular political projects of belonging and how they define the pathways to membership of particular nations. Enoch Powell, as a minister in the Conservative government in Britain in the 1970s, argued that 'the West Indian does not by being born in England, become an Englishman' (quoted in Gilroy, 1987: 46). For Norman Tebbit, a minister in a later Conservative British government, the test was not the ethnic/racial origin but loyalty to the English cricket team – he deemed those who applauded the other team as not belonging to the English (constructed as being equivalent to British in this discourse) nation, even if they were born in Britain and had British citizenship and a British education. The 'essential' characteristics of membership in the British nation as defined by David Blunkett (2002), a British Home Secretary, were knowledge of the English language as well as a belief in the values of the Human Rights Act.

Exclusionary national boundaries, therefore, even within the same nation, can be constructed and imagined in different ways and according to different organizing and categorical principles (i.e. biological origin for Powell, emotional attachment and identification for Tebbit, shared culture and value for Blunkett).

What does it mean, then, for national boundaries to be imagined? According to Benedict Anderson (1991 [1983]), nations are imagined communities 'because the members of even the smallest nation will never know most of their fellow-members, meet them, or even hear of them, yet in the minds of each lives the image of their communion' (1991 [1983]: 6).

However, this definition is problematic because such an abstract form of community is necessarily based on an imagined abstract sense of simultaneity. In such an imagination, former and future generations are necessarily excluded while they are so central in nationalist imagery, whether their organizing principle is common 'ethnic origin' or not. Moreover, as Poole comments (1999: 10), such a definition assumes that if the members could, against all odds, meet everyone in the nation face to face, imagination would become redundant. However, any construction of boundaries of belonging, of a delineated collectivity that includes some people – concrete or not – and excludes others, involves an act of active imagination. This is indeed the case, especially in the way Castoriadis discusses imagination (1987; see also Stoetzler & Yuval-Davis, 2002). According to him, the whole classificatory system of signification is imagined, often pre-experienced, and mostly pre-thought. We need a notion of the nation, which – as has been shown previously, can be constructed in many different ways – before we can determine if the people we meet belong to it or not (in the same way that we need a notion of masculinity and femininity before we determine whether the newly born baby is a boy or a girl). For Poole, the real difference between what constitutes imagined communities and a notion such as 'society' is whether or not imagining them as a community informs the way people live and relate to each other.

Understanding nationalist imagination in such a way does not contradict, however, Billig's (1995) argument, followed by Reicher and Hopkins (2001), that categorization is not a natural cognitive imperative. They argue that categorization always occurs in a context of argument *vis-à-vis* other positions. The crucial question is not the existence of the category but how it is constructed and where its boundaries pass. In the case of the politics of belonging, such an 'argumentative' approach can explain why boundaries of belonging become more salient and fierce when their hegemonic naturalness is challenged and why any social category and boundary can be – and often is – contested.[2]

It can also explain why people who are differentially located within and outside the collectivity would view the boundaries of the nation in different ways – as more or less exclusionary, as more or less permeable (e.g. many Jews saw themselves as members of the German nation while German Nazis saw them as not belonging). The question of whether or not 'there is Black in the Union Jack' (Gilroy, 1987) has been the subject of major political contestation in Britain and the recent rise of the British National Party in the UK as well as similar political parties in many other western countries presents similar contestations in regard to the inclusion of Muslims. Categorical

---

[2] A gendered example of such contested constructions of belonging can be seen in the famous case of Sandra Lovelace (see www.ichrp.org; *Lovelace vs. Canada* (30 July 1981), Com No. 24/1977, CCPR/C/13/D/24/1977, UNHRC). Sandra Lovelace, a Maliseet Indian in Canada, had married a non-Indian and left the reservation. Following her divorce, she sought to return to live on the reservation. However, under section 12(1)(b) of the Indian Act she had lost her rights and status as an Indian by marrying a non-Indian; Indian men who married non-Indian women did not face the same consequence. The Human Rights Committee decided that the most relevant claim was under ICCPR Article 27, relating to the rights of minorities. Lovelace was 'ethnically Maliseet' and had been absent on account of marriage 'only for a few years'. The HRC ruled that the Indian Act was discriminatory because it denied Lovelace her right to culture. The ruling led to the repeal of many gender discriminatory provisions in Canada's Indian Act.

imagination is always situated (Stoetzler & Yuval-Davis, 2002). Moreover, it is not just a question of the re/cognition of boundaries and categories of belonging, but also the differential emotional attachments and identifications that a variety of people would feel towards the same 'imagined community', as well as their normative value systems. Nationalist discourse does not have to relate to questions of law and order or any other political or even social questions. There might be a position – for instance, Martin Albrow (1997) – which argues that describing a certain country as British, French or German, and similarly in describing plants and birds as British or French, needs to be understood separately and outside nationalist discourses claiming a country for a particular nation. However, the mere naming of a country as Israel or Palestine, Rhodesia or Zimbabwe, Ceylon or Sri Lanka is at the heart of many nationalist projects of belonging. Describing a certain bird as 'British' or 'Scottish' or the prickly pear as Israeli or Palestinian is not external to nationalist discourses in the way that Albrow envisages. This is even more important when we label a particular person who immigrated to the UK from Pakistan as 'British', 'Black', 'Asian' or 'Muslim'.

This labelling is at the heart of the discourse that Michael Billig (1995) calls 'banal nationalism'. He points out that nations need to be reproduced continuously, not just during times of national crisis, and for this to happen 'a whole complex of beliefs, assumptions, habits, representations and practices must also be reproduced. Moreover, this complex must be reproduced in a banally mundane way, for the world of nations is the everyday world, the familiar terrain of contemporary times' (Billig, 1995: 6). This, as Billig illustrates by a variety of examples, mostly from Britain, is done by the 'constantly "flagging", or reminding, of nationhood' (1995: 8). This is performed in order to reinforce people's national identities which are, according to him 'ways of talking about nationhood'. It involves selective processes of remembrance and forgetfulness; of hailing certain occasions, artefacts, personal attributes, particular heroes and celebrities, as well as certain territories and landscapes – even the weather (about which Bhabha (1994) chose to end his essay on 'dissemi-nation') – as particular features of one's nation and nationalism and a signifier of belonging.

Many areas of state legislation, in addition to explicit state and non-state narratives, can play significant roles in these processes of reinforcing 'banal nationalism'. The selection of particular days as national holidays and of particular historical events and people as subjects of commemoration and/or study in the national curriculum; the determination of criteria for immigration and naturalization; the relationship between religious and state laws; the regulation of sexuality – these are but a few examples of the features of specific banal nationalist discourses. Needless to say such discourses tend to construct people of particular ethnic/racial origins, religious beliefs, sexualities or even classes, as deviating from the 'normal' or 'typical' members of the imagined national communities, as thus as belonging or not.

Karl Deutch (1966 [1953]) defined nations as those collectivities in which communication is easier inside their boundaries than outside them. Billig points out that there is nothing 'natural' about this process, but rather it is a result of continuing practices within various state and non-state agencies, such as the media, which reinforce this process. Reicher and Hopkins (2001) show how specific national practices and national differences are being constructed via emotive nationalist discourse in a time of national crisis and banal national 'flagging' in a time of peace. In other words, at the same time that 'banal nationalism' strives to naturalize nations and belonging to nations, it is an ongoing multi-dimensional labour of reproducing the nation and its boundaries as configured by particular political projects of belonging.

John Armstrong (1982) talks about the 'symbolic border guards' that help to maintain national boundaries. While Billig focuses mainly on discourses that are directed away from the ideological and political centre towards the periphery of the nation, these symbolic border guards relate to the whole field of cultural practices, including religion, language, gender relations and more. Armstrong argues, as does Anthony Smith (1986), that cultural myths and symbols have an enduring ability which is being reproduced generation after generation, notwithstanding changing historical and material conditions. However, this seeming endurability can be very misleading. First, because our view of it stems from a very particular temporal perspective, we can see the cultural stuff that has endured all these historical changes and survived. We cannot be fully aware, however, of how much cultural stuff has *not* survived historical changes, archaeological and historical research notwithstanding. Moreover, even with cultural stuff that has survived historical changes, their meanings can and do undergo radical changes and contestation and often these become merely symbolic markers of identity (Gans,

1979). It is true that many of these symbolic border guards have the power to evoke extreme emotions and passions, especially in times of national crisis. The cry can be to defend 'our women and children' (Enloe, 1990), or not to let 'them' 'swamp our culture and tradition', and it often does not matter that this 'culture and tradition' is among what Hobsbawm and Ranger (1983) have called 'invented traditions' and, in all appearance to the contrary, have not existed for that many years (including, for example, the Victorian inventions of Christmas trees and Scottish tartans or the much more recent import of full body veiling, including black gloves, for Muslim women in South Asia). The fact that these are 'invented traditions', however, does not affect their 'normalizing' and 'naturalizing' power.

Unifying constructions of the nation are not only constructed by cultural and symbolic boundaries but also by spatial ones in which territorial borders play the role of boundaries of social membership and belonging as well (Antonsich, 2009). Of particular importance for national emotive narratives is the construction of particular territories, usually with specific borders, as the national 'homeland' whose boundaries can also define the boundaries of national membership: 'How ... does space become place?' ask Carter, Donald and Squires in the introduction to their edited volume *Space and Place* (1993: xii), 'By being named: ... by embodying the symbols and imaginary of a population. Place is space to which meaning has been ascribed'.

'Homelands' and the construction of national boundaries and borders

The meaning of the homeland can be inscribed via its physical nature. 'What is a man who has no landscape?' asks Athos in *Fugitive Pieces* (Michaels, 1996: 86): 'Nothing but mirrors and tides'. The inscription can also be highly ideological – 'Every true republican has drunk in love of country, that is to say love of law and liberty, along with his mother's milk. This love is his whole existence', said Rousseau (1953 [1772]).

(Hetero) women/mothers are, indeed, often constructed as embodiments of the homeland. In peasant societies, the dependence of the people on the fertility of 'Mother Earth' has, no doubt, contributed to this close association between collective territory, collective identity and womanhood. Women are associated in the collective imagination with children and therefore with the collective, as well as the familial, future. Women represent the homeland, as well as the home.

A figure of a woman, often a mother, symbolizes in many cultures the spirit of the collectivity, whether it is Mother Russia, Mother Ireland or Mother India. In the French revolution, its symbol was '*La Patrie*', a figure of a woman giving birth to a baby, and in Cyprus, a crying woman refugee on roadside posters was the embodiment of the pain and anger of the Greek Cypriote collectivity after the Turkish invasion.

However, it is not the figures of the women/mothers alone that symbolize the homeland, but rather the imaginary social relations networks of belonging in which they are embedded. As Doreen Massey stated (quoted in Carter et al., 1993: introduction): 'Instead, then, of thinking of places as areas with boundaries around, they can be imagined as articulated movements in networks of social relations and understanding'.

I would disagree with Massey concerning the relative (lack) of importance of borders and boundaries of both places and collectivities (as mentioned above and see Stoetzler & Yuval-Davis, 2002). However, she does highlight the crucially important trait of the imagining of places in general and homelands in particular, as embedded in the social relations and history around which narratives of belonging are woven, and thus the same location can be constructed in totally different – and sometimes contradictory – nationalist narratives of particular political projects of belonging.

However, as we have seen in the previous chapter, borders do play a central role in the discourses of states and nations, though in reality they are nowadays less significant to the control of immigration, which may take place elsewhere. However they retain strong symbolic resonances bound up with the founding myths of the state. Claims for changing borders, 'retrieving' pieces of 'the homeland', are one of the most popular reasons why nations go to war (next to defending the 'women and children' (Enloe, 1990)). As Sahlins (1989: 271) claims, borders are 'privileged sites for the articulations of national distinctions' – and thus, of national belonging.

This central, but contested, facet of borders is in contrast with the naturalized images of homelands that assume a complete congruence (or identity) of people, state and territory. The spatial location of the homeland is endemic with assumed borders that are often signified by mountain ranges and rivers, as well as sea and ocean coasts (although the question of how far from the coast the national border is has been a cause of endless international disputes). It is an open question (historically variant) whether the national and international legality of those 'natural' borders follows on from, or rather causes, these naturalized border imaginings. Often the 'naturalized' borderlines do not correspond with the boundaries of the ethnic and national communities who live near the borders.

And it is also an open question, with different answers in different historical cases, whether the adherence to such borders relates more to strategic military and economic interests (of the states themselves or external powers as is the case in many post-colonial countries) or whether such borders are inherent to collective imaginings of particular homelands. It is important to remember, however, as has already been discussed in the previous chapter, that many international borders have not been a formalization of national imaginings of homelands. Rather, they have been the result of negotiations between imperial powers, often without any consultation with the national movements involved, controlling a particular part of the globe. Ben Anderson (1991 [1983]) discusses the construction of mutually exclusive borders as an effect of imperial western intervention in many parts of the world, although even today, in mountainous places, such as the Afghanistan/Pakistan border, these borders exist more in maps than on the ground, marked only sporadically in strategic places. Whatever their origin national borders acquire highly significant meanings in nationalist rhetoric, if not in direct relation to myths of national origin then as an expression of the legitimacy and sovereignty of the nation-state. In this way national borders become a specific form, spatially bounded, of collectivity boundaries, dividing the world into 'us' and 'them', constructing permanent residence and citizenship in particular states as the determining signifier of membership of the nation in these political projects of belonging.

Homi Bhabha (1994) tries to avoid the pre-supposition of national cultures and boundaries. He wants to write on 'the Western nation as an obscure and ubiquitous form of living the *locality* of culture. This locality is more *around* temporality than *about* historicity' (1994: 140, original emphasis). In this way, Homi Bhabha is trying to avoid assuming that any particular borders and boundaries are a given in/for any particular locality (in a way this is the antithesis of Albrow's position mentioned above), so that national rhetorics about 'the homeland' as well as about 'national history' can be interrogated without any naturalizing discourse of belonging being pre-applied to them.

Unlike in mainstream political theory approaches, in which the boundaries of the nation and the boundaries of the civil society of the state are assumed to be overlapping, Bhabha sets high store in 'the liminality of cultural modernity' (ibid.), its indeterminacy, openness and inclusivity, and in what he calls performative spaces of 'in between' and 'meanwhile' which are ambiguous and contested and thus play crucial roles in nationally fluid constructed narratives.

Bhabha's work draws attention to the fact that national narratives can play two seeming contradictory, but actually complementary, roles. On the one hand, they seek to construct national boundaries of the 'us' against the outside 'them', and on the other hand, they include discourses which provide space for cultural and other forms of difference within the nation. While the members of the nation are usually constructed as belonging to one or another nation, the membership body of the nation is never perceived as homogeneous: it is composed of and encompasses differences in terms of gender, generation, class and usually also other perceived social divisions that become the subject of a particular national rhetoric and are constructed as encompassed within its boundaries, such as ability, sexuality and – particularly relevant to the point here – of ethnicity and race. In times of rapid large-scale population movements and change, these two narratives of exclusion and inclusion tend to get mixed up and blur the hegemonic national boundary. As discussed in the previous chapter, debates about social cohesion are aimed at both resurrecting and reconciling the differentiation between these two (e.g. Cantle, 2001; Goodhart, 2004; see also Yuval-Davis, 2004a and b; Yuval-Davis et al., 2005). In some ways their measure of success in different localities and among different sections of the population might indicate the extent to which nationalist narratives can still remain hegemonic in contemporary society. This question which is embedded within nationalist discourse is related to, but different from, the question of the extent to which different states manage to maintain legitimate regimes of law and order within their populations.

As Susan Condor (2006) points out, vernacular representations of nationalist discourse often reflect these heterogeneous constructions of the nation, affected by people's differential situated gazes at the nation, their different social, economic and geographic locations, different identifications, and different normative and political value systems. On the contrary, as Condor points out, she found in her study of nationalist discourses in England that the lack of national homogeneity in Britain was perceived by most participants as a signifier – and thus paradoxically as a unifying factor – of British national superiority.

This relates to the rise of a nationalist discourse that some authors (e.g. Moallem & Boal, 1999; Hussein and Miller, 2006) have named 'multicultural nationalism', differentiating it from both civic and ethnic nationalisms which are prevalent in the literature on nationalism discussed at the beginning of the chapter. Multicultural nationalism is a nationalist ideology which recognizes the multi-origin and multicultural composition of contemporary nations and, as Condor (2006) found, even sees in this a reason for national pride, expressing the sense of conviviality of difference which has emerged in metropolitan societies and especially in cities under the social, economic and political reality of globalization (Gilroy, 2004, 2005).

Multicultural nationalism (which is closely related to multicultural citizenship discussed in the previous chapter) has to be distinguished from the cosmopolitan ideologies which are discussed in Chapter 5 (although in the writings of some authors, e.g. Michael Keith [2005] this boundary is fuzzy). They do not aspire to cancel or transcend national boundaries. They perceive the nation as multicultural in itself and see its diversity as a strength rather than a weakness. This ideology might correspond to and can be seen also as a product of multicultural policies, especially in education, but cannot be simply reduced to it. There is growing global recognition, not just in settler societies or in post-colonial and post-empire societies, that nations are not homogeneous and that regional autonomy as well as trans-border migration have shaped the composition and the boundaries of membership of the nation.

This does not necessarily mean, however, that such a recognition of the diversity of origin and celebration of a multicultural lifestyle can cancel the pressures for the ethnocization of states, for homogeneity and for clear boundaries for multicultural differences, which some have alluded to as 'thick liberalism' (Tamir, 1993). The pressures coming from the state for 'integration' and 'social cohesion' operate within civil society as well. As Sartre pointed out in relation to liberal Antisemitism (Sartre, 1989 [1944]), tolerance towards the other exists as long as 'the other' stops being different and becomes 'like us'. Otherwise, especially in the reality of 'the global war on terrorism', those who insist on remaining different and who do not show their loyalty to the national collectivity are not subject to exclusionary and racialized social attitudes and practices. While some would celebrate 'multicultural nationalism', others, as Wendy Brown (2006) and Georgie Wemyss (2006) have shown, would use tolerance as a social practice for 'regulating aversion', keeping firmly in place the boundaries between 'us' and 'them'.

Autochthonic politics

Others, however, are not only not celebrating the conviviality of difference, but are also not prepared to tolerate such 'others'. They see in them a threat and choose to construct the relationship with them as a 'zero-sum' game – it's either 'us' or 'them'.

Since the 1980s there has been a lot of discussion about the rise of what Barker (1981) called 'the new racism' and Balibar (1990) *'racisme différentialiste'* (see also Modood's notion of 'cultural racism' [2003]). Unlike the 'old' racism, the focus for these kind of racialization discourses rested not on notions of 'races' or other kinds of different ethnic origins, but on different cultures, religions and traditions which were seen as threatening to 'contaminate' or 'overwhelm' the cultural 'essence' of 'the nation'.

Peter Geschiere (Geschiere & Nyamnjoh, 2000; Geschiere, 2009), a Dutch Anthropologist working on African countries (mainly Cameroon, the Ivory coast and Zaire), pointed out that often the crucial element in the construction of the boundaries between 'us' and 'them', and thus the focus for such political projects of belonging, is of a somewhat different kind that has gained new impetus under globalization and mass immigration. It can be seen as a form of temporal-territorial racialization, of exclusion and inferiorization, that are the outcome of the relative new presence of particular people and collectivities in particular places (neighbourhood, region, country) which Geschiere sees as the global return to the local. The term Geschiere uses for this phenomenon is the Greek word *'autochthony'* (= to be of the soil), which is used in the Netherlands and in the Francophone world,[3] where the crucial difference is between the 'autochthones' who belong and the 'allochthones' who do not.

A common preoccupation of autochthonic exclusionary politics has been linking belonging to where one's ancestors have been buried, as Geschiere found in many African countries. A similar campaign has also been evolving among the Palestinians (see, for example, Hajjaj's (2007) film *The Shadow of Absence*). But such practices can be seen also among many other ethnic and national communities. A side effect of these autochthonic politics has been the growing – though very expensive – practice of flying migrants' bodies to be buried in their country of origin.

Geschiere (2009: 21–2) rightly claims that 'autochthony' can be seen as a new phase of ethnicity, although in some sense it even surpasses ethnicity (see also Yuval-Davis, 2011b). While ethnicity is highly constructed and relationally and situationally circumscribed, there are limits to these reconstructions regarding name and history. Autochthony is a much more 'empty' and thus elastic notion. It states no more than 'I was here before you' and, as such, can be applied in any situation and be constantly redefined and applied to different groupings in various ways. It combines elements of naturalization of belonging with vagueness as to what constitutes the essence of belonging, and thus can be pursued also by groups which would not necessarily be thought to be autochthone by others.

For example. a few years ago, the local theatre, Arcola, in the neighbourhood in which I live in London, ran a play called *Crime and Punishment in Dalston*. It was based on dialogues that the play's writer (Farr, 2002) had heard when he worked with local youths, which had to do with the enmity between Afro-Caribbeans, who claimed belonging to the locality, and the Turkish and Kurdish refugee communities in Dalston, whom they saw as illegitimate outsiders. I heard a similar discourse from some of my local black students when I was teaching the sociology of racism. The repudiation, accompanied by

---

[3]In the declaration of the rights of indigenous people, the UN has accepted autochthony as the French equivalent of indegeniety. Geschiere, however, differentiates between the two and after reflection, for the sake of intuitive clarity, I decided to follow him and, as can be seen below, I keep the term indegeneity mostly to apply to the discourse of marginal racialized people in settler societies claiming rights rather than to the discourse of privileged hegemonic majorities defending access to privileges and resources, although as will become clear I view these two constructions as interpenetrating each other and one cannot totally differentiate between them in many historical locations.

various 'descriptions' of the refugees as dirty and lazy – and having
come to take our housing and our jobs – was of a very similar character to what the white working class used in order to repudiate these
blacks and their families fifteen or twenty years earlier. This is, of
course, not a unique phenomenon, and the growth in gang warfare
among different groupings of young people from both majority and
various minority groupings in most global cities can be seen as one
form of expression of such autochthonic politics of belonging.

The notion of autochthonic politics of belonging is very important
when we come to understand contemporary extreme right politics
in Europe and elsewhere. The people who follow these politics continuously argue that they are not racist, although they are very much
against all those who 'do not belong'. In some cases, such as in the
case of the English Defence League, the organization has formally
adopted both Jewish and Gay sections, as well as Hindu, Sikh and
Afro-Carribean supporters, [4] something unimaginable in the older
kind of extreme right organizations with neo-Nazi ideologies. In
France, Marine Le Pen who is the current leader of *Front National*,
originally led by her father, goes to great lengths to deny that her
party is racist, anti-Semitic or homophobic. She claims that 'the
right-left divide makes no sense anymore. Now the real division is
between nationalism and globalisation'. Thus she warns of the 'dilu-
tion' and 'wiping out' of the French nation and civilisation, under
threat from 'never-ending queues of foreigners'.[5]

Autochthonic politics of belonging can take very different forms
in different countries and can also be reconfigured constantly in
the same places. Nevertheless, like any other forms of racialization
and other boundary constructions, their discourses always appear to
express self-evident or even 'natural' emotions and desires: the protection of ancestral heritage, the fear of being contaminated by foreign influences, and so on – although, as Geschiere points out, they
will often hide very different notions of ancestry and contamination.

The discourse of autochthony is closely related to that of indigeneity, although, as we have seen in the case of Dalston, it expresses
a politics of belonging that can also be adopted by those who would
not necessarily be considered, especially by others, as indigene. To be

---

[4]See http://theenglishdefenceleagueextra.blogspot.com/2010/11/jewish-gay-join-us-english
extremists.html

[5]*Guardian*, 22 March, 2011

an indigene means to 'really' belong to a place, and to have the most 'authentic' claim for rights over it. The discourse of 'indigeneity' has been used by hegemonic majorities who have utilized it as an exclusionary means to limit immigration, prevent citizenship rights, call for repatriation, and in its most extreme form, for 'ethnic cleansing'. In such a discourse, the immutable links of people, state and territory are formulated in their most racialized forms. It is a discourse with growing political impact across Europe and in other western countries with the rise of globalized neo-liberalism and in some ways this has become even more so with the global economic crisis within that system. Like autochthony, it can be interpreted as one kind of 'defensive identity community'. Castells (1997) has talked about it, as mentioned above, although it must be emphasized here that while the feelings are real and the effects of neo-liberal globalization produce a certain sense of people losing control over their lives in the ways discussed in the previous chapter, they do not reflect the realistic anxieties of the hegemonic majorities being 'swamped' by the immigrants and their cultures.

It is important to re-emphasize, however, that this phenomenon should not be seen as being confined only to the West. When I visited Gujarat in India in 2002 as part of an international feminist delegation to investigate the gendered effects of the inter-communal violence there (IIJ, 2003), I heard the repeated claim by the BJP (Bharatiya Janata Party) supporters that Muslims had no legitimate place in Indian society, as they were not indigenous but rather had come there as invaders (500 years ago ...). Even less surprising, such claims of indigeneity are common in post-colonial societies – among the recent and most virulent ones have been those promoted by Mugabe in Zimbabwe[6] as well as in other societies in the South that are torn apart by different forms of ethnic conflicts.

And yet, the discourse of 'indigeneity' has also played a central role in the politics of inclusion and recognition, of claiming rights.

Indigenous politics of belonging

The 2007 UN Declaration on the Rights of Indigenous People affirms a long list of rights to which indigenous people are entitled, from their

---

[6]The 'real' indigenous people in Zimbabwe, the Bushmen of the Kalahari, who are a racialized minority in Zimbabwe, are not, needless to say, those who are 'defended' in the rhetoric of Mugabe and his people.

right not to be discriminated against by other people, to their right
to keep their own cultural traditions, to be able to use their territorial and other traditional resources and keep their self-determination
(as communities or nations). What this declaration neglects to do,
however, is define who these 'indigenous people' are.

The global movements of indigenous people, or of 'first nations',
have grown out of resistance movements of groupings of the population who are the racialized descendants of the inhabitants of various
European Settler societies. Many of them have been nomadic tribal
societies; most, but by no means all, were part of stateless societies;
all have suffered discrimination, inferiorization, displacement and
dispossession to varying degrees.

However, the boundaries of who is entitled to call themselves
'indigenous people' have been fuzzy and are expanding all the time.
This will largely be discussed below. However, in order to demonstrate the double-edged character of indigeneity, one needs to
remember that the extreme right BNP (British National Party),
and similar political organizations in other western countries,
have called themselves movements of indigenous people and have
claimed protection under the terms of the UN declaration to what
they believe is the threatened existence of 'indigenous Caucasian
people' in Britain.[7]

The UN and human rights advocates' championship of indigenous
people, however, is due to the fact that the discourse of 'indigeneity'
is generally used by movements of the largely excluded, dispossessed
and marginalized remnants (although, as in some Latin American
countries, they can still constitute the majority of the population) of
the societies that existed before or on the margins of settler and other
nation-states (Feldman, 2001; see also Blaser et al., 2004). They are
frequently seen, by themselves and by others, as an 'organic' part of
the land and the landscape, and all other inhabitants as part of the
'imposing society' (to use an Australian Aboriginal expression) who
dispossessed them. A major focus in their struggles is the call to recognize their 'land rights' over where they used to reside and worship
before the European invasion (even when the indigenous people are
located in Europe itself, as in the case of the Saami in Scandinavian
countries). As they had often been stateless nomadic populations
with no written records of the territories they customarily used, they

---

[7]See, for example, http://isthebnpracist.co.uk/

had no official land titles registered to their name, as would be the case under a bureaucratic state apparatus. As the lands they claim are now often privately as well as state-owned, their claims have frequently been met with fierce resistance by settler societies and states, as well as endorsed by human rights discourse and eventually, with reservations, also international law.[8]

One of the questions that arises in the attempts to define who are the indigenous inhabitants of a particular territory concerns the temporal dimension. Although frequently in the narratives of indigenous people's movements, 'they have occupied a specific territory from time immemorial' (Abu-Saad & Champagne, 2001: 158), usually the crucial date of authenticity is fixed as that of occupation at the time of European colonization. This can prove to be Eurocentric. It constructs the past as if history started when the contact with the Europeans was established, and covers up previous population movements and colonizations (as happened in Algeria, for instance, with the Arab settlement in Berber lands, and with the Amerindians, in empires such as the Aztec and the Mayan). Another question, however, even more central to our discussion here, concerns the form of ownership to be claimed by those 'land rights' movements. Should it be given to individual members of the 'first nation', in a way that would not limit their freedom to sell the land? And to individual families (in which case the ownership would usually go to the male heads of households) or to each individual adult which would also include the women as land owners? Or should the 'land right' be transferred collectively, as a Trust (and who should have the decision-making powers in these Trusts)? And most importantly, should their rights to the land be exclusive, or could other members of the society (as well as the state itself) continue to have rights on that land as well? What are the political, let alone the economic, conclusions of indigenous land claims? These are important questions not just in relation to the nature of plural legal systems which are being adopted in various settler societies as the result of (a partial) recognition of the indigenous people's collective claims, but also in relation to our discussion here on different kinds of nationalist rhetorics. Contestations regarding the boundaries of indigenous people

---

[8]The 1989 ILO Convention 169 Concerning Indigenous and Tribal Peoples in Independent Countries, especially Articles 8 and 9, obliges signatory states to recognize indigenous laws – 'where these are not incompatible with fundamental rights defined by the national legal system and with internationally recognized human rights'. Building upon this, in September 2007, after more than two decades of debate, the UN Declaration on the Rights of Indigenous Peoples was approved.

often focus on those who live in urban areas as non-'authentic', who should not share in the entitlements of membership which should be confined only to those who live in traditional 'homelands' or reserves (Ramirez, 2010).

Although indigenous people movements have adopted national-ist discourses and are known collectively as 'First Nations', they are virtually always divided into separate kinship and tribal groups with different languages and customs and with claims to different terri-tories within the settler state. One of the most divisive practices that is taking place in various settler states, such as in Canada, the USA and Australia, is the use of DNA tests among indigenous people in order to determine who are 'authentically' (or 'autochthonally') descendants of the local claimants and who are descendants of other kinship groups that were displaced into these territories by the set-tlers and as such have no part in the land (including mineral) rights of the local indigene. This is only one of the ways in which construc-tions of belonging to 'first nations' prove to have differential effects on different members with different social and economic locations.

This practice casts a shadow on what is considered to be Indigenous people's 'spiritual' unity with the land: 'We are the land. More than remembered, the Earth is the mind of the people as we are the mind of the earth ... It is not a means of survival ... It is rather part of our being, dynamic, significant, real' (a Laguna author, quoted in Tsosie, 2001: 184).

Feldman (2001) would argue that such claims are part of criti-cal transformative pedagogy – a 'strategic essentialism', to use a well-known expression of Gayatri Spivak (1993) – which can pre-pare the ground for an exclusive claim on the land when enough political power has been accumulated for self-government as an enclave within the nation-state, if there is not enough power/num-bers of people to claim a full 'take-over' of the state (as happened in Algeria, Zimbabwe and, in a somewhat different manner, in South Africa; see Stasiulis & Yuval-Davis, 1995). If this is the case – which I believe it often is – then indigenous people's movements need to be considered as simply a sub-category of nationalist rhetoric.

However, there are also arguments (e.g. Reynolds, 1996) that the aboriginal perception, for instance, that 'they belong to the land', rather than that the land belongs to them, paves the way for an alter-native, non-exclusive, mode of ownership and sovereignty in which more than one ethnic/national collectivity can co-exist.

Such a claim, for an alternative nationalist discourse, has also been argued by Gilroy (1997) and others (e.g. Boyarin, 1994; Raz-Krakotzkin, 1994), as applying to diasporic discourses.

Diasporism as an alternative discourse of belonging

Gilroy attempted to contrast nationalist sentiments based on 'notions of soil, landscape and rootedness' with the idea of diaspora as 'a more refined and more worldly sense of culture' (1997: 328). Avtar Brah (1996) incorporated into her normative notion of 'diaspora space', not just racialized diasporic minorities but also all sections of the society, including the hegemonic majorities of western societies, who should all occupy decentered and non-privileged positionings in civil society. Postmodernist discourses on 'travelling cultures' (Clifford, 1992), 'nomadism' (Bradiotti, 1991), 'hybridity' (Bhabha, 1994) and 'living at the border zones' (Anzaldúa, 1987; see also Lavie & Swedenburg, 1996), have inspired and echo these constructions of diasporism.

Some of the critiques of such literature (e.g. Helmreich, 1992; Yuval-Davis, 1997a; Anthias, 1998; Ifekwunigwe, 1999) pointed out that the binary, naturalized and essentialist ideas about kinship, nature and territory, that are so characteristic of more traditional nationalist rhetoric, nevertheless often creep in 'through the back door' in these theorizations. Moreover, diasporic politics very often tend to have a very different set of values and political dynamics from the ideal type described above. Unlike the Simmelian (1950) and Schutzian (1994 [1976]) constructions of 'the stranger', which only focus on the context of the stranger in her/his new environment and their relations with and positionings in that society, members of diasporic communities are often also engaged in narratives of belonging, or of yearning to belong, not (or not only) in relation to the country/society where they live, or even a 'cosmopolitan' boundary-less humanity, but in relation to their country, nation and/or state of origin. As Sara Ahmad (2000) pointed out, the construction of 'the stranger' is a form of fetishism that is produced in the naming and is devoid of any real human characteristics. It is just a reflection of the gaze of the one who has named her/him as such.

As Robin Cohen (1997) has shown, diasporas are much more heterogeneous than the above theories would have us believe. Moreover, as the NGO document of the 2001 World Conference Against

Racism in Durban pointed out, western people working in the Third World are often described as 'ex-patriates' while Third World people living in the West are described as migrants or immigrants (their average class location in the corresponding societies also tends to be very different). The hegemonic western gaze has prevailed in this, as in so many other instances.

Also, what Gilroy and some others do not take into account is the effects that 'diaspora yearning and ambivalence' can have on 'the homeland'. Mechanisms of identity regulation, which have a symbolic meaning as boundary reproduction for the members of the diaspora in the countries where they live, can have serious effects on the continuation of national and ethnic conflicts in 'the homeland' (Yuval-Davis, 1997a; Anthias, 1998). Skrbiš (1997) has commented on the changing relationships between diasporas and home countries, from passivity to active interactions, around times of rising conflict and war in the homeland, in his case Croatia. Contributing funds to various 'causes' and struggles in the homeland can often be the easiest and least threatening way for members of the diaspora to express their membership and loyalty to the collectivity. Such acts of symbolic identification, which are part of contemporary identity politics, can, however, have very radical political and other effects in the 'homeland', a fact that might often be only of marginal interest to the people of the diaspora.[9] As Ben Anderson (1998) has pointed out, diasporic politics are often reckless politics without accountability and without due democratic processes. At the same time, as more and more ethnocracies develop, in Central and Eastern Europe as well as in the South, laws parallel to the Israeli and German 'laws of return' are being developed, and states are constructed that see as their body of citizens all the members of their ethnic collectivity rather than those who are living in their state territories. In states like Lithuania – but also Ireland – presidents of the state will have lived all or most of their lives, until they were called to fill the post of president, outside the borders of the state.

As Pnina Werbner (2002) argues, the structure of diasporas in different countries and the relationships among themselves as well as in

---

[9] A good example of the above are the funds raised for Hindutva political projects in India (see AWAAZ South Asia Watch's tracking of Hindutva funds in Britain, http://www.countercurrents. org/comm-awaz270204.htm). Similar studies were done also on Hindutva fund raising in the USA as well as Irish and pro-Israeli Jewish.

relation to the homeland can be chaotic and often there is no clear hierarchical structure or even a formal one. Nor should one construct all members of a particular diasporic community, let alone all those who originate from them, as sharing an homogeneous membership in the same diasporic or national community. And yet, diasporic communities as a whole, and political leadership within them in particular, fulfil crucial roles in various political projects of belonging in both the countries where they live and in their countries of origin.

The development of transport and communicative technologies in the second half of the twentieth century has produced new possibilities for maintaining contact between diasporas and homelands. The spatial/temporal shortcuts in the communication between diasporas and homelands have intensified the level of information as well as the level of interaction between the two. Maybe even more importantly, they have enabled people in the diaspora who were previously isolated from each other new possibilities of getting together and might have changed discourses of belonging. In some nationalist struggles, such as in Kosovo, for example, it enabled a quick 'delivery' of nationalist diasporic young male 'volunteers' to constitute the bulk of the Kosovar forces (the ANA, Albanian National Army) that fought the Serbs in Kosovo in 2001 (Kaldor, 2007: 12).

In others (or in the same communities at times when there is no acute armed conflict), the effects can be very different. Diasporic communities, whether of Mexicans, Indians or Israelis, actually become more transnational when a large number of their members continually commute between 'the homeland' and their country of official residence or often official citizenship, thereby becoming part of the globalized market.

However, as will be discussed further in the next chapter, such transnational commuting can also take place in order to reinforce, or often even to create, a cultural and religious embeddedness in members of young diasporic generations as a mode of counter-defensive identity collectivity constructions. And even more importantly, discussing diasporic politics of belonging should not make us forget that the same people have also developed various forms of belonging – practical, emotional and/or ideological – to the countries where they live, and thus should always be considered within such a multi-layered context.

Before turning to discuss religious politics of belonging I would like to briefly describe, as is the case at the end of each chapter of the book, the various feminist politics which developed in relation to different kinds of nationalist political projects of belonging.

Feminism and nationalism

If in the western world women started organizing in order to claim their full and equal citizenship rights, in the colonial South or wherever national liberation struggles were fought, feminists became engaged in the general national struggle. Kumari Jawayardena (1986) traced some of the major feminist movements of this type since the time of the first wave of feminism in countries like Egypt and India. They argued that there was no sense in fighting to be equal to the men in their societies, if even the men were not free citizens of their own national collectivity and state. Similar, more elaborate arguments of this nature were expressed by such feminists in more recent national and revolutionary struggles, such as in South Africa, Palestine and in the Kurdish movements.

At the same time, and especially where more of them have been in touch with feminists from other countries, feminists have tended to resist those people, usually men, who argued for a 'revolution in stages' – i.e. first national liberation and then women's liberation. They argued that as women constituted about half of the nation, no national liberation could take place without them, and they fought men's attempts to prevent them from receiving an equal share of post-liberation resources (see, for example, Connell, 1998, on the Eritrean and South African women's movement; also Alexander, 1994, on the Caribbeans). The Palestinian feminists even went so far as to call for a 'women's parliament'[10] in order to debate such issues. There have also been similar women's organizations among both Diasporic and Indigenous peoples' movements. For reasons that will be discussed more in the next chapter, such internal feminist struggles have not always been successful, but even when confronting such internal opposition, these feminist movements basically see themselves as part of the national struggle and not opposing it.

The relationship of western members and members of other hegemonic national collectivities (such as in Israel and in Apartheid South Africa) to their collectivities has usually been very different.

---

[10]See http://www.peacewomen.org/resources/OPT/ModelParliament.html

In Chapter 5 we will be discussing cosmopolitan feminism, but even when the women themselves felt embedded in their national community, they developed a certain ambivalence towards it as a result of feeling empathy with the oppressed collectivity. Jawayardena's (1995) book actually describes such women who went to India, to help with the plight of those oppressed. Not all of them were feminist, but some were, seeing their feminism as part of a larger emancipator human struggle.

Cynthia Cockburn (2003, 2004, 2007) has carried out a whole series of studies – in Israel/Palestine, Northern Ireland, Bosnia, Cyprus – where she had studied feminists engaged in peace activism across borders and boundaries. She described these feminists as being engaged in transversal politics (Cockburn & Hunter, 1999, but see also Yuval-Davis, 1997a, 2006c). Transversal politics are dialogical politics in which all the participants in the dialogue see themselves not as representatives but as advocates of particular collectivities and social categories. They share similar values but operate according to the principles of 'rooting' and 'shifting', i.e. being reflexive as well as staying grounded in one's own social location, while also empathizing and imagining what it means to be in the dialogue partners' shoes. Transversal politics will be discussed in more detail in Chapters 5 and 6 in relation to cosmopolitanism and ethics of care. What is important here, however, is that the relationships of the feminists participating in such dialogue are often not symmetrical, that some of them are more critical of their national collectivities than others, but they all share feminist politics, respect each other and look for ways to transcend, if not to transform, their national and ethnic conflicts. Some of them feel more than others that they belong in their collectivities, but they are all critical of the construction of women in nationalist rhetorics. Their attitudes to armed struggle might be different – seeing guns as 'toys for the boys' (Enloe, 2000) can be a sign of privilege even when women from oppressed national collectivities might not always agree that armed struggle is the right way.[11]

Conclusion

Nick Bisley (2007: Chapter 7) reviews the literature which examines the ways neo-liberal globalization has affected nations and nationalist discourses. Several different, as well as opposing positions

---

[11]For a further discussion of women and the military, please see Chapter 5 in Yuval-Davis' *Gender and Nation* (1997a).

have been taken by different scholars on this question. One trend, to which ethno-symbolists like Smith (1995) and Guibernau (2001) belong, claims that globalization does not diminish the role of nationalism as a hegemonic contemporary identity, but rather often makes it more attractive as a haven from its effects as well as providing new mechanisms (via media and transportation technology) that can even enhance it.

A second view (e.g. Delanty & O'Mahony, 2002) sees globalization as providing opportunities for nationalist resurgence movements against established states as well as producing 'new nationalisms' (Kaldor, 2004) that, while basing themselves on pre-modern ideologies, are the creations of the contemporary age. These are the Castells' (1997) 'defensive identity communities' kinds of nationalist rhetoric.

The third trend sees globalization as the source of cultural processes of hybridization that dilute the power of nationalist ideologies (Ozkirimli, 2005). Globalization facilitates 'long-distance nationalism', 'portable nationalism' via diasporic politics (Østergaard-Nielsen, 2001). But as Anderson (1998; see also Yuval-Davis, 1997b) has shown, diasporic politics can also promote very right-wing extreme nationalist ideologies which do not have to undergo the test of *real politics*.

I do not see these trends as diagnostic alternatives, but rather as complementary. Globalization has contributed to the growing separation of nationalism and the state, as well as made it both more necessary and more difficult for the state to use nationalist 'social cohesion' discourse as a major tool of its governmentality. However, I would argue that in some ways the most important observation regarding this question is the partial transformation of what nationalist issues actually are in the contemporary world, and a certain fusion of nationalist issues with other identity politics issues.

It is illuminating that at the first conference on self-determination of the UN, which took place in August 2000 in Geneva,[12] many of the cases discussed would not have fallen under the more 'traditional' struggles for national self-determination but would have concerned racialized minorities (like the African Americans and the Indian Dalits) or indigenous people (like the Canadian first nations or the Saamis in northern Europe). The more 'traditional' cases included the Kashmiris and the Irish. Significantly, the demands of the conference were not formulated in terms of national independence but

---

[12]See http://www.tamilnation.org/selfdetermination/00conference.htm & http://i-p-o.org/self-determination.htm. A second conference took place in 2004: http://libris.kb.se/bib/11368146

rather – as Professor Ramon Nenadich from Puerto Rico defined it at the time – that self-determination was a form of 'collective restorative justice for the malformation of many multinational states created through exercise of the now discredited historical right to conquest and domination'.[13]

In this way, self-determination is being shifted from a nationalist discourse to become part of a global movement for collective, as well as individual, human rights (see the discussion in Chapter 5). As befits the era of neo-liberal globalization, the demands have often been formulated in monetary terms, whether it is reparations for African Americans or mineral rights for indigenous people in Australia. One of the insolvable issues in this regard concerns the question of who is the 'self' that should be compensated or endowed. As discussed in Chapter 1, there is no difference in identity politics between individual and collective identity – any 'authentic' member is constructed as both essentially the same and therefore as representative of the collective 'as a Black', 'as a woman', etc. While this operates well as a political mobilization discourse, it is more problematic when the issue concerns property rights.

It is still somewhat early to say whether or not this transformation will lead to a further separation of nations and states. Nations are becoming just one more format of identity community of belonging while states continue to transform to become a mediating tool between territorial, global and non-state governance organizations. The rise of particularly virulent kinds of autochthonic politics, however, where states seem to be particularly weak, might be symptomatic. What is nevertheless clear is that there is a growing awareness by people all over the world that nations are not homogeneous, that states also govern people who do not 'belong' to the 'indigenous' nations, and that much more complex and multi-layered constructions of political communities of belonging are the ways in which people negotiate their identities and attachments as well as the ways different political projects of belonging assume authority over them.

One such type of contemporary political projects of belonging, albeit one with a very long history – indeed longer than nationalism's – is that of political religion, which is the subject of the next chapter.

---

[13]See http://www.amazon.com/Pursuit-Self-Determination-Collected-Papers-International/dp/ 0932863329, and a more detailed report: http://www.coax.net/people/lwf/GG_HC.HTM

4

The Religious Question: the Sacred, the Cultural and the Political

Introduction: the breakdown of the secularization thesis

In the previous chapter we examined how different constructions of collective identities relating to nations, ethnicities and other collectivities relate to contemporary political projects of belonging. The focus of this chapter is religious collectivities and political projects of belonging which often partially, at least, overlap with those discussed in the last chapter but also add additional elements of transcendent meaning and authority.

On the surface, one of the more surprising facets of contemporary politics of belonging is the revitalization of religion, both as an identity and as a political project, within the overall context of neo-liberal globalization. Modernity, capitalism, liberalism have all emerged historically as part of the enlightenment project which also included the rise of secularism as a hegemonic ideology (Martin, 1979). August Comte, whom many see as the founder of modern sociology, developed the alternative project of religion of humanity (Wernick, 2001) and Karl Marx (1977 [1843]) saw in religion 'the opium of the masses', which, while soothing the pain of those who suffer, brings with it great dangers of its own. Although both Durkheim (1968 [1912]) and Weber (1905) saw religion as being central to social life, there has been an underlying assumption in most modern social sciences that religion is going to wither away. As Weber expanded in his (1905) 'Protestant Ethics' thesis, particular forms of religious ideologies and practices had originally facilitated and energized the rise of modern capitalism. However, these forms of religion, predominantly Christian Protestantism, could do this because of the way they transformed their primary orientation and pursuit of salvation from the sacred and the afterlife spheres, so central to previous forms of Christianity, into the here-and-now secular world, while at the same time retaining the ability to postpone immediate gratifications – and thus could use profits for reinvestments rather than just consumption.

Against the predictions of the secularization thesis, however, religious devotion and neo-liberalism can still go hand in hand. This is especially clear in the Neo-Con USA, although – as we shall see later on in the chapter – they are by no means unique. Much of the popularity of contemporary religious zealousness can be seen as a reaction, a means of comfort, as well as a mode of resistance to some of the effects of neo-liberal globalization (Karner & Aldridge, 2004; Meyer, 2006, 2008), but at the same time it is important to realize that its technological and communicatory powers are being appropriated and instrumentalized by their leaders (Imam et al., 2004).

This chapter starts with a general discussion of what constitutes religion – a more complex question than it might seem at first glance. It also discusses the different relationships between the religious and the political in general and the politics of belonging in particular.

It then moves on to examine more specifically relationships between religion and nationalism, both in the West and in the post-colonial world, and the ways that religions, as a result, can play central roles in both war and peace rhetoric, conservatism and social change.

The next section of the chapter turns to explore the phenomenon of what is known as 'religious fundamentalism' or 'absolutism' (Bhatt, 2006), which has arisen in all major contemporary religions, and how this relates to global discourses of civilizations (both clashing and dialogical) as well as to more glocal technologies of governance and belonging.

This is followed with a discussion of the effects 9/11 has had on the religionization of contemporary politics of belonging and the gradual transformation of some facets of multiculturalist discourses and politics into multi-faithism as a naturalized discourse of legitimate diversity.

The chapter ends with a brief discussion of religious and anti-fundamentalist feminisms.

What is religion?

In order to understand the religious phenomenon, one needs to relate to, and yet also to differentiate it from, the notions of both culture and power.

Elsewhere (Yuval-Davis, 1997a: Chapter 3), I rejected both universalistic and relativistic notions of culture which share an essentialist view of 'culture' as having a specific, fixed inventory of symbols, ways of behaviour and artefacts which coherently and unproblematically constitute cultures of specific national and ethnic collectivities. Internal differentiations and differences in the positionings of different members of these collectivities to 'their culture and tradition' cannot be a accounted for in either of these two approaches, which view them as fixed and homogeneous.

Instead, following other scholars such as Chatterjee (1993 [1986]), Bhabha (1994), Bottomley (1992), Hall (1992) and Friedman (1994), I adopted an alternative approach which, using discourse analyses inspired by both Gramsci and Foucault, views cultures as dynamic social processes operating in contested terrains in which different voices become more or less hegemonic in their offered interpretations of the world. This recognizes that often cultural discourses will resemble more a battleground for meaning than a shared point of departure.

It is important to note that two contradictory elements co-exist in the operation of cultures. On the one hand, there is a tendency towards stabilization and continuity, and on the other hand, perpetual resistance and change. Both of these tendencies grow out of the close relationship between power relations and cultural practice (Bourdieu & Nice, 1977; Asad, 1986; Bottomley, 1992). As Friedman points out (1994: 76), cultures are not just an arbitrary collection of values, artefacts and modes of behaviour. They acquire, to a greater or lesser extent, 'stabilizing properties' which are inherent in the practices of their social reproduction. Cultural homogeneity in this view would be a result of hegemonization, and it would always be limited and more noticeable in the centre rather than in the social margins, being affected by the social positioning of its carriers.

It is important to note also, however, that these processes of social reproduction are not just processes of cloning, but also of social interaction in which motivation and desire play their part – as we have seen in the previous chapter in relation to post-colonial national movements and their constructions of 'culture and tradition'. As a result, cultural models become resonant with subjective as well as collective experience. They become the intersectional ways in which individuals experience themselves, their collectivities and the world, and thus often occupy central spaces in identity narratives.

In all of these ways the religious domain bears a close relationship to that of culture, although the two cannot be reduced to each other.

Religion relates to the sphere of the sacred, of the ultimate meaning (Tillich, 1957; Durkheim, 1965; Geertz, 1966; Luckman, 1967; Beyer, 1994; K. Armstrong, 2007). Moreover, religious discourses supply the individual, within specific social and historic contexts, with explicit or implicit (related) answers to the three basic existential questions people have to grapple with – what is the meaning/purpose of one's life?; what happens to us when we die?; and what is good and evil?

The relations between the world of everyday life and the sacred religious domain are usually indirect, although in most religions there will be specific times and places which will be dedicated to the realm of the sacred. Spatially, places such as churches, mosques, synagogues and temples are designated places of worship, while specific holy-days like the Muslim month of Ramadan, the weekly Jewish Sabbath or church services, or praying at several times of day in different religions also play a part. So these times and places are sharply differentiated and delineated from the secular by specific performative religious acts, such as praying or fasting or lighting special candles. However, these dichotomous constructions are far from being so in everyday life. Many of what Luckman calls (1967: 58) the 'graduated strata of meaning' will mediate between the trivial and 'profane' and the 'ultimate' significance of a biography or a social tradition, and thus practices from sexual relationships to food to judgements can be more or less religiously enhanced and sanctified. In a pluralist society all of these do not even have to come from the same religious sources.

Specific religious institutions and a belief in god(s) are common, but by no means a necessary ingredient for religion to be defined in this way. As Karen Armstrong (2009) argues persuasively, religions are more about performativity – i.e. regular repetitive practices that gain their internal as well as social authority with repetition (Butler, 1990) – than about implicit beliefs, although this differs even formally between religions. For example, Christianity is generally much more about specific beliefs than Judaism, for instance, the orthodox version of which instructs its (male) followers to follow 613 'mitzvot' (religious practices). Saba Mahmoud (2005) also argues strongly that the conceptual relationship between the body, self and moral agency differs in the ways in which these are constituted within different ethical-moral (cultural and religious) traditions. Armstrong also points out that different people differ in their talents and ability to immerse themselves in religious spirituality, as is the case with people's differential artistic and poetic capabilities.

However, once these 'transcendent superordinated and integrating structures of meaning are socially 'objectivated', to use Luckman's terminology (1967: 25), i.e. a personal spirituality becomes a religious institution, a paradoxical situation often develops. Because of their ultimate meaning, religious practices and beliefs can become some of the most intractable and inflexible symbolic border guards for belonging to specific collectivity boundaries and cultural traditions – so much so that Durkheim (1965) saw in religion the most basic socially cohesive act, in which symbolically society worships its own 'collective conscience'.

As religions often present their answers as pertaining to the whole human condition and not just to members of a specific collectivity, they would tend to include an expansionary missionary element in them. This might mean not only a sense of membership of a collectivity (which can often become also a political community) which crosses borders and boundaries, but also an engagement in the voluntary or involuntary conversion of members of other collectivities, who would culturally and politically (as well as racially and ethnically) be excluded in most other ways but would definitely be doomed to hell if they didn't convert.

At the same time, however, the same religion (whether it is Christianity, Islam or Buddhism) also becomes incorporated into hegemonic traditions of the different collectivities and acquires specific cultural signifiers which would associate it with those collectivities (e.g. the differences between Russian and Greek Orthodoxy, Pakistani and Saudi Islam, Indian and Chinese Buddhism). This definition of the religious arena also includes ideological constructions of individuals' identities who would not define themselves as religious, however – hence the association (constructed in very different ways and excluding smaller or larger sections of the population) between Catholicism and Irishness, Islam and being Bosnian, Judaism and being an Israeli.

The role of religion in contemporary political projects of belonging can also be an alternative to rather than an enhancer of such projects. While the examples in the previous paragraph are those where specific religions are incorporated into specific nationalist discourses, religious people of different religions have been known to risk their lives and to give essential support to persecuted people who were not of their belief, whether they helped escaped slaves in nineteenth-century USA, hid Jews in Europe during the Second World War, or are contemporary activists fighting for the right of sanctuary for asylum seekers in anti-immigration legislation campaigns and migrant and refugee support organizations.[1] While racist religious zealots persecuted, imprisoned, carried out pogroms and lynched racialized Others in the name of religion, liberation theologies of all kinds have been part of various social revolutionary and national liberation struggles, whether in Latin America, the Middle East or Africa. The battle for meaning, as well as the battle for domination, has spread to all contemporary religions, even Catholicism, in which, at least formally, there should be a monopolistic, hierarchized order of power. The organization 'Catholics for Free Choice', for example, has argued – and their argument was accepted as legitimate in the preparatory meeting to the UN 1994 International Conference on Population and Development (ICPD) – that they represent, just as the Vatican does, the millions of Catholics all over the world, as their positive policy towards the use of contraceptives is more popular among Catholics everywhere than the inhibitory one of the Pope.[2]

In addition to all versions of institutionalized religions, there has also been a rise in various new 'alternative' and 'New Age' religious movements, from Scientology to the Moonies to the Japan-based Seicho-No-Ie. Even more popular are various hybrid and syncretic forms of religions, such as the myriad of churches led by charismatic/ evangelical/Pentecostal individual preachers which are based on Christianity but also include older African forms of African worship practices (Ugba, 2009). Such syncretism, as Nandy (1983) and others have pointed out, has always been popular in pluralist societies, in which local, regional, national or empire gods were worshipped in non-exclusionary ways. In the colonial world, in spite of the efforts of many missionaries (and the tolerance of others), Christianity, Islam and Budhism were also worshipped in ways where more traditional religious practices have been incorporated in and this is what made them so conducive to being incorporated into national, ethnic and

---

[1] Of course, the motivation for doing so would not necessarily be part of someone's religious beliefs but as a result of sharing with them other communities of belonging, from neighbourhood and village to professional and business connections as well as more diffused feelings of care and empathy. However, religious discourse can be used and is being used on such occasions just as it can be utilized for exclusion and damnation.

[2] An argument that has finally started to be accepted by the Vatican also when the Pope granted limited permission for the use of condoms in the fight against AIDS.

even racial (e.g. the Ku Klux Clan) political projects of belonging. Luckman (1967), however, talked about an even more eclectic mode of personal religions in contemporary western consumerist societies, in which people, in a similar way to gathering various goods into their personal baskets in the supermarket, will also gather different practices and beliefs from various religions to construct their own personal version of religion.

The notion of God, unlike the notion of the sacred, has never been a common denominator for all religions – Budhism and Confusianism, for example, are 'godless' religions. The notion of 'secular religions', however, does not only exclude God, it also signifies movements and ideologies – from communism to ecology – that have constructed total worlds of meaning, including the answers to the three existential questions above (of the meaning of one's life, what happens after death and what is good and bad), without establishing a separate realm of 'the sacred'. Nationalism has been considered by many to be an archetypical 'secular religion'. However, before turning to examine more closely the relationships between religion and nationalism, we need to explore the notion of the secular.

Secularism

In the introduction to our book *Refusing Holy Orders* (2001 [1992]), Gita Sahgal and I differentiated between two very different notions of the secular. Emphasizing the difference between these two notions is vital, both analytically and politically.

One meaning of secularism is that of atheism (denial of the existence of God) or, at best, agnosticism (indifference to the existence of God or a belief that God's existence either way can never be proven). This denial or indifference rejects a construction of a separate, transcendental or sacred sphere and sees this as an irrelevance at best, or as a dangerous illusion at worst, as the title of Christopher Hitchens's (2007) book states: *God is Not Great: How Religion Poisons Everything*.

This kind of secularism relates to a view of the world which is associated with the 'age of enlightenment', of scientism and extreme rationality. What cannot be observed, at least in principle, does not exist or is meaningless. Therefore, there is no meaning to the notion of God except for the various roles – social, emotional, political and economic – this has played in people's lives. We need to assume, therefore, that there is no afterlife except for the transformation of

our body matter into physical corruption. Any morality and principles of good and bad, if these exist, need, according to this perspective, to be anchored in other ontological bases than that of God.
This can be the moral system which bases all moral judgements on
their ability to help in the fulfilment of life's well-being and hap-
piness, as developed by Aristoteles, or in the UN Declaration of
Human Rights, but these are up to human rather than transcendental legitimation. Therefore, there is no ultimate meaning to life
except the one aspired to by the individual (or their collectivities)
and their particular systems of beliefs.

This meaning of secularism is related to, but also vastly different
from, the second meaning, which is basically political, rather than
existential-philosophical, and concerns the principle of the separation of religion from the state.

The most known example of such a principle can be found in
the constitution of the USA – a constitution which was written for
a society which was largely established by religious communities
but with no one hegemonic religion. This meaning of the secular
is not unique to the American constitution, however. It has been a
basic political principle, applied in different ways, of other pluralistic
states, such as India and South Africa, where the motivating drive for
it has not been atheist, secular ideologies, but rather, like in the USA,
religious and communal pluralism.

The principle of the separation of religion from the state in the
USA is anchored in the constitution's First Amendment, which is
part of the Bill of Rights. This prohibits the establishment of any
one religion and guarantees freedom of religion (along with freedom
of speech and of the press). How different this sense of secularism is
from the first one can be shown in the fact that 'In God We Trust' is
the official motto of the USA and has appeared on various American
federal documents and artefacts, including coins.

In India, the term 'secularism' was officially added to the Preamble
of the Indian Constitution only in 1976. However, the whole notion
of India as a secular state, which is there for all its citizens and not just
for members of one of India's religious communities, is basically what
has differentiated the establishment of the Indian state, 'the largest
democracy in the world', from Pakistan, which was constructed during the 1948 partition as a state for South Asian Muslims, although
Hindus and Christians as well as tribal people continued to live there
and be citizens of the state.

The 1996 South African Constitution has grappled with the question of how best to respect the country's vast array of races, ethnicities, religions, languages and cultures, with individual rights. The collective and consultative process which preceded the writing of the constitution[3] has produced many innovations (including being the first national constitution which officially included the defence of gay and lesbian rights). Its secularism does not even require the complete separation of religion and the state, while it avoids giving any religion a specific status within the state. Rather, Article 15(2) states that 'Religious observances may be conducted at state or state-aided institutions, provided that those observances follow rules made by the appropriate public authorities: a) they are conducted on an equitable basis; and b) attendance at them is free and voluntary.' The South African Constitution also provides for the establishment of a Commission for the Promotion and Protection of the Rights of Cultural, Religious and Linguistic Communities.

India and South Africa take quite different approaches to religious education in schools. Basically, the Indian Constitution doesn't permit religious education in state-funded schools (with the exception of state-administered schools founded through religious trusts), whereas South Africa has developed a policy not of relig*ious* education but 'relig*ion* education' which tries to teach children all about each others' religions. In the USA, the role of religion in the classroom (and the curriculum) has provided one of the longest-running battles in public policy.

Historically in Europe, the principle of the separation of religion and the state emerged as a result of two distinct stages. First to appear was the principle that local political authority could determine the religion of its population. The Latin phrase *cuius regio, eius religio* (whose realm, his religion) comes from the Peace of Augsburg in 1555, which ended a battle between Catholicism and Lutheranism and allowed German princes to choose whichever religion they wanted within their domain. The space for Protestantism and secularism was further enhanced after the Thirty Years' War of 1618 to

---

[3]I was invited to one such consultative conference, when some ANC women leaders became worried that the draft of the constitution was giving equal weight to a 'non sexist South Africa' and 'respect for culture and tradition'. They invited women from other post-colonial countries to hear of their post-independent experiences in this area. Following that conference, the ANC women managed to get official recognition of the priority of women's rights to 'respect of culture and tradition'. What actually happened in Post-Apartheid South Africa is a different, and very complex, story, of course.

1648, in which large parts of western Europe broke away from the power of the Vatican, although until today there is no full separation of religion and the state in most of Europe.[4]

While different political rulers and Christian religious leaders struggled over domination, members of non-Christian minorities, most notably the Jews, were excluded from this discourse and were not considered part of the political community. The debates on the emancipation of the Jews emerged at a time when atheist and secular 'enlightenment' ideologies were gaining prominence, and eventually, after the French revolution, this brought about the second stage of separation in which individuals could be of different religious belongings and yet still have full citizenship rights. The first country to emancipate the Jews and grant them equal rights on a par with Gentiles was France in 1791[5], with the Netherlands following in 1796, but this continued until 1923 when Romanian Jews were finally emancipated.

Epistemologically, therefore, the two kinds of secularism are historically connected. Politically, however, the separation of religion and the state has enabled the privatization of religion in civil society, which paradoxically could protect, under certain circumstances, religious communities from atheist secularization (for instance, in determining the curriculum in private religious education). It was a different story in the republics falling under the grip of the Soviet Empire and the Eastern Bloc states, in which religious institutions were either repressed or tightly controlled by the state where no significant autonomous civil society space was allowed. Even here, however, religion survived in intimate and familial environments and traditions[6] and in post Soviet times has often become closely

---

[4]I am working on this chapter while staying in Umea in Sweden where only in 2000 there was an official separation of church and state (although even today employers automatically deduct tax from their employees, 2% of which goes to the church unless employees specifically ask for it not to do so).

[5]It is important to note, however, Talal Asad's (2004) argument that what has happened in France in recent years around issues of Muslim women's headscarves, forbidding wearing 'the veil' in public schools (except the publicly subsidized religious schools), actually represents a return to the older tradition of *cuius regio, eius religio*. The public domain stops being a social domain in which particular subjects are formed as morally independent and socially responsible and becomes subject to the political will of the political sovereign (see also Yuval-Davis, 2005c).

[6]See, for example, Marfua Tokhtakhodjaeva (1995) who pointed out that what survived as religion in Uzbekistan under the Soviet rule was largely cultural practices such as circumcision, the celebration of Muslim festivals, and discriminatory attitudes towards gender roles that were justified with reference to religion, including secret polygamy by ranking party leaders and other influentials.

attached with nationalist and ultra-nationalist movements (e.g. Aitamurto, 2007; see also Skrbiš, 2005, regarding Croatia; Zubrzycki, 2006, regarding Poland; and Mihelj, 2007, regarding Slovenia). In most places, religion was one of many organized but scattered and insubstantial forms of resistance which gained power only in the years when things were *already* unravelling and there was a power vacuum. However, in Lithuania, for instance, the Catholic Church was an organized and substantial voice for public opposition, while in Poland the influence of the Catholic Church never really waned and was intimately tied to national identity. In 1956 it reached a sort of coexistence agreement with the Polish Communist leadership.[7]

Religion and nationalism

Historically, therefore, religions have had several contradictory relationships with nationalist movements and states which often shifted historically even in relation to the same national collectivities – of conflation and exclusion as well as of coexistence in different social and political spheres.

According to most 'modernist' theorists, nationalism constitutes a modern alternative to religion, which emerged at the time of enlightenment and will, eventually, make it redundant (Althusser, 1971; Gellner, 1983; Hobsbawm, 1990). Ben Anderson, when wanting to explain the power of nationalism, did so in quasi-religious terms – that its emotional powers and the willingness of people to kill and die for it are exactly because there is no instrumentalist value of self-interest in it, but rather it is sacred (Anderson, 1991 [1983]).

This view of religion, however, is problematic in several different ways. First, it denies the implicit reliance on religion as a hegemonic cultural tradition which plays an important part even in states with secular constitutions – whether in determining national festivals, national symbols or civil exclusions. The debate on the possible inclusion of Turkey, whose population is mostly of Muslim rather than Christian origin, for example, within the EU has highlighted this relationship and brought back to public memory the fact that the original 1957 Treaty of Rome, which ushered the European Economic Community, later the EU, into existence, was blessed by the Pope. There was an implied assumption then that Europe was a

---

[7]See http://www.opendemocracy.net/democracy-protest/polish_democracy_2782.jsp

Christian continent or even more narrowly Christian – Catholic and Protestant – thus virtually excluding the Orthodox forms of Christianity that had characterized Eastern European societies under the Byzantine Empire (with the notable exception of Greece, the 'cradle' of 'European civilization' and enlightenment, which was the only Orthodox Christian country considered for EU membership, and even then only in 1979).

Moreover, when we view the states of the world as a whole, only a minority of them can be considered fully secular. Even when there is no formal incorporation of at least some arenas of religious laws into state laws, and there exists an explicit secular republican ideology as in France, there is a reliance on Christian festivals, for example, as the formal state holidays (after the abortive attempt during the French revolution to provide alternative 'festivals of reason'). There have been numerous cases where nationalist movements, rather than distancing themselves from local hegemonic religions, relied upon these to legitimize themselves as representing 'the people' and to launch wars against the 'enemy' and/or 'foreign oppressors'. This was true in Ireland and Poland, as well as in India and Algeria, and the Jesuit order in Paraguay. Some national movements presented themselves as modernizing agents of religious as well as other cultural traditions (as in the cases of both the pan-Arab national movement and the Zionist movement) and have often fought with traditional religious leaderships for domination of the civil as well as political domains. In recent years, however, these power relations seem to be undergoing a significant reversal.

This can be easily understood if we remember Chatterjee's (1990) analysis, mentioned in the previous chapter of the processes involved in the construction of post-colonial nations and the precedence of the cultural production of the nation over the political one, which involves complex processes of mimicry and distancing from colonial cultures and the search for 'cultural authenticity' which is often expressed in religious terms. This is of extreme importance when we discuss the rise of new religious 'fundamentalist' movements, not because these movements themselves were fundamentalist – which they were not – but because their discourse opened the door to a legitimation of these later political developments.

This is so, especially as the hegemony of the modern nation-state in the post-colonial world has often been very limited and was mostly confined to urban centres and the upper classes. The use of cultural and religious traditions as symbolic border guards has enabled, to a large extent, the continued coexistence of the 'modern' centre with the pre-modern sections of society. At a later period it also enabled, in many cases, the rise of a new generation of leadership which could turn to those same customs and traditions and use pre-modern terminology while developing modern ethnic and national projects of a very different kind from either the previous nationalist or the previous religious ones. In such projects, what symbolized progress and modernity in the older projects was now constructed as European cultural imperialism. As an alternative, a fundamentalist construction of 'the true' cultural essence of the collectivity has come to be imposed.[8] These constructions, however, are often no more similar to the ways people used to live historically in these societies than the previous 'national liberation' ones, and neither have they abandoned modernity and its tools, whether this is the modern media or high-tech weaponry.

Even more than in the construction of the modern nation, these movements tend to exclude and often persecute ethnic, and especially religious and sexual, minorities. In Pakistan, for example, in order to get a passport one has to make a declaration that Ahmedis are not Muslims and to sign that Mirza Ghulam Ahmad Qadiani is an impostor prophet and an infidel and also must consider his followers, whether they belong to the Lahori, Qadiani or Mirzai groups, to be non-Muslims.[9]

Women, sexuality and gender relations, in general, occupy an important role in these projects. If in times of liberation and modernization the changing roles and the education of women were seen as the symbols of change, in this new discourse women are constructed in the role of 'carriers of the tradition'. The symbolic act of unveiling which played centre-stage in the emancipatory projects is now being surpassed in the campaigns of forced veiling, as happened, for example, in post-revolutionary Iran or in Hamas' Gaza. Even practices such as Sati in India can become foci for fundamentalist movements which see in women's following these traditions the safeguard of a national cultural essence, operating as a mirror image of the colonial gaze which focused on these practices to construct

---

[8]As Marieme Helie-Lucas (2006) points out, in such cases the 'reinvention of tradition' constructs a homogeneous cultural, religious and dress-code tradition where originally a much richer and diversified culture existed.

[9]See http://en.wikipedia.org/wiki/Passport

Otherness but with their actual targets being the post-colonial modern secular state (Mani, 1989; Chhachhi, 1991). The rise of ethnic and religious fundamentalist movements affects, therefore, not only the hegemonic cultural project of the nation but also its boundaries. If modernist nationalist projects are inherently fixed around the triad relations of people, state and territory, in these projects there is the fourth element of tradition and religion which operate as exclusionary tools that are much sharper than secular nationalist projects. Religious and cultural minorities are not just marginal in these political projects of belonging, but are actively excluded and often persecuted as polluting the nation and are thus closely related to projects of ethnic cleansing, whether this is the persecution of Muslims in BJP-dominated Gujarat or the Christian Copts by Islamists in Egypt. However, religious fundamentalist (or absolutist) movements can have aspirations that transcend the boundaries of their nation or state and the boundaries of their politics of belonging are planetary, as are the boundaries of 'the global war on terrorism', which has been declared by the USA and its allies against one such fundamentalist project, Al-Qaeda, after 9/11. In the next chapter we shall examine the nature of the political project of 'humanitarian militarism' which is behind the 'global war on terrorism'. Here, however, we still need to examine more closely the nature of those religious fundamentalist movements.

Religious fundamentalism

There is a tendency to accept fundamentalist movements' own rhetoric and to view these as basically religious, as basically pre-modern, and as always resisting contemporary social and political order. However, as I and others have commented elsewhere (e.g. *Contention*, 1995; Yuval-Davis, 1992a and b; Sahgal & Yuval-Davis, 2001 [1992]; Imam et al., 2004; Balchin, 2008), fundamentalist movements all over the world, with all their heterogeneity, are basically political movements which have a religious or ethnic imperative (often both) and seek in various ways, in widely differing circumstances, to harness the modern state, weaponry and media powers to the service of their creed. This creed, which can be based on certain sacred texts or evangelical experiential moments linked to a charismatic leader (like the Jewish Lubavitche Rebbe or the Iglesia ni Cristo in the Philippines), is presented as the only true and valid form of the religion and/or the ethnic culture. Religious fundamentalist movements, therefore, need to be differentiated from liberation theologies which, while deeply religious and political, see themselves as part of a pluralist society rather than attempting to impose an absolutist truth (more on this in the next chapter on the cosmopolitan question).

The first modern religious groupings to be called fundamentalist were American Protestant churches which, in 1919, established the World Christian Fundamentalist Association after the publication of the 'Fundamentals' – based on a series of Bible conferences which took place between 1865 and 1910 (and a 1910 publication *The Fundamentals: A Testimony to the Truth*, edited by A.C. Dixon). Some people (like A. Sivanandan, the Director of the Institute of Race Relations in London[10]) would argue that therefore only Christians can be called fundamentalists, just as others reserve that name for Muslims only. However, as Cass Balchin shows (2008: 32), fundamentalist movements in different religions also emerged around the same time in early twentieth century: 'In Poland, World Agudath Israel (World Jewish Union) was founded; in 1925, the Hindu fundamentalist Rashtriya Swayamsewak Sangh was founded; and in 1928, the Muslim Brotherhood was founded in Egypt and (Catholic) Opus Dei was founded in Spain'.[11]

While the specific historical and cultural circumstances of each religion are significant, heterogeneity and contestation exist within the different religious traditions as well as between them. Moreover, the construction of 'a strict adherence to the text' is always selective. All great religious scriptures include internal contradictions (although, of course, strict believers would see these only as apparent contradictions) and therefore specific choices are always exercised in the interpretation of texts into daily practices. Probably the name 'fundamentalist' is therefore not the most suitable one, and Chetan Bhatt's (2006) term of 'absolutist' may be more relevant. However, here I stick with using that term, not only because of my own long association with the organization 'Women Against Fundamentalism', but also because this is the term which has come to be known and understood in popular culture.

---

[10]See http://www.irr.org.uk/2008/november/ha000016.html, 'Catching History on the Wing', the speech by the IRR's director, A. Sivanandan, at the IRR's 50th celebration conference on November 1, 2008.

[11]She adds (personal correspondence) that since then she has also found that the African Independent church, the Kimbuists, was founded in 1921, and Iglesia ni Cristo, the largest independent church in Asia, in 1914 – i.e. *all* around the same time.

Fundamentalism can align itself with different political trends in different countries and manifest itself in numerous forms. It can appear as a form of orthodoxy – a maintenance of 'traditional values' – or as a revivalist radical phenomenon, dismissing impure and corrupt forms of religion to 'return to original sources'. Jewish fundamentalism in Israel, for example, has basically appeared in two forms, for which the state has very different meanings. On the one hand, as a form of right-wing Zionism, in which the establishment of the Israeli state is in itself a positive religious act, and on the other hand, as a non-, if not anti-, Zionist movement, which sees in the Israeli state a convenient source for gaining economic and political power to promote its own versions of Judaism. In Islam, fundamentalism has appeared as a return to the Quranic text (fundamentalism of the *madrassa*), and as a return to the religious law, the *sharia* (fundamentalism of the *ulama*). In the USA, the Protestant fundamentalist movements include both fundamentalists in the original sense – those who want to go back to the biblical texts – and those who are 'born again Christians' who rely much more on emotional religious experiences (see, for example, Maitland, 1992; Jones, 2008; Blumental, 2009).

It is necessary to differentiate here between fundamentalist movements of dominant majorities within states, which look for universal domination in society (such as the evangelical New Right in the USA, Khomeini's Iran or Serbian Yugoslavia) and fundamentalist movements of minorities who aim to use state and media powers and resources to promote and impose their vision primarily within their specific constituencies, which are usually defined in ethnic terms (such as the Jewish fundamentalists of the Lubavitche Hassids and Hindu and Sikh fundamentalists, as well as some African churches in Britain). Identifying various heterogeneous forms of fundamentalist movements, however, does not invalidate the use of the term fundamentalism for identifying specific social phenomena. All major social movements – such as national, socialist, and feminist movements – have been similarly heterogeneous.

The recent rise of fundamentalism, almost a century after the initial fundamentalist movements were established in the early twentieth century, is linked to the crisis of modernity (broadly characterized as the attempt to build and maintain a social order based on the principles of the enlightenment – rationalism and progress). After a period of optimism following the Second World War, when the global South gained political independence from its colonial masters, it became clear to people all over the world that neither capitalism, communism nor nationalism were fulfilling their material, emotional and spiritual needs. The accompanying feelings of despair and disorientation sharpened with the demise of the Soviet Union, the end of the Cold War, and the growing hegemony of neo-liberal globalization. The growing sense of insecurity that results from the locus of decision making shifting further and further away from people, and the deepening poverty that widens divisions between haves and have-nots and fuels the competition for limited resources, pushes people into finding new ways of coping. As Birgit Meyer (2006, 2008) claims, convincing religious images with stylistic aesthetics can 'create a shared sensorial perception of the world' (2006:7), a holistic sensorial experience which, by being shared by the broader community, can overcome the *Zerstreung* (which in German means both 'distraction' and 'fragmentation') of the modern world, thus evoking a sense of 'authentic belonging' in the midst of a fragmented world. Fundamentalist forms of religion, with their repetitive authoritative performative version of the only 'true' version of religion, are especially good at constructing such holistic sensorial experiences.

This is closely linked to the rise of collective identities defined by religion, ethnicity or culture, each projecting itself as the only way to protect its (willing or unwilling) members and gain access for them to power and resources. As Manuel Castells (1996–98) argues, in times where people stop being sure that they will be able to continue to live where they live, with their family, and doing the work they do, they will turn to what he calls 'defensive identity communities', which are constructed as primordial and unchanging. Religions provide people with a compass and an anchor. Ethnic nationalisms provide them with fixed identities and impermeable community boundaries. Overall these fundamentalist ideologies and their resolute construction of fixed and absolute truths have provided a source of comfort, solace and even a sense of empowerment to people. They also provide a compass and an anchor which give people a sense of stability and security, as well as a coherent identity. This shifts the centre of the strucuturation of meaning away from the individual towards the religious leaders and institutions.

The religious Right is increasingly playing a crucial role in identity politics everywhere. The linkages that exist among politico-religious groups and between them and various other right-wing forces, from the local to the international levels, both within given countries and communities and outside them, are increasingly clear. For instance, the Vatican, Syria and Iran have voted consistently on the same side in international forums, from the ICPD (the United Nations International Conference on Population and Development held in Cairo) in 1994 to Beijing+5 in 2000. It is also increasingly clear that there are links between mainstream politico-religious groups of the Right and the extremist groups (whether spawned by them or not), which work strategically to reinforce each other in pursuit of their common ends, even when these links are denied.

The control of women and the patriarchal family are usually central to fundamentalist constructions of social orders. These are often seen as the panacea for all social ills:

> A widespread evangelical conviction is that stability in the home is the key to the resolution of other social problems. Once wanderers came 'home' and the poor acquired the sense of responsibility found in strong Christian familiality, poverty would cease. (Marsden, 1980: 37)

And women's desertion of their proper social role might mean a social disaster:

> Woman has such a degree of biological disability and such huge family responsibilities, as to preclude her leaving purdah in a well ordered society. (Purdah Mandrudi, quoted in Hyman, 1985: 24)

One of the paradoxes associated with fundamentalism is the fact that women collude, seek comfort and even gain at times a sense of empowerment within the spaces allocated to them by fundamentalist movements (see the chapters by Yasmin Ali, Elaine Foster, Sara Maitland and Nira Yuval-Davis in Sahgal & Yuval-Davis, 2001 [1992] as well as IIJ, 2003). It is a well-known fact that in spite of the general subservient place women occupy generally in religious institutions, they constitute the majority of their active members. This can be seen as linked not only to religion as a source of solace to the oppressed but also to the emotional division of labour between the genders in which women, as part of their role as guardian of the emotional and moral well-being of their family members, would also be active in the religious domains (Beth-Halakhmi, 1996). In Chapter 6 we shall discuss the implications of this for the feminist political project of 'the ethics of care' (V. Held, 1993; Tronto, 1993). Here, it is important to note that being active in a religious movement allows women to have a legitimate place in a public sphere which otherwise might be blocked to them, and which in certain circumstances, by constructing 'religion' *vs* 'tradition', they might be able to subvert for their purposes, as in, for example, the relationship between young girls and their parents (e.g. in Britain young women claiming a 'pure Islamic' identity, shorn of the impurity of the 'backward custom' of their parents, have mobilized religion to support their assertion of their right not to be forced into marriage). At the same time, it can also be less threatening but still a challenge and a space for personal accomplishments to which unskilled working-class women and frustrated middle-class women might be attracted. For women of racial and ethnic minorities, it can also provide the means by which to defend themselves as well as to defy the racist hegemonic culture. However, the overall effect of fundamentalist movements has been very detrimental to women, limiting and defining their roles and activities and actively oppressing them when they step outside of the preordained limits of their designated roles (AWID, 2009).

As Michael Mann (2005) has pointed out (see also Sahgal & Yuval-Davis, 2001 [1992]: 512–13), the attraction of fundamentalist movements is also aided by the hollowing out of liberalism into neo-liberalism, which has weakened the appeal of liberalism and liberal democracy in less successful parts of the South (and among those who feel threatened in the North). There is a sense of collective empowerment which is caused by the rise of claims to 'theo-democracy' – claims to political rule by 'we, the religious people'. The paradox of religious fundamentalism is that it allows space for only one version of 'the truth' and at the same time seems as a grass-roots movement to be some kind of divinely directed democratic government. However, as was seen after the Iranian revolution, and in spite of recent attempts to revise such a turn, the centre of power in a post-revolution of that kind has moved quickly from 'the people' to those who are seen as the representatives and interpreters of God's will. It is also important to note that fundamentalist movements not only use modern communication and military technologies, but have also benefitted from developing new economic markets that might seem anti-capitalist or neo-liberal, such as 'non-profit Islamic banking'. Actually, these have proved to be an amalgamation of new wealth for particular fundamentalist leaderships, and TV evangelists in American TV stations are known to have accumulated vast fortunes as a result of their mass mobilizations.

Identity politics, discussed in the previous chapter, have also paved the way for the rise and legitimation of religious fundamentalist and other absolutist movements. The reification and essentialization of identities, which are linked to fundamentalist politics, have also been presented as a defensive reaction to the processes of globalization. Both Stuart Hall (1996) and Verena Stolcke (1995) talk about cultural fundamentalism (although, considering its strong emphasis on immutable collectivity boundaries it might be preferable to call it ethnic fundamentalism). Given the rise of global capitalism and the growing sense of disempowerment in a political world system in which political autonomy and sovereignty seem to mean less and less, more and more people feel the need for what Stuart Hall calls a symbolic retreat to the past in order to face the future.

Religion, civil society and the political

One of the reasons for the relative success of religious political movements in recent years both locally and globally is the fact that in most modern states, especially secular ones, religion was seen either as non-political or as a neutral political force whose agenda does not compete or threaten the political agendas of the ruling parties. In Israel, for example, different governments used to rely, especially before the 1967 war, upon the religious parties as convenient coalition partners with no autonomous agenda except for getting more resources for their educational institutions. It was only many years later that it became clear that many of the graduates of these schools and *yeshivot* constituted the popular basis of settler fundamentalist movements. Similarly, in India, although a member of the RSS (Rashtriya Swayamsevak Sangh) murdered Gandhi, it was not until many years later that graduates from the schools of this religious movement were at the forefront of the rise of the BJP (Bharatiya Janata Party), the political wing of the RSS, originally founded in 1951, as an alternative hegemonic political project in India in the 1990s. This ignorance also applied to the ways religious movements were used by external political powers. The USA funded the *mojahidins* who fought against the USSR in Afghanistan (including Osama Bin Laden) and thus created the political climate which allowed the Pakistani military (largely with Saudi money) to fund the *madrassas* which then became the basis for the training of the Taliban and other movements associated with them and Al Qaeda. Similarly, it was the Israelis who originally funded and trained Hamas, as a counter political power to that of Fatah and the PLO among the Palestinians. They indeed became such a power, and won the Palestinian elections, to the chagrin of, and consequent economic and military conflict with, the Israelis, who found them much less malleable than Fatah.

A somewhat similar phenomenon can also be seen in the economic arena where international economic and international aid organizations and bilateral and multilateral aid agencies have developed growing bonds with various religious organizations (not usually differentiating between fundamentalist and non-fundamentalist organizations) as part of the wider phenomenon in which NGOs are often seen and used not only as part of the civil society but also as *the* civil society. Religious NGOs are gradually being seen as the more sustainable civil society organizations. The most visible sign of influence of the religious Right on development aid was through George Bush's PEPFAR: President's Emergency Plan for AIDS Relief,[12] which prohibited funds going to organizations (and countries) that supported abortion rights, and instead actively promoted abstinence programmes rather than sexual health and education programmes and the promotion of condom usage. Inevitably these policies meant denying funding to progressive NGOs and extending funding to religious – mostly Christian – NGOs.[13] But Christopher Pallas (2005) describes how this process has also been taking place in the World Bank and traces its beginning to the growing interest of the World Bank in civil society and poverty and the naturalized association between poverty and religious organizations as those which are engaged in various civil society welfare activities among the poor.

And indeed, in addition to education, part of the populist attraction of fundamentalist and other religious movements is the fact that so many of these are engaged in and are committed to welfare services in the community, especially in societies and communities where state services are either non-existent or very poor.

---

[12]See http://www.pepfar.gov/about/index.htm

[13]Please see critiques of this in Balchin (2003) and http://www.huffingtonpost.com/jodi-jacobson/obama-asks-abstinence-onl_b_157169.html

Regular charity activities – both financial and in the form of personal involvement – are often seen as religious duties as well as a way of reaching potential new recruits for the movement. The sanctuary movement in the USA and elsewhere has played a major role in defending and rescuing migrants and refugees since the time of slavery.[14]

At the same time, these charity activities can be very exclusionary and directed only towards those who belong – actually or potentially – to their constituency. It is well known, for example, that Mother Teresa's organization in India refused to take care of girls who had been damaged by illegal abortions. In addition, the individualistic nature of such charity work also means that it is not usually seen as relating to the overall political goals of those religious organizations.

As the AWID (2009) reported after their 160 countries' comparative action research:

> Women's rights activists in Egypt, Iraq, Pakistan, Turkey and Uzbekistan list numerous examples of religious fundamentalisms providing basic services where the state has failed to do so or where social divisions breed structural poverty. Many note, however, that such remedies are temporary and superficial, do not address the root causes of inequality and create dependency among those served by humanitarian or charity drives. Although service provision appears to be a relatively more popular recruitment strategy in the Middle East and North Africa region, it is also a feature of Catholic and Christian fundamentalisms. Evangelical Christian sects active in communities in Latin America, Asia and the former Soviet Union provide food as well as employment and educational opportunities to disaffected groups.

Fundamentalism, the 'clash of civilizations' and inter-religious cooperation

Although religious fundamentalist militarist activism has been on the rise since the 1980s, the attacks on the World Trade Center towers

---

[14] For example, see http://newsinitiative.org/story/2007/07/27/sanctuary_old_idea_new_movement; Lippet, 2005.

in New York and the Pentagon in Washington, DC, September 11, 2001, marked the 'official' launch of the 'global war on terrorism' and the official demarcation by President Bush of all states and societies as constituting part of axes of good or of evil. Many used the notion of the 'clash of civilizations', written about by Samuel Huntington (1993), to describe the global processes involved. Only relatively few know that 2001, the year in which 9/11 occurred, had been designated by the UN as the year of 'dialogue between civilizations' and that this dialogue had been initiated and promoted mostly by the Islamic Republic of Iran, ruled at the time by the reformist President Khatami.[15]

Whether clash or dialogue, the notion of separate civilizations reifies boundaries of belonging between people, homogenizes each civilization, assumes a similar attachment and practice by all people from the same civilization in basically the same 'culture and tradition', and most of all, assumes a non-overlap between the different civilizations. This, of course, ignores the synthetic nature of all contemporary cultures, their appropriations of symbolic artefacts and meanings from other civilizations and their own internal heterogeneity discussed at the beginning of the chapter.

Huntington himself distinguished between around nine different major civilizations.[16] However, in the 'global war on terrorism' – and in the minds of Islamist fundamentalists – the world is dichotomized between the good and the evil – and who is what depends on which side you are on.

And yet in various UN and other global forums this popular imagery is often subsumed by another dichotomy of belonging – one between the secular and religious, where coalitions of conservative religious political powers, such as the Vatican and the Iranian government, collude against women's reproductive rights, for instance, in the UN 1994 Cairo conference, a coalition which was more solid in the ICPD +10 meeting and in its opposition to any UN declaration on sexual orientation which unites Muslim countries, most African countries and the Vatican.

---

[15]See http://www.un.org/Dialogue/background.html.In 2010, Iran officially abolished this initiative. Thanks to Mastoureh Fathi for drawing my attention to this (BBC Persian, September 21, 2010), http://www.bbc.co.uk/persian/iran/2010/09/100921_l38_iran_calender_event.shtml

[16]Western, Sinic, Orthodox, Budhuist, Japan, Latin America, Hindu and Islamic, although Ethiopia, Haiti and Israel seem not to be part of any of the above in his scheme.

The inter-religious coalitions can have an even more convoluted logic than just a tactical alliance in the struggle for a specific UN resolution. For example, Hindu fundamentalists are prepared to accept Sikhism, which they encompassed as some kind of indigenous Indian religion, as long as they are also prepared to be their allies against the 'invading Muslims',[17] while Christian fundamentalists have been funding Jewish settler *yeshivot* on the West Bank because they believe that a precondition to the return of Jesus is the return of all Jews to the Holy Land. Then they will be given the choice between converting to Christianity or extermination. The Jewish fundamentalists who believe that the Messiah will come once all Jews have 'returned' do not care that the Christian fundamentalists are basically anti-Semitic and want all Jews who refuse conversion to be exterminated in the future, and happily receive their financial aid now for their own purposes.[18]

The dichotomy of religious versus secular, however, is spreading even further and in less formalized ways. While it might not be surprising, given the rise in religious-based politics of belonging, that Sudanese refugees in Britain send their wives and children to other Muslim countries like Egypt or Saudi Arabia if they can afford it, it is interesting that Catholic schools in France opened their doors to Muslim girls who wanted to continue to wear headscarves after they were forbidden to do so in secular state schools, given the scarcity of Muslim schools in France.[19]

Moreover, these coalitions are often determined by other political reasons and can create some unpredictable alliances. Chetan Bhatt (2007), for example, has shown how the same fundamentalist militias which are fighting the West were also cooperating with them in humanitarian aid after the Kashmir earthquake.

Ecumenical organizations, of course, have been active in a whole range of charity and peace activities, in which religion has been assumed to be the foundation of moral accountability (Brewer et al., 2010). Recently, however, since the failure of the Left in the post-Soviet era, there is a growing popularity in various countries of coalition bodies in which

---

[17]This construction, however, can also be found in the India Constitution Article 25 which subsumes Sikhs, Jains and Buddhists in 'Hindu'.

[18]For example, http://www.npr.org/templates/story/story.php?storyId=105310088; see also Fisk, 2002.

[19]See http://www.nytimes.com/2008/09/30/world/europe/30schools.html

both religious and secular community organizations take part, and in which religious organizations are seen as the most sustainable form of organization in civil society (e.g. in the UK, 'Strangers into Citizens'[20] in London or the 'City of Sanctuary'[21] in Sheffield). It is difficult to know, at this stage, whether this mode of organization is stable or just a phase in the struggle by religious and civil organizations for the domination of a civil 'Big Society'. It is even more difficult to know whether this means a reconfiguration of religious belonging as a facet of activist citizenship construction or (or as well as) whether it is one of the 'warning signs of fundamentalisms' (Imam et al., 2004) in which political-religious groups seek to widen their membership base and their political powers. It is significant, however, that recently there have been a couple of national and international initiatives by atheist secularists who have discovered the need to organize a defensive campaign against what they see as the religionization of public life, such as 'the International Bureau of Laicite,[22] initiated by Women Living Under Muslim Laws in December 2009.

Multiculturalism and multi-faithism

As mentioned in the previous chapters, certain changes have taken place in the governmentality of difference and diversity as well as of migration in western societies – associated with but not wholly determined by the aftermath of 9/11 – which have meant that the transatlantic project of multiculturalism has been transformed as a form of common sense, even where it has not ended officially. Paradoxically, the alternative political projects that emerged in its stead promoted assimilation and religious (rather than ethnic and cultural) diversity at the same time. On the one hand, there has been a growing pressure, under the notion of 'social cohesion', for immigrants and ethnic minorities to assimilate into the hegemonic majorities. At best there would be a provision of 'efficient' generic services for migrants and immigrants from everywhere (which would dichotomize between the locals and the immigrants while no

---

[20]See http://strangersintocitizens.blogspot.com/

[21]See http://www.cityofsanctuary.com/

[22]See http://www.wluml.org/zh-hant/node/5768

longer funding projects in specific migrants' communities[23] and at a time where there will also be growing pressure to 'cap' the number of immigrants and deport the 'undesirables' from the South, or – as especially but not exclusively happened in France – the Roma[24]). On the other hand, there is a growing legitimation and naturalization of segregated faith communities, faith schools and often also – with more or less successful and/or legitimate incorporation of legal pluralism, especially, but not exclusively – in the realm of personal law.[25]

'Faith' (unlike 'race' or even country of origin when it comes to members of the national collectivity) becomes the legitimate naturalized signifier of difference and a separate community organization in the 'post-racist' era, although of course in reality this has been to a large extent a euphemism for constructing 'Muslims' as the insiders' outsiders. This came out very clearly, for instance, in Tony Blair's speech in December 2006 on multiculturalism.[26] Probably the most surprising aspect of this speech was Blair's suggestion that the way forward for a social cohesion of members of different faith communities was to organize mutual visits and common activities between classes from the different faith schools which were being encouraged by the British government while not challenging at all the naturalized boundary of people of different faiths as the only legitimate sub-communities of the British social cohesive national community. Some, like Tariq Modood (2003), see in the separate organization of 'faith communities' a form of active/ist citizenship and a way for collective integration to take place within a multicultural Britain. Others, however, in having to watch the reconstruction of

---

[23]Sometimes, as was the case with the Southall Black Sisters (SBS) in London, the local council tried to stop their funding, claiming that this was discriminating as they were not serving the whole population. The Supreme Court, on July 28, 2008, rejected this claim, emphasizing that sometimes in order to get equality of delivery, as the Race Relations Act demands, there is often a need for special agencies to cater for the social needs of sectors of the population and there is no dichotomy between cohesion and specialist services.

[24]See Moran (2010).

[25]See ICHRP (2009).

[26]See http://www.number10.gov.uk/Page10563. It is important to note, however, that the spread and funding of faith schools or private academies run by various religious and fundamentalist groups and individuals is being ever intensified under the Conservative/Lib-Dem coalition government which came to power in 2010.

minorities into religious subjects at the same time as the re-centring of the White Christian hegemonic majority, find themselves almost nostalgic about the 'good old days' of multiculturalism with all its problematics (discussed in the previous chapter).[27]

The centrality of faith organizations in its civil society structure has made British society more similar to the American model, but all over Europe religion and religious organizations have come to occupy more central and salient roles in civil society, especially when it comes to Muslim communities. In France, for example, when Sarkozy was Interior Minister, he created in 2003 the French Council of the Muslim Faith (*Conseil Français du Culte Musulman*), into which quite fundamentalist organizations, such as the Union of Islamic Organizations of France, were also incorporated. In Eastern Europe, in the post-Soviet era, where the restructured state left a vacuum in many social services areas, there has been an explosion in the involvement and visibility of religious organizations in many countries both in terms of service delivery and politics.[28] As discussed above, in the South, religion was often never replaced as the signifier of boundaries and the culture of social solidarity but even there, with the combination of rising political power and funding from outside aid organizations, these political movements have become stronger. Part of the reason for their success is the processes of decentralization/privatization/removal of the state's 'bread for the poor' with its privatization and neo-liberalization. However, this does not always necessarily work. In both India and Kyrgyzstan, for instance, 'tradition' has been mobilized to justify the withdrawal of the state (Galanter & Krishnan, 2004; Beyer 2007) and yet it is quite clear that people want more, not less, state provisions in this economic crisis.

Another side to this enhancement of faith organizations in civil societies is the parallel rise in the persecution of religious minorities where visions of pluralism and multi-faith threaten fundamentalist visions, whether this is the Muslims in India and in the West or the (local) Christians in Pakistan and the Middle East.

---

[27]Please see the Southall Black Sisters' (SBS) and the Women Against Fundamentalism's (WAF) submission to the Commission on Social Cohesion, http://www.womenagainstfundamentalism. org.uk/WAF_SBS_report.doc

[28]See http://www.awid.org/eng/Issues-and-Analysis/Library/Fundamentalism-Threatens-Women-of-Eastern-Europe

Religion and feminism

From the discussion above, it is clear that gender relations on the one hand, and feminist ideologies on the other hand, are quite central to contemporary debates around questions of religion and religious fundamentalisms and their relations to contemporary political projects of belonging.

Feminist movements have emerged in all the major religions, although Judith Plaskow (1990) probably expressed some common apprehension of them all when she claimed that in order for Judaism to transform into a religion which was not patriarchal, it would need to undergo as great a revolution as it did when it transformed itself from a religion focused around a temple in which animals were sacrified into the abstract monotheistic religion of the Jewish diaspora.

During the week in November 2009 when I was writing this section of the chapter, a member of the Jewish feminist group 'Women of the Wall', was arrested in Jerusalem when she tried to pray in front of the 'Wailing Wall' with a 'talit' – the white praying shawl in which Jewish men wrap themselves when praying – as apparently she had transgressed the by-law which commands that all those praying near the wall be dressed 'appropriately'. In the past, members of such groups were arrested when they tried to lead prayers at the male section of the Wall.

As mentioned earlier in the chapter, many religious feminists attempt to use the discourse of 'religion' versus that of 'tradition'. For example, Jewish feminists have argued that it is not that women are not allowed to lead prayers, but that to do so is not allowed in mixed audiences – so as not 'to distract' the men from their praying – and therefore women leading prayers in 'women only' audiences are not breaking any rules.

The issues, of course, are much more serious than that and indeed concern, the ability of women to separate traditional religious discourses from a core religious essence in which they can participate as equals. As Karen Armstrong (2009) argues, this is an impossible mission because all sacred texts are embedded in allegorical ambiguities. In *Gender and Nation* (Yuval-Davis, 1997a: Chapter 3), I relate to the debate on that question which focused around the possibility of 'post-modern' piecemeal feminist practice in Iran and elsewhere, which took place between Afsane Najmabadi (1995) and Deniz Kandiyoti (1991). My argument there was that to a great extent such practice might be the only way of struggling for women's equality where there are no secular spaces, but then, where there are no such spaces, work and the achievements of years can be destroyed in moments within authoritarian religious environments, if the supreme religious authority decries that those are not valid/permitted according to the religious laws. It is interesting that Saba Mahmoud (2005, 2009), writing more than a decade after these debates have taken place, and after studying young Muslim women who have been part of the Muslim revivalist movement in Cairo, has come out against the notions of 'liberation' and 'resistance' as being necessarily central to feminism, especially in the non-western world. She reached this conclusion after observing the pious women she studied organizing themselves around self-fashioning and ethical conduct rather than the transformation of juridical and state institutions. I wonder, however, to what extent one can construct these women as autonomous political subjects and what are the political implications of such 'politics of piety'. With all the differences, but given contemporary politics in Egypt and the role of various groupings associated with the Muslim Brotherhood in these, I cannot avoid thinking of the 'born again' American hippy Jewish women I studied in the 1970s who found themselves, while practising a subjective praxis of piety, becoming part of the settlement project of the occupied Palestinian West Bank and the overall fundamentalist Jewish political project of belonging in Israel (Yuval-Davis, 1992b).

The boundary between politics of piety and transformative religious feminism is far from being clear, however. In the years since the publication of *Gender and Nation*, religious feminism, especially among young Muslim women, has arisen considerably all over the world and has a lot to do with contemporary political projects of belonging. In the West especially, but not only, where the use of headscarves became forbidden in public spaces, wearing a headscarf, and sometimes even the full cover of the *niqab*, becomes a way of declaring one's loyalty to one's community of belonging, as well as a way of claiming power within that community. Similar things happen among 'born again' Jewish and Christian women who join fundamentalist versions of the religion, which gives them identity security as well as more often than not the personal support of their community of belonging in which their families can be included or, often initially at least, excluded.

At the same time, in non-fundamentalist religious developments, often generic human rights and women's rights discourses prevail and women have gradually been allowed more and more access to leadership positions, in spite of vehement opposition by the more conservative elements within a religious organization. At the time of writing this section of the chapter, there was a discussion among conservative bishops of the Anglican Church whether or not to accept the Pope's invitation to join the Catholic Church as a mark of protest against the inclusion of women bishops within that Church.

As the Anglican Church was originally created by Henry VIII as a device for securing a divorce (although, of course, it was also partly a nationalist/class project in which he and the English aristocracy appropriated the wealth and power of the Catholic Church in England), it would be interesting to see whether these days sexual politics would prove to be stronger than the nationalist politics of these conservative Anglican bishops.

Another kind of feminist politics which relates to the religious sphere is the various feminist organizations that were established in different countries as well as internationally in order to fight against the effects of fundamentalist religious political movements locally and globally. These organizations are not usually anti-religious but are worried that particular forms of religion have growing powers in the public sphere; these have often been very detrimental to women's rights, even when they have given them subjectively feelings of empowerment and support. Both Women Living Under Muslims Laws (WLUML)[29] and Catholics for Free Choice have local associated organizations in many countries as well as a global organizing group, and their networks have been very active in the UN and other global forums as well as locally in campaigns aimed at allowing women freedom of choice in regard to their sexualities and reproductive rights in addition to their overall social and political equality. WLUML has produced over the years a large body of literature which illustrates how Muslim laws, while perceived as 'the one truth', actually operate differently in the various Muslim societies and states.

Contesting religious absolutism has also been the task of Women Against Fundamentalism (WAF),[30] which was established in the UK at the height of the Rushdie Affair. Unlike the other two organizations, members of WAF are from different ethnic and religious backgrounds and have seen their role as being to struggle against sexism and fundamentalism in all religions as well as to promote the

---

[29]See http://www.wluml.org/

[30]See http://www.womenagainstfundamentalism.org.uk/

transformation of Britain into a secular, anti-racist state, in which there is a full separation between religion and the state. While one of their targets – the British blasphemy law, which privileged Christianity – was removed by the New Labour government, they still had to fight against the inclusion of a clause in the new British Equalities law which they[31] see, to a large extent, as expanding the notion of blasphemy to all major religions. Also, their struggle for a secular education is not hugely successful in a time of British multi-faithism in which a third of state schools are now religious schools (Runnymede, 2009[32]).

Under the Bush administration feminists all over the world, and especially in the South, suffered greatly as a result of the 'gag rule'[33] which forbade funding to any organization which gave information about, let alone practised, abortions. This is just one of the reasons that the largest international women's organization, AWID (Association for Women's Development and Human Rights), decided to carry out a comparative action research study, obtaining information from feminist development workers and human rights activists from the 160 different countries in which they have members. The results (AWID, 2009), some of which have been quoted in this chapter, have given the international and global women's movements (which will be discussed in the next chapter) their first systematic data on how different fundamentalist religious organizations in different countries and from different religions have been operating and how these have affected women's rights in these countries.

Conclusion

Religious belongings, as has been discussed and illustrated in this chapter, far from 'withering away' with modernization and liberalization, have remained engaged throughout as important elements of nationalist, ethnic and other political projects of belonging. In recent years, religious political projects of belonging have also become more and more autonomous, constructed as providing an alternative empowering way of belonging to marginalized and threatened

---

[31]I'm a founder member of WAF.

[32]See http://www.familyandparenting.org/Filestore//Documents/consultations/runnymede_faith_schools_consultation.pdf

[33]Consequently removed by Obama as one of his first symbolic acts when entering the White House.

people, in the South and in the North. The Iranian Islamic revolution is probably the first popular revolution since the French revolution that did not follow nationalist and socialist enlightenment models as a way of achieving national liberation and social justice. However, even that revolution and other Muslim, Jewish, Hindu and Christian absolutist or fundamentalist religious political movements, in spite of their often anti-western rhetoric, did not reject but rather benefitted from and pursued the latest technologies for armaments and communication and the support of global financial institutions such as the IMF.[34]

The greatest strengths and causes of the sustainability of religious movements are that in spite of this, they work well on both local and global bases, on individuals and communities, and in spite of their *de facto* exclusionary and hierarchical social relations regarding women, ethnic, religious and sexual minorities they can provide discourses of both empowerment and moral accountability that in times of growing instability under globalized neo-liberalism seem for many to be the best anchors to depend on, both in terms of ascribed identities and in terms of guidance for social and political action, for a growing section of numerous populations in different parts of the globe.

In the next chapter we turn to explore political projects of belonging for which the need for ascribed identities often comes second to ascribed moral values as ways to transcend borders and boundaries and also – as I shall be arguing – to often reconstruct them in other ways.

---

[34]See http://www.mees.com/postedarticles/finance/iran/a45n33b02.htm

5

The Cosmopolition Question: Situating the Human and Human Rights

Introduction

Ulrich Beck stated in one of his writings that 'to belong or not to belong is the cosmopolitan question' (2003; cited in Calhoun, 2003a: 244). As will become clear in this chapter, I believe the cosmopolitan question/s to be much more complex than that. This chapter explores, however, some of the main issues in the relationship between cosmopolitanism and belonging, as well as the politics of belonging. If Favell (1999) defined politics of belonging as 'the dirty work of boundary maintenance', cosmopolitan projects seem to counter-weigh such political projects of belonging and challenge the notion of boundary itself. As such they seem to have become particularly popular in recent years. Indeed, it can be argued that the kind of political projects of belonging most suitable to the age of globalization would be the cosmopolitan ones. Mary Kaldor (2003) even went so far as to construct a typology according to which only a cosmopolitan politics of belonging could provide the right antidote to those who initiate and maintain the endless new wars so typical to the contemporary era. Like globalization, however, cosmopolitanism is not a new phenomenon, although it has undergone a revival since the end of the Cold War. Like other political projects of belonging, cosmopolitanism is not an homogeneous project and affects in differential ways people situated in differential social positionings.

This chapter opens with an exploration of the notion of cosmopolitanism and the different ways in which it has been constructed and debated. It then focuses on the extent to which cosmopolitanism presents an alternative mode of belonging in the contemporary world to more bounded modes and what this actually means. Different kinds of cosmopolitan discourses will be examined in relation to this – 'situated', 'rooted' and 'rootless' cosmopolitanism, as well as what Mica Nava (2007) and others have called 'visceral' cosmopolitanism. The chapter then explores cosmopolitanism as a political project both from above and below. First, it examines cosmopolitanism as a form of supranational and global governance and its relationship to the UN form of governance, and it then examines both the legislative and demotic discourses of 'human rights' and 'human security' as probably the most important contemporary cosmopolitan discourses. It heightens some of their strengths but also discusses some of their problematics.

The chapter turns then to examine what many, following the 2000 article in *The Nation* on the legacy of the mass protests in Seattle[1] (Brecher et al., 2000), have called 'globalization from below' and its differential effects on various groupings of people across the globe. It discusses various social movements which have used human rights and related discourses as their mobilizing and normative base, from ecological to anti-capitalist and international solidarity movements, secular and religious. It explores how the different new technologies of communication and travel have affected these movements as well as the extent to which they have developed alternative political modes of belonging. As in previous chapters, it also briefly discusses feminist politics that have been considered to be cosmopolitan.

The chapter concludes by looking at the general question of the relationship between universalism and belonging.

What is cosmopolitanism?

Overall, cosmopolitanism is a slippery concept. Looking at the literature, it is very difficult to find a clear definition of it. Most of those who write about it assume the reader already knows the meaning of the term. One definition that attempted to catch this illusive characteristic of cosmopolitanism has been by Pollock et al. (2002). In the introduction to their volume on cosmopolitanism, they claim that it:

> may be a project whose conceptual content and pragmatic character are not only as yet unspecified but also must always

---

[1] The mass protest gathering that took place in Seattle in November 1999 around the time of the meeting of the World Trade Organization.

escape positive and definite specification, precisely because specifying cosmopolitanism positively and definitely is an uncosmopolitan thing to do. (Pollock et al., 2002: 1)

The first to use the term cosmopolitanism, however, was the Greek philosopher Diogenes, who defined himself as 'cosmopolitan', 'a citizen of the world' (Diogenes Laertius: VI63, cited in Vieten, 2007: 8), in contrast to the citizen of the *polis*, the city-state. This definition includes the two elements around which much of the discussions on cosmopolitanism have focused – cosmopolitanism as boundariless politics of belonging and cosmopolitanism as a participatory mode in supranational polity. While these two modes are usually closely related, they are also very different and irreducible to each other. As Eleonore Kofman (2004) argues, the first tends to produce a literature which constructs cosmopolitanism as a form of belonging which is detached, fluid, and which avoids any fixed notions of boundaries. A representative approach to cosmopolitanism of this type is that of John Urry's 'cultural citizen' (1995) who operates on the surface, travels frequently, and feels at home everywhere and nowhere.

The second is based more on local attachments in which the national expands into the international and the transnational. Here is where discussions on global citizenship and human rights legislations belong, such as those promoted by David Held (1995) and Mary Kaldor (2003), which are discussed below.

However, as Calhoun (2006), Fine (2008) and others have shown, the literature and constructions of cosmopolitanism have been more complex than that.

One basic differentiation that they, but especially Etienne Balibar (2006), make is between cosmopolitanism as an ideological utopia, in the Kantian way (1998 [1795]), that like all other ideological utopias can establish a moral and political trajectory rather than as a realizable practical project (as can be seen, for example, in Marta Nussbaum's work on cosmopolitanism (2002 [1996]) in which it is seen as a universalist moral imperative), and cosmopolitics, which specifically refer to a cluster of political projects which one can relate to globalization, human rights, socialism, etc. (as will be discussed later on in the chapter).

Against such a dichotomous approach to politics and morality we have Ulrich Beck's (1998) 'cosmopolitan manifesto', in which he calls for the moral political project of global citizenship enhanced by a new kind of social cohesion which should be based on the recognition that individualization, diversity and scepticism are written into our global culture. He argues that there is a new dialectic of global and local questions which do not fit into national politics. He sees liberty, diversity and tolerance as the cosmopolitan values.

A construction of cosmopolitanism which is neither political nor moral is what Mica Navas (2007) 'visceral cosmopolitanism'. 'Visceral cosmopolitanism' operates on an inarticulated emotional experiential level, in which a person (and as Nava points out, more often than not that person is a woman) might be open to sexual as well as emotional attachments to 'the other' that cross ethnic, racial and other social boundaries. As she demonstrates, such visceral cosmopolitanism can coexist without necessarily breaking away from racial, national and other forms of prejudice, as was the case with some of the British white women who had sexual and emotional relationships with black GIs during the Second World War, for instance.

There is a continuum of visceral cosmopolitanism between such curiosity, which includes the emotional readiness to open oneself to get close to 'the exotic other', 'the stranger', and what Szerszynki and Urry (2006; Urry, 2002) call 'banal globalism', a result of the pro-liferation of global symbols and narratives made available through the media and popular culture. Although this can and does hap-pen everywhere, it is especially developed in contemporary urban metropolitan life where a multicultural conviviality has developed (Gilroy, 2004). Richard Sennet (1977) describes the cosmopolitan as one moving comfortably within diversity, a common phenom-enon in urban life. A similar but more structural approach has been developed by Michael Keith (2005: 3) where he speaks about how the cosmopolitan city does not merely curate the exotica of differ-ence, but also raises transnational or global politics in its streets and neighbourhoods and reveals the contested and limited nature of the national settlement in its schoolrooms and town halls. It involves naturalizing living side by side as well as befriending and develop-ing intimate relationships across cultural, religious, racial and other forms of social diversities – what Patricia Hill-Collins (2009) calls 'the new politics of the community'. In other contexts, as will be discussed later in the chapter, such visceral cosmopolitanism can make people risk their lives for others outside their collectivities of belonging, as in international solidarity movements or under the Nazi occupation.

However, cosmopolitanism does not mean that people stop belonging to particular collectivities or that all their identifications are a result of free choice. Within the multicultural conviviality, ascription, discrimination and forced identities continue to exist and thus affect in differential ways various members of the same society, even if normatively and politically they are of a similar mode. As Calhoun (2006: 537) emphasizes, when the limits of belonging to specific webs of relationships are transcended, this is not into a free-dom from relationships but into a different organization of relation-ships. And Tania Murray Ki (2000:246) goes even further and argues that these days there is 'a global conjuncture of belonging' in which 'cosmopolitanism and parochialism are no longer opposed; they are linked and [mutually] reinforcing.'

It is for this reason that Homi Bhabha's (1996) notion of 'ver-nacular cosmopolitanism' (see also Werbner, 2006) is so important. As cosmopolitanism does not mean abstractions of identities and belonging, it also does not mean abstractions of specific cultural context/s and resources. Although Bhabha emphasizes the 'impu-rity' and hybridity of concrete cultural constructions, the importance of the 'third space' (Bhabha, 1990b) and 'border zones' (Anzaldúa, 1987) in any social and political change, this is definitely not about the abstraction of the individual and her location.

Therefore, another important differentiation when we discuss cos-mopolitanism relates to the situatedness of cosmopolitan projects (Yuval-Davis et al., 2006). Who are their carriers and where/how are they located intersectionally, locally and globally? Are they located only in cities, where traditional communities largely no longer exist and people live in 'communities of strangers'? Do they carry with them their own assumed boundaries, and how do they relate, more generally, to different cultural, political and economic habitus (Bourdieu, 1984)?

In other words, when we study particular cosmopolitan projects, we need to understand both their actual social situatedness and their political and normative message regarding the issue of being rooted in such particular context.

Situated cosmopolitanisms

In her (2007) dissertation on 'Situated Cosmopolitanisms', Ulrike Vieten[2] explores specific cultural and philosophical traditions relating to

---

[2]One of my ex-PhD students at the University of East London.

cosmopolitanism and notions of 'the other' in Britain and Germany. Recognizing the uniqueness of the voices of the various scholars she had studied in both countries, as well as the inevitable mutual (although not symmetrical) cross influences of their works on each other, she nevertheless argues that historical, political, economic and cultural traditions help to establish differentiated hegemonic discourses within which specific intellectual visions emerge. She also argues that in the case of Britain, the overall context in which the idea of cosmopolitanism first emerged has been the rise and fall of the British Empire, which produced a specific kind of commercial cosmopolitanism, first formulated in the work of Adam Smith in (1998 [1776]), which outlined his vision of commerce as a tool to sustain peace among nations. As Mica Nava (2007) has also demonstrated in her work on Selfridges, national boundaries and closures can be seen as obstacles to the serious work of doing business. Obviously the British Empire invested a great deal in accumulating military power and engaged in frequent warfare in order to guarantee that no political borders would block the smooth operation of British business, even if it was exporting opium to China. Once imperial governance was ensured, however, other forms of ethnic, religious and cultural boundaries were not seen as obstacles for this encompassing vision. In Germany, on the other hand, the situation was quite different. Unlike the British case in which domination, rather than homogenization, was the primary political goal within the British Isles as well as globally, in Germany the focus was on the unification and homogenization of the German people, and by implication, 'civilized Europe' as a whole, focusing on issues of national culture and faith. Vieten (2007: 50) quotes Fichte (1806), who saw cosmopolitanism as the next step to patriotism in what can be called a revolution by stages: first the nation, then humanity (or, at least, those people who are considered to be human) as a whole, as represented by a united Christian Europe.

While Ulrike Vieten focused on the situatedness of cosmopolitanism in dominant nations such as Britain and Germany, Jansen (2008) and Vidmar Horvat (2011) settled on the cosmopolitanism of more marginalized nations who traditionally constituted parts of larger empires, such as the Ottoman and Habsburg. Jansen focused his ethnographic work, conducted between 1996 and 1998, on Zagreb and Belgrade, while Vidmar Horvat relates more generally to what she calls 'a Western Balkan perspective'. Within such a political context, cosmopolitanism, rather than being seen, like in Fichte's work, as the next step to patriotism, is viewed in the context of nationalist conflicts as signifying the break-up of the national ranks and a sure sign of treason and disloyalty. At the same time, in the Former Yugoslavian context, for urban ordinary cosmopolitans this term evoked a nostalgia for a past 'normality' that came to an abrupt end with the eruption of the armed conflict.

For Kwame Anthony Appiah (2006), focusing on Ghana, the country in which he grew up before becoming a professor of philosophy in Princeton University, the relationship between nationalism and cosmopolitanism is much more harmonious but in a very different way to that of Fichte's. Appiah vehemently rejects the often perceived equation between cosmopolitanism and westernization, and brings up his father as an example of a 'cosmopolitan patriot' to whom loyalty to the Ghanian nation was not a contradiction to his loyalty to humanist values.

'Rooted' and 'rootless' cosmopolitanism

As discussed in Chapter 1, the importance of belonging to particular communities and identities has a rich political as well as sociological and psychological tradition. Such a normative approach has also been applied to the issue of cosmopolitanism (see, for example, Robert Merton, 1957). In socialist, especially post-colonial studies, however, such an approach has acquired an additional edge. Appiah's (2006) standpoint on cosmopolitanism is seen as an example to what Sidney Tarrow (2003) and others have called 'rooted cosmopolitanism'. While many, including myself, would see socialism and communism as belonging to the cluster of cosmopolitan political projects, cosmopolitanism, usually accompanied with the prefix of 'rootless', has been a derogatory swear word within communist discourse, and often a euphemism for anti-Semitic disclosure directed against the Jews.

Interestingly, it was the Stalinist communist party in Russia which polarized the relationship between patriotism and cosmopolitanism (editorials in the newspaper *Pravda* in 1949 are often mentioned as a classical example of this[3]). The carriers of 'rootless cosmopolitanism', then, were not just non-patriots but also the Jews who (at that time)

---

[3] See http://www.cyberussr.com/rus/chernov/chernov-cosmo-e.html

had no homeland of their own and were blamed as having no loyalty to the states in which they were resident or even citizens.

For the same reason that Stalin (1941 [1917]) and even Otto Bauer (2001 [1924]), who believed in the separation of nations and states, would not recognize the Jewish collectivity as entitled to national self-determination, the construction of the Jews as a diasporic collectivity (before the establishment of the state of Israel in 1948 and the hegemony of Zionism as the Jewish nationalist ideology) earned them the title of being 'rootless'.

As can be seen from the writings of Appiah and Tarrow and many others, in spite of the growth of post-colonial diasporas as both empirical and political phenomena, 'rootedness' is valued today no less than in Stalin's or even Fichte's times, although for somewhat different reasons. In earlier days the discourse of 'rootless cosmopolitanism' has been often used as an inferiorizing and exclusionary discourse against the racialized Other – mainly Jews and other diasporic minorities in Europe. In the post-colonial and neo-liberal globalized world, it has been mainly adopted as a discourse of resistance against western hegemony, a 'McDonaldian' (Barber, 1995) commercialism that homogenizes, as well as transcends, boundaries of belonging as in earlier imperial times. In order to 'decentre' the West, there is a perceived need to deconstruct the equation between westernization, modernization, globalization and cosmopolitan ideologies which transcend boundaries of belonging.

And yet, it is important to emphasize that 'rootless cosmopolitanism' is as situated, as vernacular, as that of the 'rooted' variety and that the latter perspective concerning cosmopolitanism can easily neglect the plight of the most marginal, excluded and racialized as irrelevant to the main concerns of cosmopolitan discourse. Moreover, the situatedness of the supposed 'rootless others' is important not only in relation to racialized minorities to whom cultural hybridization and transcending boundaries of cultural, emotional as well as geographical belonging might be a question of survival (Werbner, 1999a), but also in relation to professional and academic 'nomads' (Braidotti, 1994) and privileged ex-pats. As Mike Savage and others have shown (e.g. Savage et al., 2004; Knoweles, 2006; see also Bauman, 2005; Szerszynki & Urry, 2006), 'banal globalism' is often very firmly embedded in their suburban urban neighbourhoods where the families of those 'cosmopolitans' live and their attitudes are not that different from that of their neighbours who do not spend very much time travelling and working abroad. Moreover, when they do live for shorter or longer periods in other countries, the ex-pats or the professional international workers, as Knoweles and others have shown (Knoweles & Harper, 2010; O'Reilly, 2000), will often live in separate 'compounds' with other western or professionals and thus their 'feeling at home' everywhere (as is the case with most tourists) is cushioned by facilities which most of the 'natives' do not possess or have any use for.

Thus, cosmopolitanism is always situated, although not always rooted, and intersectional social locations, of which national origins and formal citizenships are only part of the constituting factors, affect profoundly cosmopolitan gazes. As feminist standpoint theorists have shown (Haraway, 1991), there is no 'view from nowhere'.

It is especially necessary to explore the boundaries in belonging in those cosmopolitan projects which construct themselves as universal political projects. We shall turn, therefore, to briefly examine the UN, the closest existing political institution of world governance, and also examine more closely issues and discourses of human rights and human security which are part of its cosmopolitan political agenda.

The UN and world governance

As mentioned above, ideas about 'citizenship of the world' can be found already in ancient Greek philosophy, as well as in later western philosophies, most notably Kant (1999 [1795]), who imagined that perpetual peace would be possible only with the application of one common rule of law for everyone. This is the case as most of the political narratives on social contract and social order assumed national or imperial states' boundaries, while in the interstate arenas relations were largely dictated by conflicting interests that were settled by various power mechanisms including war. International peace congresses attempting to find alternative normative arrangements to handle such conflicts and international non-governmental organizations (such as the Red Cross) started to appear in the second half of the nineteenth century, but it took the First World War and the enormous losses on all sides for the first suprastate governance organization to be established under the Versailles Treaty – the League of Nations, which at its height had 58 state members. While its basic aim was to prevent another world war by working together to negotiate for peace and to defend human rights, its structure did not reflect the differential powers of the different states and there was no right of veto for the superpowers, which eventually resulted in its desolution with the rise of fascism and Nazism and eventually the Second World War (Zimmern, 1936; Walters, 1952; Ostrower, 1996; Bell, 2007).

The United Nations,[4] which does include in its structure this decision-making mechanism via the Security Council, that includes permanent (the superpowers) and non-permanent members, has managed to survive since 1948 when it was first established, including the Korean and the Cold Wars, and has today 192 member states. In addition to the General Assembly, the Security Council and the Economic and Social Council, the UN has a long list of associated organizations which operate in different international arenas, from health, to refugees to labour and trade as well as the World Criminal Court and military peace-keeping forces. While the World Bank and the International Monetary Fund were established already in 1944 in Bretton Woods,[5] they still work closely with the UN.

Opinions vary as to the effectiveness of the UN, especially its general assembly, which some critiques have tended to belittle as just 'an expensive talking shop'. Others see it as little more than the USA's tool for legitimating its international hegemony, especially after the end of the Cold War.

When David Held (1995) talked about cosmopolitan democratic world government, he had in mind a much more unitary, state-like governing apparatus than the UN, with much more developed decision-making powers. Although he claims that such a governance institution would not replace national ones, its authority would clearly override them in cases of conflict – the major difference between his proposed world governance and that of the UN today. Indeed, when, towards the end of the millennium, an attempt was made to reform the UN – not only to make it more efficient for today's world, but also to give it some more decision-making powers – this ended in failure. The relatively marginal roles the UN has been playing in the wars in Iraq and Afghanistan have added to this feeling. Even the millennium development goals,[6] seen by many as a possible realization of the best global aspirations for the benefit of humanity organized and promoted by the UN, have been put in doubt in the context of the global economic crisis.

---

[4]See http://www.un.org/en/index.shtml; Schlesinger (2003); Chesterman (2005).

[5]See http://www.dailyreckoning.com.au/bretton-woods-agreement/2006/11/29/

[6]See http://www.un.org/millennium/sg/report/

It is quite clear (and this has also been seen on the regional level of the EU) that in spite of the development of various suprastate mechanisms and institutions of governance in and around the UN, it cannot be described as a cosmopolitan mode of governance, because although it speaks using the rhetoric of universal principles of justice, the political projects of belonging that dominate it remain on the level of the state and state-like clusters of interest, although these are multi- or rather transnational corporations – using international financial organizations but also some state ones, do, of course, have growing powers on that governance level as well as in more local ones. The fact that the intersectional interests of many of the citizens may often deviate from those represented by the so-called 'representatives' of their states, who negotiate and/or block various international agreements, often seems to be constructed as irrelevant except as a rhetorical legitimating device.

This issue has been at the centre of consideration for those who have called for a cosmopolitan world governance which would not only involve, as in the Held model, a world government, but would also heavily engage a global civil society, transcending borders and boundaries, in which civil dialogue instead of military conflict would determine global policies (Kaldor, 2003). The rise in numbers, funding and political involvement in the international arena of NGOs[7] (non-governmental organizations) has been precisely because they were seen as representatives of this global civil society. I have heard UN officials boasting, for example in the 1999 annual conference of the Academic Council of the United Nations (ACUN) in Oslo, that they indeed now involved global civil society in their policy consultations, and as proof of this mentioned two NGOs they had asked to participate in their meetings. Some of us gently pointed out that these NGOs, good as they were, could not be considered as representative of civil society – at most they were advocates of some particular interests within it. This is so not only because they were created by a particular group of people who were not mandated by any section of the population to represent them, but also because they were hand-picked by UN officials who thought they would be good to work with and thus cannot be seen as really independent political agents. Although in more recent years the problems of NGOs' accountability has started to be noted and various ways have been

---

[7]See http://www.ngo.org/links/list.htm

suggested to resolve or minimize the effects of these issues, the real accountability for most NGOs continues to be to their funders rather than to their constituencies.[8] Moreover, rather than opening the UN to an even more inclusive global civil society, it has been observed that the opposite is true and both in the April 2009 Durban Review Conference (of the 2001 World Conference Against Racism), which took place in Geneva, and in the World Summit on Climate Change in Copenhagen in December 2009, NGOs, let alone wider numbers of international protesters, have been excluded from the dialogue.

The professionalization and legalization of much of the NGOs and other international and global activist organizations and networks have not managed (yet? I somehow doubt it) to break the barrier between global citizenship and global governance. In any case, human rights discourse has occupied the centre-stage in these processes and struggles.

Cosmopolitanism, human rights and 'the other'

At the beginning of the chapter, I quoted Beck's statement that 'to belong or not to belong' is *the* cosmopolitan question. I would argue, however, that the other central cosmopolitan question is whether 'the other', and not just me/us, can/should belong. Above all, this concerns the question of whether belonging is (always, or even most of the time) a question of personal choice and who is included, or not, in the boundaries of belonging, even as 'a human'. In a lecture on refugees, Agamben (1994) pointed out that refugees (one of the ultimate 'others' in any society) are constructed around a major paradox, i.e. 'that precisely the figure that should have incarnated the rights of *man par excellence*, the refugee constitutes instead the radical crisis of the concept'.

Following Hannah Arendt (1943), Agamben claimed that 'in the nation-state system, the so-called sacred and inalienable rights of man prove to be completely unprotected at the very moment it is no longer possible to characterise them as rights of citizens of a state'. As such, as discussed in Chapter 2, Agamben looks (somewhat anachronistically, given the changes in the legal status of refugees since the Second

---

[8]See http://www.gdrc.org/ngo/accountability/index.html

World War) at the refugee as a modern embodiment of 'bare life', which in the *ancien régime* belonged to God and in the classical world was clearly distinct (as *zoe*) from political life (*bios*) which in the modern world relates to person's nationality. The refugee as such

> represents such a disquieting element ... because by breaking up the identity between man and citizen, between nativity and nationality, the refugee throws into crisis the original fiction of sovereignty. (Agamben, 1994: 2)

Agamben's reflections on 'bare lives' are very important and illuminating, especially when we are discussing the governability issues as well as the human rights of all kinds of 'people on the move' (to use the UN Secretary-General, Kofi Annan's definition), documented and non-documented, 'internally' or internationally displaced and migrating in different places on the globe. I would argue, however, that we have to be careful not to view even the most vulnerable categories of 'people on the move' just as 'bare life', to the extent that this category is defined not just as those who have no rights, but as those who have no political life, identity, subjectivity and belonging. Such a construction equates all polities with the 'nation-state' and all citizenships with citizenship of the nation-state. This was never true, and, as discussed in Chapter 2, is becoming less and less so. This should not be confused, however, with the very valid point that Agamben also makes which is that refugees threaten by their mere existence the principle of the nation-state as the exclusive principle of sovereignty.

If historically, under the French revolution, the rights of both the citizen and the (hu)man subjects were constructed together, these two kinds of rights have been clearly differentiated – if continually related – in later periods. However, their relationship is far from being simple or homogeneous. As Seyla Benhabib (2007) pointed out, cosmopolitan human rights law is differentially institutionalized across the world. This creates global citizenship stratification in which people with the same citizenship status would be entitled to different rights in different parts of the globe. This global citizenship stratification system intersects with another in which those who own particular passports would generally be awarded with more rights, formally or informally, in different countries (discussed in Chapter 2). It also intersects with the citizenship status stratification which exists in each country, from the 'super citizen' who fully belongs, via those who have full formal citizenship status but are subject to economic and/or racial discrimination; denizens, who have only part of these citizenship rights; the sub-citizens – refugees or asylum seekers – who have no legal right for employment and no security rights; to the un-citizens – the undocumented migrants and other forms of Agamben's 'bare life'.

The relationships between human rights and citizenship rights have not just expressed themselves in top-down manner of incorporating human rights to state law. The UN Declaration of Human Rights and its offshoots legislations have also been playing pivotal roles in various emancipatory struggles. Like other cosmopolitan projects, different kinds of human rights political projects tend to vary and be ambiguous on the extent to which cosmopolitanism is an alternative governance or governmentality project, involving a supranational global polity and even militarism, or whether it is a global identification communal resistance project, specific to particular social movements such as environmentalist and anti-capitalist.

The multiplex and controversial character of the human rights discourse

As Hannah Arendt argued in her classic writing on 'the rights of Man' (1986 [1951]), the human rights discourse is not anchored in any supranatural 'god' authority but in people's humanity. Shortly after its establishment in the aftermath of the Second World War, the 'universal declaration of human rights' was produced by a multinational, multicultural team working under the leadership of Eleanor Roosevelt at the newly established United Nations. While some would argue that the declaration was in actuality the USA exporting the principles of its own constitution to post-fascist Europe and the rest of the world (Sharma, 2006), for many others, and probably in a not mutually exclusive way, the declaration became a secular basis and a yardstick to assess and fight for liberty and justice all over the globe.

As Herman claims, the original declaration talked about different kinds of human rights:

> The original design of the UN members who passed the Universal Declaration of Human Rights in 1948 was to

consolidate the rights listed in the declaration into a single treaty encompassing civil, political, economic, social and cultural rights. US lobbying resulted in the division of the implementing covenant into an International Covenant on Civil and Political Rights and one on Economic, Social and Cultural Rights (16 December 1966). From that time onwards, the US official position has been to relegate the latter rights to a lower status and view them as something to be 'achieved progressively' rather than implemented immediately. (Herman, 2002: xiii)

Of course, the fall of the Soviet Union and the end of the Cold War have only exacerbated this differentiation. It was not until after these events, when alternative liberatory discourses such as socialism and Marxism became unfashionable, that human rights discourse became a major hegemonic discourse both official and demotic (G. Bauman, 1994). In 1994 a major UN conference was organized around the theme of human rights in Vienna, and more and more civil society organizations were established or declared themselves to be pursuing human rights goals.[9] At the same time there have been unprecedented developments in international human rights legislation, with its formal incorporation into various regional and national legislations as well as new supranational human rights organizations such as the International Criminal Court.[10] There has also been a certain reintegration of the different kinds of human rights and international organizations of human rights, such as Amnesty International, for instance, who have incorporated economic, social and cultural human rights into their aims.[11]

However, at the same time that human rights seemed to have become more and more a hegemonic discourse, when greater numbers of politicians and lawyers, as well as activists, have been dealing with this and incorporating it into the mainstream state as well as international legislation, others have become more and more critical of that discourse. Some critiques have come from the Right. For example, David Cameron, the leader of the British Conservative party, committed himself, when in opposition, to removing the

---

[9]This includes also the USA itself, in which there has been a surge in human rights – and not only civil rights – organizations since the 1990s.

[10]See http://www.hrw.org/legacy/campaigns/icc/

[11]See http://www.amnesty.org/en/economic-social-and-cultural-rights

Human Rights Act from British law once he came to power and substituting it with a 'British specific' version of a 'Bill of Rights and Obligations'.[12] Others, more extreme, object to it altogether, viewing any such Act as a supranational, or suprastate, legal imposition as well as introducing an ethical and a legal code, which is not 'indigenous' and has a moral authority that stems from its moral universality claims.

However, critiques of that discourse have also come from other directions, rejecting human rights as western, as individualistic, as legalistic (Sharma, 2006). Costas Douzinas, the Head of the Human Rights Centre at the Birkbeck Law School at the University of London, argues in his book *The End of Human Rights* (2000) that these days we see the end of human rights because

> human rights are the necessary and impossible claim of law to justice ... [with a] tradition of resistance and dissent from exploitation and degradation and a concern with a political and ethical utopia, an epiphany of which will never occur but whose principle can stand in judgement of the present law. When human rights lose that element, they remain an instrument of reform and, occasionally, a sophisticated tool for analysis but they stop being the tribunal of history. (Dousinas, 2000: 380)

He views human rights as getting lost currently 'in ever more declarations, treaties and diplomatic lunches' and argues that the end of human rights comes 'when they lose their utopian end' (ibid.).

Interestingly enough, Michael Ignatieff, when heading the Centre for Human Rights at Harvard University, saw these being threatened almost for the opposite reasons. For him, the proliferation of declarations and treaties is also dangerous but not because human rights have been losing their utopian appeal, rather because they have been losing their pragmatic appeal. Giving as a title to one of his Tanner lectures at the University of Princeton 'Human Rights as Idolatry', Ignatieff warns of 'elevating the moral and metaphysical claims made on behalf of human rights' (2001: 53). For him, 'human rights' is a specific form of politics with a minimalist kernel that is aimed at defending people's rights to free agency, the ability to make decisions and to be protected from abuse and oppression.

---

[12]See http://www.conservativelawyers.com/Bill%20of%20Rights%20and%20Obligations06.pdf

The equation of human rights with negative freedom (to use Isaiah Berlin's (1958) term) sounds too extreme and minimalist even to Amy Gutman, the Princeton professor who has written the introduction to Ignatieff's book. She points out that 'the right to subsistence is as necessary for human agency as a right against torture. ... Starving people have no more agency than people subject to cruel and unusual punishment' (in Ignatieff, 2001: ix). However, Ignatieff claims that there has never been mass famine in a democratic society where people could have objected to unreasonable government policies, such as the Chinese 'Great Leap Forward' that caused mass starvation in China, and therefore does not feel such an objection as contradicting his overall approach.

Of course, such a definition of human rights goes well with neo-liberalism and the spread of the free market and many in the Third World have felt that this stance 'reflects the elite basis of liberal thought in which having enough to eat is taken for granted' (Herman, 2002: ix). Herman points out that much of the debate at the UN 1994 conference on human rights in Vienna had been focused on what has been called 'Asian values'. And while much of the same debate has been interpreted to have been on what is known as 'cultural rights' (see the discussion later on in the chapter), it can also be constructed as being between individual rights to freedom and collective rights to development. These relate to the economic and social rights which have been marginalized in much of the human rights discourse and which, as mentioned above, have slowly been reclaimed as part of the human rights discourse in the post-Cold War period.

This, however, has not been the only major change in international human rights related policies. Another, even more major controversial issue has been the right – or even the duty – of the UN, or some states, to intervene forcefully in the affairs of other states in which human rights violations take place. Overall, the basis of international relations as well as of the UN has been constructed as international (or, rather, interstate), not transnational, and thus there has been no space for intervening in what is considered the internal affairs of other states or that which would threaten the stability of an international state order. Nonetheless, the impetus of the establishment of the UN and especially of the Universal Declaration of Human Rights has been the will for the atrocities of the Nazi regime not to be allowed to happen ever again. A new international relations discourse started to emerge in which the failure of the international community to intervene in Rwanda in time to prevent the major genocide there in 1994 has been seen as an event that cannot be allowed to be repeated.

After the end of the Cold War, the ability of international military intervention, without posing a major threat to international stability, has grown. Ignatieff argues (2001: 40) that in the late 1990s three criteria emerged for the rationing of military interventions:

1   the human rights abuses at issue have to be gross, systematic and pervasive;
2   they have to constitute a threat to international peace and security in the surrounding region; and
3   military intervention has to stand a real chance of putting a stop to the abuses.

He also adds that in practice there is a fourth criterion, which is that the region in question must be of vital interest, for cultural, strategic or geopolitical reasons, to one of the powerful nations of the world and another powerful nation is not opposed to it. It should be noted that Ignatieff is one of the major human rights professionals who has supported the invasion of Iraq. His recognition of the *realpolitik* basis has not prevented him from being one of the staunchest supporters of the developing, so-called 'humanitarian militarism' which has cost much in human lives, especially of those who were supposed to be rescued, as has been exposed more and more with each additional war, from Bosnia to Kosovo to Afghanistan and Iraq.

The normative basis of this so-called 'humanitarian militarism' is not only built on the notion of universal human rights that have a higher normative value than that of state sovereignty, but also on the twin notion of the need to fight terrorism. 'Terrorism' that is promoted either by rogue states or by other groups that certain states are too weak or are 'failing' to deal with therefore needs outside intervention in order to keep local and global security. Although already hailed by the Reagan government as the core of US foreign policy, it has become the inseparable 'twin' of 'human rights abuses' as a rhetorical device for the justification of international intervention especially during the years after 9/11. However, such policies suffer from major shortcomings, especially in terms of a reconstruction rather than deconstruction of the social and political order and their reliance on justifying these military interventions in terms of securing the security of the West from terrorist attacks rather than bringing peace and democracy to the local populations. As a result, the disenchantment of human rights activists as regards the so-called 'humanitarian militarism' has grown massively. Moreover, as Mary Kaldor and Shannon Beebee (2010) have shown, the strategies of such military interventions, including post-war policies of peace, are often based on active support of the fighting opponent organizations reaching agreements on shared governance, and often end up by only intensifying the nature of those wars and militarized conflicts as a mutual enterprise in which networks of criminals and political extremists supposedly on different sides are able to mobilize political support and also develop war related businesses.

The search for an alternative or complementary cosmopolitan discourse which would not stumble into the pitfalls of 'human rights' discourses and especially their militarized forms, had started already earlier, and much of it, especially among activists in UN NGO forums, had come under the umbrella of the related discourse of 'human security'.

'Human security'

'Human security' became a buzzword during the late 1990s. A product of the post-Cold War era, it gained special resonance with the growing security mania after 9/11. However, the notion of 'human security' relates to concerns that have been growing since before that. Some of these concerns relate to the field of military security. There are claims that 'human security' represents 'the cardinal mission' of the United Nations (the International Commission on Intervention and Sovereignty, mentioned in Alkire, 2002: 4). This has grown out of the UN's 'agenda for peace' (A/47/277-S/24111) and reflects the growing move by security concerns from inter-state to intra-state concerns and from national territories to ethnocized and racialized communities, both local and transnational. However, the agenda of 'human security' as it has developed has become much more radical and encompassing than that, partly, as mentioned above, pushed along by the growing participation of NGOs in international conferences (although in the 'Durban + Ten' World Conference Against Racism, the NGOs with their alternative policy goals started to be marginalized again in the post-Kofi Annan UN). A significant role in the development of the 'human security' discourse has also been played by the growing sophistication of Peace and Conflict Studies (of which the above mentioned book by Beebee & Kaldor, 2010 is but one good recent example). It also reflected the growing unease not only with the spread of ethnic conflicts and wars, but also with the growing poverty and inequity under the neo-liberal globalized market and the recognition that military intervention as such cannot solve such systemic problems. As the 1994 UNDP report stated, 'human security' is 'articulating a preventative "people-centered" approach that is focused jointly on "freedom from fear and freedom from want"'(Alkire, 2002: 4). Or, to use Kofi Annan's, the then UN Secretary-General, more detailed declaration: '"human security" can no longer be understood in purely military terms. Rather, it must encompass economic development, social justice, environmental protection, democratization, disarmament and respect for human rights and the rule of law' (UN Millenium Report, 2000: 43–44).[13] It is interesting to remember that Ignatieff points to Kofi Annan as one of those for whom 'human rights' means idolatry.

The field of 'human security' has thus not necessarily rejected the notion of 'human rights' but rather has incorporated it into a wider discourse which includes critiques and concerns not only from the arena of international relations but also from the field of development. At the same time, as Kristen Timothy argues (2004), the agenda of human security was seen as part of the 'peace dividends' of the post-Cold War era when it was thought that part of the monies that used to be directed to military budgets could now be redirected towards the development of the Third World and this would also play a preventative role in militarized conflicts in these countries. This is also the reason it has been marginalized as a mainstream discourse after 9/11 during the rise of the 'global war on terror' discourse (Basch, 2004) and that in spite of paying lip service to 'make poverty history',[14] no major global changes have materialized in most of the areas which the 'millenium development goals' aimed to radically transform and improve.[15] However, growing frustration with the way the wars in Iraq

---

[13]See http://www.un.org/millennium/sg/report/

[14]An international campaign led by international pop stars Bob Geldof and Bono which gained the formal support of the G8 leaders in their 2005 meeting. See http://en.wikipedia.org/wiki/Make_Poverty_History

[15]Most of these goals seem now not to be realizable, although in some areas, such as health, important developments have taken place. In September 2010 a high-profile international meeting took place to evaluate the state of affairs (see http://www.un.org/millenniumgoals/sept_2010_more.shtml).

and Afghanistan have been going seems to bring human security back into more mainstream attention (Caldor & Bebbe, 2010).

The 'human security' approach to development can be seen as a cosmopolitan moral and political project of belonging in which the actual well-being of humans, as well as their formal rights, are what counts. It is for this reason that it has been heavily influenced by the capabilities approach developed by Amartya Sen (1981, 1992a) and later on by Martha Nussbaum (Nussbaum & Sen, 1993; Nussbaum, 2000). This approach rejects the discourse of rights and entitlements as well as of general measures of opulence, such as GNP per capita, and instead focuses on the ways people positioned in all groups in society are capable of achieving a quality of life in terms of achievement and freedom. It argues that resources have no value in themselves apart from their role in promoting human functioning. Martha Nussbaum claims (1995: 5) that the capabilities approach is compatible with cultural relativism – the supposed lack of which has been a major source of critique of the 'human rights' discourse – although she argues that they are not necessarily with subjective preferences, as they 'may be deformed in various ways by oppression and deprivation'. Its main focus, however, has been to develop a list of universal functions of human beings that are most worth the care and attention of public planning the world over (Nussbaum, 2000).

The link between the 'capabilities' approach and the 'human security' approach is not only ideological but also personal. Amartya Sen himself has adopted the mantra of 'human security' (2000a) and has been a major inspirational figure in this field. The notion of 'human security' has attempted to answer critiques of the various development studies and women and development studies paradigms (e.g. Bhavnani et al., 2003), avoid Eurocentrism and tackle questions about specific cultural constructions.

While many are attracted to the transformative implications of the 'human security' approach, there is only a partial agreement as to what constitutes 'human security' and what the issues are that need to be tackled in order to achieve it. Various scholars, activists and agencies have defined 'human security' in somewhat different terms. The Harvard Program on Humanitarian Policy and Conflict Research compiled a list of more than 20 different definitions of 'human security' by various UN, government and academic institutions and scholars.[16]

---

[16]Harvard Program on Humanitarian Policy and Conflict Research, 'Definitions of Human Security (http://www.hsph.harvard.edu/hpcr/events/hsworkshop/list_definitions.pdf)

Sabina Alkire, who prepared a conceptual framework of 'human security' for the international 'Commission on Human Security' (2002), argues that a working definition of 'human security' should do no more than identify a certain 'vital core' to be protected from 'critical pervasive threats in a way that is consistent with long-term human fulfilment'. She identifies three categories of rights and freedoms in this 'vital core' of 'human security' – those pertaining to survival, to livelihood, and to basic dignity. Beyond these, she claims, the definition should not be more specific, as 'the task of prioritizing among rights and capabilities, each of which is argued by some to be fundamental, is a value judgement and a difficult one which maybe best undertaken by appropriate institutions' and wide-ranging public participation'. The final report of the Commission on Human Security defines human security in the following terms:

> Human security means protecting vital freedoms. It means protecting people from critical and pervasive threats and situations, building on their strengths and aspirations. It also means creating systems that give people the building blocks of survival, dignity and livelihood. Human security connects different types of freedoms – freedom from want, freedom from fear and freedom to take action on one's own behalf. To do this, it offers two general strategies: protection and empowerment ... [that] are mutually reinforcing, and both are required in most situations. ... Human security complements state security, furthers human development and enhances human rights. ... Promoting democratic principles is a step toward attaining human security and development. It enables people to participate in governance and make their voices heard. This requires building strong institutions, establishing the rule of law and empowering people. (2004: intro)

Although Sadako Ogata, the former UN High Commissioner for Refugees (1999), talks about 'human security' as guaranteeing to all people all the rights 'that belonging to a State implies', the right to/ notion of belonging as such to a national or ethnic community is not referred to explicitly in any of the various definitions of 'human security' I have seen or in the report. And yet the relationships between individuals and communities are central to the discourse of 'human security'. One can see this whenever the notion of human dignity is associated with people's right to exercise solidarity (e.g. Sen, 2000a) or practise their cultures (e.g. Ogata, 1999), and whenever their right for 'human security' is linked with their rights to a sustainable sense of home and social networks (Leaning and Arie, 2000). Probably most significantly, in the various definitions and discussions on 'human security', the carriers of rights are sometimes constructed not just as human individuals but also as 'their communities' (Alkire, 2002: 2).

This brings us back to the issue of 'collective rights' in human rights discourse. There is no interrogation as to how these relations of ownership between certain individuals and specific collectivities have been constructed or what the boundaries are for these 'imagined communities' (Anderson, 1991 [1983]). And yet, civil wars and ethnic strife are considered to be major threats to 'human security' (two chapters of the Report are dedicated to societies in violent conflict and in post-conflict situations) as are the more general questions of racism and social exclusion.

It is in this intersection of the various constructions of 'human security' and the intersected needs and/or rights of people to belong to particular collectivities and communities and to defend them when they consider their communities to be under threat, where some of the problematics raised in this chapter regarding cosmopolitanism and human rights arise.

David Chandler (2002) argues, and recent historical experience justifies his claim, that although 'human rights' discourse talks about human empowerment and recognition, in reality it often offers less to people than what old-fashioned international aid used to offer. As relevant examples he brings the withdrawal of the UN World Food Program of aid from Afghanistan after the 9/11 bombing, the suspension of relief from Sierra Leone after the military coup, and the fact that after the 'humanitarian intervention' in Kosovo and Iraq people have had less access to food than before. While in Kabul some women have been able to take off the chador (many preferred not to) and, more importantly, to go to school and work, in most of Afghanistan little if anything has changed in this respect, except that now the gangs which control the opium trade that the Taliban have banned have more power than ever. The 2009 elections in Afghanistan, which showed an extreme combination of corruption and very low participation as a result of the successful terrorization of the people by the militias fighting the official government and its western allies, have highlighted the situation and exposed it globally – which only brought about a further intensification of the militaristic strategies of western powers.

Chandler (2002: 119) anchors these developments in what he calls an inherent flaw of the human rights discourse and its

> inability to establish a foundation for the substance and character of the new rights it proclaims. The redefinition of rights from neutral means to ethical and value-laden ends, or claims on an external authority, removes the universality and democratic content of rights. Neither the discussions over the substance or content of human rights, nor the means of implementing and guaranteeing them, are resolvable through democratically accountable mechanisms because these political questions of power and distribution are reposed as moral absolutes open to external or juridicial interpretation through international institutions or domestic and international courts.

In other words, like Douzinas, Chandler relates 'the end of human rights' to the growing power of judicial authorities in this field. Unlike him, however, he sees this as part of the growing hegemony of the normative discourse, rather the end of it, and unlike Ignatieff he sees the spread of human rights politics as disabling rather than facilitating human agency.

Part of my own and many others' critique of identity politics, including feminist identity politics, has been its inherent 'tyranny of structurelessness' (Freeman, 1970), which conflated representation with advocacy and assumed that there could be only one politically correct position on any question, if one's consciousness is 'raised' high enough (Yuval-Davis, 2006c). Chandler basically argues that this tyranny of structurelessness has now spread to the 'human rights' and 'human security' industry. Although his book was published in 2002, he would not be surprised that in the name of 'freedom' and 'human rights' a non-authorized coalition of mainly the USA and Britain has launched the first major colonial war of the twenty-first century (as well as, paradoxically, suspended parts of human rights legislations in many different states, including their own). And yet, to discard normative and ethical principles for political action, to give up the thrill of global (if not cosmopolitan) political activism and the ideal of global citizenship that encompasses differences rather than discounts them, and to go back to prioritizing national if not even more primordial identities, might prove to be a cure that is worse than the original disease. But then that is what is implied from what Chandler says about the 'human rights' discourse.

Is there any recognition of the above problematics in the demotic contemporary cosmopolitan movements which attempt to promote various ecological, anti-capitalist and feminist goals from below? And how do they deal with issues of borders and boundaries which are at the heart of the cosmopolitan question of belonging?

Of course, given the plethora of such organizations and groupings all over the world, I can only discuss here several examples. For this purpose I shall briefly discuss contemporary global social movements such as the ecological and anti-capitalist movements and end this part of the chapter by discussing what Reilly (2008) calls 'cosmopolitan feminism' (but see also Antrobus, 2004). Of particular importance while discussing these examples would be the roles and the significance of the virtual worlds of the internet and its social networks' by-products (e.g. *Facebook* and twittering) for the ways issues of borders and boundaries are dealt with in these contexts.

Contemporary global social movements

There have been discussions on 'new social movements' (e.g. A. Scott, 1990; Larana et al., 1994; Melucci, 1996) which broke away from the traditional 'old left' socialist and revolutionary movements since the students' movements of the late 1960s and then the identity politics movements of Blacks, women and other marginalized and disadvantaged groupings. Although many of these crossed and transcended ethnic and national borders and boundaries, they did not necessarily see themselves as cosmopolitan or even particularly inclusive. And although not many of them used DNA tests, as some indigenous people groupings have been doing, I remember bitter debates on 'who is Jewish?', 'who is Black?', and whether women originating from various countries were to be allowed into a conference of 'black women' in London?

The global social movements which are the focus of this section of the chapter are very different and have sometimes been called 'globalization from below'. The mass protests in November 1999 at the Third Ministerial Meeting of the World Trade Organization in Seattle (J. Smith, 2001) are often mentioned as the symbol and inspiration of these movements. This was the place where both national and transnational movements and organizations came together to protest in a specific location against a global phenomenon – neo-liberal capitalism. In recent years, whenever high-profile international meetings of world political and economic leaders have been taking place, such as the G8, the G20 or the WTO, such mass protests (and often also teach-in camps) have become almost a tradition in their own right.

At the time this section of the chapter was being written, there were reports of police brutality in Copenhagen against the latest wave of demonstrations against the shortcomings of the World Summit on Climate Change in December 2009. Indeed, global warming, climate change and ecology in general seem to be at the centre of this global movement. It is global, not just because people of many countries are involved in the networks and activities of this movement, but also because the issue itself is perceived by all as not being caused by just one country (although the industrial West is blamed for mostly exploiting and polluting the natural resources of the globe) and cannot be resolved on a national level either. What gives these movements their cosmopolitan flavour is that their basic assumption is that all human beings depend on each other as well as that they all matter and are 'unexpendable'.

This more social rather than ecological focus of such a contemporary global movement was highlighted in the mass demonstrations and the campaign of 'Make Poverty History'[17] surrounding the G8 summit of 2005 which focused on the world's, especially the Southern world's, poverty. Again, although states were called to do their parts in solving the problem, it was conceived to be relevant to all, as poverty was seen as infringing on the basic human rights and human security of all.

Neo-liberalism has been perceived by the more radical parts of these movements as the underlying cause of much of these issues (as well as the heritage of the colonial past). The 'Global Social Forum' (e.g. Teivaiunen, 2002; Waterman & Sen, 2003), which now meets in different parts of the world each year but for the first few years took place in Porto Allegro in Brazil, was originally conceived as an anti-Davos forum. (Davos in Switzerland has been the location of an annual conference of the 'World Economic Forum',[18] in which civil and political leaders of the global neo-liberal economy gather in order

---

[17]See http://www.makepovertyhistory.org/

[18]See http://www.weforum.org/en/index.htm

to discuss the ways the global anti-capitalist or, rather, anti-neo-liberal, can struggle against it in their various local contexts).

The virtual technology of the internet, the web and more recently social networks such as *Facebook* and Twitter, have proved to be very effective as mobilizing tools in the organization of these new social movements, facilitating transnational and global participation in an unprecedented way, although, like in the NGO Forums of the UN, there is no escaping the internal stratification of those activists who actually get to travel to those global conferences and the many who stay behind, unless the conference happens to take place in their region. However, the implications of this issue concern not only who is participating in these new global meetings or actions, but also whether these can lead to any long-term alternative global or cosmopolitan community of belonging.

The Global Social Forum is a contentious site, in which diverse but broadly 'leftist' political and identity groupings from all over the globe meet to discuss the social, political and economic effects of global neo-liberalism. While some of its more traditional 'leftist' activists (e.g. Santos, 2006) would like to transform it into a decision-making organization along the lines of traditional socialist Internationals, others insist that any attempt of imposing a 'party line' would damage the spirit of the post-modern contested, diverse and fluid terrain which is the real strength of the Forum. Moreover, many who participate in it, especially its attached 'Women's Forum', have grown weary of dealing with mainstream politics, such as in the UN, and feel that this is the only way an organic alternative global civil society can grow.

'Cosmopolitan feminism'

In some ways, feminists, especially western feminists, have always strived to 'global sisterhood'. As many Black and subaltern feminists pointed out (e.g. Mohanty, 1986; hooks, 1989; see also Anthias & Yuval-Davis, 1983; Yuval-Davis, 1997a: Chapter 6), often such views were coloured by a racialized ethnocentrism in which western, liberated women were there to liberate and civilize their oppressed sisters in the South. Such views persisted beyond the colonial period and, as Zillah Eisentein (2004) and others (e.g. Al-Ali & Pratt, 2009) pointed out, have played a significant role in the 'militarized humanitarianism' drives for recent western military interventions in Iraq and especially Afghanistan. However, at the same time, with the growing success of black and post-colonial feminist movements, there has been also a growing change which has facilitated locally and globally growing 'rainbow' and 'transversal' feminist solidarities (see the discussion of this in the next chapter) across borders and boundaries.

One of the most important fronts of such solidarity focused around a series of UN conferences since the 1990s (Antrobus, 2004; Reilly, 2009). A transnational coalition of feminist organizations and NGOs from a wide range of countries in both the North and the South gained wide recognition around the 1994 Vienna UN Conference on Human Rights in 1994, where feminists adopted the slogan 'Women's Rights are Human Rights', aiming at incorporating a gendered interpretation to human rights discourse and highlighting issues which were until then excluded from that agenda. A feminist lobby, a feminist tribunal and other outlets at the NGO Forum of that conference, as well as, for the first time, statements on the subject which were made before the official delegates, managed to make some important gains, which were reinforced in subsequent UN conferences, especially the ones on population and development in Cairo in 1994 and the 1995 Fourth World Conference on Women in Beijing. There was a growing recognition of women's rights as independent subjects where they were not recognized as such before (for example, in relation to issues such as reproductive rights and rape in war).

Human rights have been in this case and many others a rallying cry for recognition and the entitlements of people all over the world, not as citizens of specific states or as members of specific cultural or religious community, but as part of the human race. Although feminists have been pointing out the masculinist construction of that subject of rights ('the Man') and fought against it, they nevertheless saw an inherent potential in the universal principle of the human rights discourse and, like other groupings of marginalized and racialized people who have been excluded from 'the human', have used it as a major instrument for resistance and the claiming of rights. A major focus for this mobilization in recent years has been the International Criminal Court, for which both feminist and other human rights international activists have been fighting. It is important to point out that in all these forums Southern women's groups have probably been the most organized and powerful components of these coalitions, and definitely it was not a case of them just following western leadership but of working together with mutual respect and a sense of equality.

A major issue for contestation and debate in all these conferences, which became even stronger in the +5 and +10 smaller follow-up conferences, has been the role of 'culture and tradition' *vis-à-vis* 'human rights' as the legitimate principle to establish roles and treatment of women in various societies. This debate has been wider than just that of gender relations, although those have occupied centre-stage, as so often cultural differences have been marked by differential symbolic gender relations. As was mentioned earlier in the chapter, in the name of human rights, in what came to be known as the debate on Asian values in the Vienna conference, there has been a claim for prioritizing women's cultural roles to that of their human rights. This, as discussed in Chapter 4, continues to be a major focus for feminist struggles everywhere. The success of the feminist movement in these UN conferences, however, has been the establishment of the basic right of women to be free of violence – domestic, communal and militarized.

Charlotte Bunch, of Rutgers University's Centre for Women's Global Leadership, discussed in a brainstorming seminar which took place at the National Centre for Research on Women in June 2005, that the discourse of women's rights as human rights started as a tactical tool in the preparations for the 1994 UN conference. She claimed, however, that this took over and gained its own authority in the following years, because it managed to touch on so many women's lives across the globe and gave them a legal as well as a political tool in their struggles, for instance, in the struggle against violence against women. A major achievement has been the acknowledgement that rape is not a crime against honour (of the males in the family, community, nation) but a mode of torture, a crime against humanity (Copelon, 2003). A related major campaign has been for the recognition of what has been known as Korean 'comfort women', who were kept by the Japanese military during the Second World War as the enslaved victims of war crimes.[19]

Another factor that Charlotte Bunch mentioned as a reason for the popularity of the discourse of 'women's rights as human rights' has been that after the fall of the Soviet Union, other cosmopolitan or universalistic discourses, such as the socialist ones, became marginalized and lost their popular appeal. As I have commented elsewhere, however (Yuval-Davis, 2006c), part of the success of that discourse has been linked to the professionalization as well as the

---

[19]See http://ipsnews.net/news.asp?idnews=48065

NGOization of feminist activism, similar to that of human rights activism as a whole, and such a discourse was useful for legal as well as popular mobilization struggles.

Sentiments of global solidarity and common political action continue to develop among feminists in different parts of the globe. However, in recent years, the focus of such activities has turned, to a certain extent, away from the UN, as it became clear in the follow-up UN conferences that endless energies were required by the feminists attending the conferences to defend the feminist achievements of earlier conferences from the threats of the growing influence of right-wing Conservatism, which was especially religious, across the globe. In the +10 follow-up conference of the 2001 World Conference against Racism, which took place in Geneva, it also became clear that the opening up of UN conferences to NGO Forums as agents of civil society is becoming a thing of the past, as NGOs were not allowed to directly intervene any more in the formal discussions. It is in global feminist organizations such as AWID[20] and the Women's Forum,[21] attached to the Global Social Forum, as well as in other global campaigns, much of them using internet technologies, that feminist cosmopolitan activism continues to be engaged.

Conclusion

The chapter discussed some of the major debates on the notion of cosmopolitanism as well as some of its major current manifestations as a political project of belonging. One element of cosmopolitan and humanitarian discourse needs further clarification, however. It has probably been stated most clearly by Appiah (2006), who argues that two elements are necessary components in a cosmopolitan approach.

First is the idea that we have commitments towards other human beings, even those with whom we have no familial or friendship relations, or even just of common citizenship. The second element is that we need to respect not just other human beings in the abstract, but also specific human beings, with specific beliefs and practices that give their lives meaning, without expecting or wishing all people and all societies to become the same. Appiah argues that the two

---

[20]See http://www.awid.org/

[21]See http://www.womens-forum.com/

cosmopolitan ideals, the universal one and the respect for legitimate difference, have inner conflicting tensions, and therefore cosmopolitanism should not be seen 'as the name of the solution but as the name of the challenge'. Appiah's double-edged construction of the cosmopolitan idea reflects Michel Wieviorke's dilemma on 'why is it so difficult to be anti-racist' (Wieviorke, 1997). Wieviorke argues that not so long ago it was not difficult to differentiate between racists and anti-racists. However, today there are divisions among those who see themselves as anti-racist and those who accuse each other of encouraging racism if not of actually being racist themselves.

The reason for this basic disagreement is that there are two visions of non- or anti-racist society. One vision is universalistic – all people need to be treated the same, especially in the public sphere. The other vision is based on the politics of recognition and claims public acceptance of multicultural and affirmative action practices as a precondition for reaching a non-racialized society.

The universalist position sees in the public acceptance of forms of difference a form of racialization, a reification of boundaries and discrimination. The pluralist position accuses the first camp of recognizing and legitimizing only majoritarian discourse, which are usually westocentric, heterosexist and middle-class in nature, and of rendering as invisible the standpoints and interests of excluded minorities. This position has been argued not only by anti-racists, but also by feminists and other identity social movements. In his article, Wieviorke does not really resolve this dilemma except by saying that neither extreme position is valid.

I would argue, however, that this dichotomy of universalism/relativism is a false one. We need to look at 'the universal' in the same way Dipesh Chakrabarty does. He points out (in Pollock et al., 2002: 105) that 'The universal ... can only exist as a placeholder, its place always usurped by a historical particular seeking to present itself as the universal'. The aim of emancipatory and anti-racist politics is to aspire to establish a universal which would be as inclusive as possible, at the same time knowing that this is a process and not a goal, and that therefore, as Pollock et al. (2002: 1) claim, 'specifying cosmopolitanism positively and definitely is an uncosmopolitan thing to do'.

We cannot – and should not – construct an homogeneous, or even a unified, political order. Rather, we should engage in a transversal dialogue (Cockburn & Hunter, 1999; Yuval-Davis, 1994, 1997a, 2006b) that is bounded by common political values, informed by recognitions of our differential locations and identifications, and led by a global discourse in which translation, rather than a unitary language, is seen as the cosmopolitan political tool and political projects of belonging are multi-layered, with shifting, contested and porous boundaries.

The question of belonging, however, does not only relate to the boundaries of belonging and the different signifiers that construct collectivity boundaries for different political projects of belonging. The question is also what kind of relationships should exist among different members of the collectivity – or humanity – or all living beings. This is the question which preoccupies feminists and others who have developed the political project of 'the ethics of care' – the subject matter of the next chapter.

6

The Caring Questi
Emotional and the P

At the beginning of the introduction to this book, the qu.   .s
raised about the significance of the surprise and discom. . that
many British people felt when they discovered that some of the
major participants in the 7/7 terrorist attacks on London transport
in 2005 were British citizens who, moreover, were born, raised and
educated in Britain.

In the previous chapters, various political projects of belonging
were presented and discussed which would have helped to answer
that question. The naturalization of boundaries of belonging of citizenship, of national, ethnic and religious communities, and as members of the human race, would assume a shared belonging which
normatively would make such acts not just individual criminal acts,
but also acts of betrayal for at least some of the various collectivities to which they belong. On the other hand, in the book, we have
also considered the exclusionary as well as inclusionary boundaries
of belonging, which would naturalize the loss of application of common moral rules and practices towards those who are outside these
boundaries. It was commented on that even in the widest cosmopolitan discourses there were those who stood outside the situated
boundaries. Although, as will be explored below, not every form of
'othering' is dehumanizing, it is worth mentioning that even when
the inclusionary boundaries include, at least in principle, also non-
humans, as in the case of animal rights movements, the construction
of the enemy Other could allow killing in the name of life, hating in
the name of love, exclusion in the name of inclusion.

In the introductory chapter it was also pointed out that belonging
and the politics of belonging are located in the intersection of the
sociology of power and the sociology of emotion. In her ground-
breaking book *The Cultural Politics of Emotion* (2004), Sara Ahmed
claims that all emotions are politicized and bound up with the securing of social hierarchies. She sees emotions as working to shape
the 'surfaces' of individual and collective bodies, to delineate their

boundaries and thus take on the shape of the very contact they have with objects and 'others'. She illustrates the various emotions which are involved in the various political projects of belonging and how they work. If she would have written on the case of the 7/7 terrorists, she would have looked at the spatial politics of fear that are aimed at creating distance from external objects of fear and especially the politics of disgust, which would demand that the bodies/objects of disgust should be ejected from the collective body. She speaks of the workings of shame and love in which the objects of emotion not only circulate but also get 'taken in' or 'taken on' as 'mine' and 'ours', and targeting particular objects or people as carriers of shame (as has been the case for members of the British Muslim community who oppose terrorism) can at the same time construct the ideal of love even when the shame announces the failure of that ideal in the past.

Thus, the politics of belonging involve the full range of human emotions and passions, from pain and grieving, via fear and disgust, to shame and love. As Hannah Peterse (1998) argues, love (and I would add all other emotions) is not only pre-moderm, or the remnant of pre-modernity in contemporary society and politics, but, rather, at the heart of contemporary political projects of belonging. Corinne Squire (2001) argues that we are being continuously immersed by publicly performed emotions and in the book she edited with others (6, Perri et al., 2007) they show how what they call 'public emotions' are part of everyday public life and culture as well as politics and law.

While a lot of the discussions in the previous chapters focused on assumed and constructed boundaries of the different political projects of belonging, focusing on the emotional and cognitive 'others', in this last chapter of the book I would like to examine the sociology of emotions and how it intersects with the sociology of power, by especially focusing on the emotions of caring and love which underlie what can be seen as the feminist political project of belonging, i.e. the ethics of care, and, through this, the extent to which caring and love can counteract other emotions as the normative basis of political action. The question of boundaries does come into it, as will be explored later on in the chapter, but the point of departure is not whether one belongs or not, but rather how. As we have seen throughout the book, there have been feminist interventions as part of and in resistance to virtually all forms of political projects of belonging. The ethics of care, however, developed as an attempt to demonstrate – as well as to transcend – gendered constructions of belonging, a morality which encompasses, rather than filters out, caring emotions as guiding interpersonal, familial and community relations.

Moral approaches of this kind have, of course, also developed outside feminist discourse, and long before feminism appeared historically for the first time. They would be found within various religious discourses, but have also come to be valued as autonomous philosophical and political ideologies. Alison Assiter (2009) claims that such a perspective involves alternative metaphysical assumptions about personhood to those that are at the base of a liberal theory of citizenship.

The chapter starts with a discussion of feminist ethics of care and that alternative metaphysical 'picture' of the person, which Assiter sees as inspired by Kierkegaard but going back also to elements of Aristotelian and Spinozist, as well as Levinas' approaches.

It will then turn to examine the relationships between love and power, inclusion and exclusion, which are inherent in these discourses of care, focusing on issues which concern notions of boundaries and difference.

The chapter ends with a discussion of the relationships between ethics of care, belonging and feminist transversal politics

Feminist 'ethics of care'

Although many would point to the contributions of women social reformers such as Jane Adams[1] and the transitional role of women as public political actors from mothers to charity organizers to public and feminist citizens (Werbner, 1999b), much of the literature on 'ethics of care' refers to the work of Carol Gilligan (1982) as its starting point in feminist theory. Gilligan, a feminist psychologist, criticized the masculinist framework of the hegemonic model of moral development in psychology at the time, especially the model of moral development stages constructed by Kohlberg (1973). Like other feminists of the day (e.g. Harding, 1986; Haraway, 1991), she aimed at exposing the situated knowledge from which scientific models have assumed universality. She argued that girls' experiences have been ignored in the construction of the 'universalist' moral development framework that was based on observation of males' moral development. She pointed

---

[1]See http://womenshistory.about.com/od/addamsjane/p/jane_addams.htm

out the paradox that women were seen as being morally deficient as they seem to be 'stuck' in the third stage (out of a total of six) of moral development, which is conceived in interpersonal terms and in which goodness is equated with helping and pleasing others.

As Gilligan (1982) points out, the paradox is that the very traits that traditionally defined the 'goodness' of women – their care and sensitivy for others – are those that also mark them as deficient in moral development.

The sixth stage of the Kohlberg model, which assumes a full maturation of morality, she claims should be seen as male morality. It is guided by what Gilligan calls the justice principle – emphasizing equality, universal fairness, rights, impersonal procedural rules, formal obligations and non-interference. Females' morality, however, she sees as being guided by the care principle which prioritizes intimacy, attachment and cooperation.

It is this morality, constructed around the notion of care, which has come to be associated with Gilligan, although in her work she actually emphasized that the two views of morality should be seen as complementary rather than oppositional, and that mature morality is constructed around a certain convergence of the two, or, rather, a dialogue between rights and responsibilities. She quotes Mary Wollstonecraft's *A Vindication of the Rights of Women* (1792), in which she claims that liberty is the mother of virtue since enslavement causes not only abjectness and despair but also guile and deceit. Moreover, in claiming rights, women claimed responsibility for themselves and were able to consider it moral to care not only for others but also for themselves.

> When assertion no longer seems dangerous, the concept of relationships changes from a bond of continuing dependence to a dynamic of interdependence and thus the notion of care expands from the paralyzing injunction not to hurt others to an injunction to act responsively towards self and others and thus to sustain connection. (Gilligan, 1982: 149)

Gilligan's work has been received by other feminist scholars somewhat ambivalently, as she has been accused not necessarily of being essentialist – as she emphasized that the model of female morality she is describing is a result of differential socialization – but as universalizing women's sense of morality from her own situated gaze which assumes particular racial and class assumptions of a 'women's morality' (e.g. J. Mansbridge's and D.L. Rhode's articles in Phillips,

1998). Notwithstanding this, the basic differentiation that Gilligan makes between morality based on justice and morality based on care and affection has become the starting point for the feminist ethics of care project and is reflected also in other similar political projects.

Care as an alternative metaphysics

Several authors (e.g. Gregory, 2008; Assiter, 2009) emphasize that 'ethics of care' as a political theory – whether feminist, Christian or otherwise – share a basic critique of common liberal discourse which includes conceptions of autonomy that find little room for dependency and vulnerability and conceptions of rationality and duty that find little room for effectivity and emotions except as natural energies to be constrained by reason (Gregory, 2008: 151). Following their critique of liberal epistemology, identities and belonging need to be constructed primarily not as autonomous rational attitudes but as relational and dialogical (Bakhtin, 1981, 1984; see also Yuval-Davis, 2010). Such an approach also implies that notions of care and solidarity need to be perceived as better virtues than utilitarian and formal universal justice principles.

Assiter (2009: 66) suggests that such an alternative metaphysical model of self can be derived from the work of Kierkegaard who, she claims, offers a different version of universality from the Kantian one, which begins by examining the interactions of individuals with others, rather than by defining the moral boundaries of self-interested individuals as in liberal theory.

The question of the relational universality of this alternative metaphysical model will be discussed below, when the issue of the boundaries of care is examined. What is important here is that this model of self is constructed as 'embodied, needy and as dependent on others ... an amalgam of stories, formed by the relationship between it and various others' (Assiter, 2009: 67) (see also the somewhat similar embodied notion of 'social flesh' that Beasley and Bacchi [2007] put at the heart of their 'new politics for ethical future').

Relationality, therefore, is not necessarily symmetrical. This is exactly the nature of the disagreement between Levinas (1999: 100–3) and Buber (1947). In his writings, Buber differentiates between the alienated 'I–It' relationship and the caring 'I–You' relationship, which is a relationship of subject to subject. However, Levinas argues that the reciprocity assumed in the Buberian relationship of 'I–You' transforms the relationship from one based on generosity and care into a commercial relation of mutual expectations and trade. His model of an ethical relationship is that of non-symmetry, in which the 'I' does not expect anything from the 'You' but rather the 'I' assumes an obligation and responsibility towards the 'You'.[2]

It is this asymmetrical relationship which is assumed in some of the main feminist theories of 'ethics of care', like those of Sarah Ruddick (1989) and especially Virginia Held (1993, 2005), who develop their model of ethical care and belonging from what they conceive to be the 'mother–child' relationship.

Care as a maternal project

Virginia Held (1993; see also Ruddick, 1989) holds the bond between mother and child as the starting point for an alternative model of moral reasoning to that of the autonomous rational man, in which dependence and nurturing are constructed as basic for moral relations. Mutual respect and equality of status in spite of asymmetrical needs and other differences are perceived to be more important than contractual principles based on legal rights.[3] Connection, trust, compassion and affectivity should be recognized, according to Held, as important sources of moral reasoning. She argues that the principle of non-intrusion, which Hannah Arendt (1958), for example, promoted as a condition for moral justice, is unsatisfactory as a primary moral principle, because it precludes the possibility of dependent people's needs becoming the focus for moral deliberation. Moreover, the perspective offered by the mother–child relationship throws a different light on privacy and personhood. Instead of the model of atomistic, self-sufficient individuals assumed in liberal theories of moral justice, she argues that ethics should start from processes of connection and individuation. Moral reasoning should also be regarded as a contextual activity, directed at the evaluation of different ways of understanding and judging.

---

[2]A different interpretation of the Levinas–Buber differences is discussed towards the end of the chapter.

[3]Some feminists in family law reform, however, would argue that practices such as mutual respect can in fact never be separated from the fact of legal contractual principles. Laws don't guarantee one rights but it's most probably harder to get men to behave in the absence of contractual principles. Ethics of care, however, deal with normative rather than empirical realities.

Virginia Held, therefore, transformed Gilligan's description of the differentiated moral development of boys and girls into the basis for a new feminist morality which she constructs as a binary – and superior – opposite to masculinist morality based on the liberal principle of contractual justice.

Although in her later work (2005) Held emphasizes that her model of ethics of care can be used also in global politics, her starting point of having the mother–child bond as the model relationship of ethics of care, necessarily prioritizes intimate, if not just familial, relationships. Thus as a political project of belonging it can be seen as potentially colluding with more exclusionary, if not primordial, boundaries of belonging. Similarly, as discussed in *Gender and Nation* (Yuval-Davis, 1997a: 111–14), Ruddick's assumption that, as mothers, women would be more careful of human life and anti violence and war does not always pass the test of reality, as the behaviour of many women in the Rwandan genocide and in many other instances too (such as in the Gujarat anti-Muslim pogroms) can testify (IIJ, 2003). Caring for one's own children can sometimes be seen as conditioned by doing away with the lives of children of others or, at least, being indifferent towards their plight (Brecht's classical play *Mother Courage* is a good illustration of this).

Caring and loving, even of dependents, are not always cast in the form of a maternal model. Caring and loving can take place in relation to other adults, such as the sick, disabled and elderly, without transforming them into 'honorary children', as well as between adult friends and lovers. Indeed, another trend of feminist 'ethics of care' constructs care not as an extension of the women's/mother's familial role but as an inherent part of citizenship duties.

Care as a feminist citizenship project

Joan Tronto (1993; see also Robinson, 1999) develops her version of ethics of care as an essential component of citizenship. Unlike some other feminists, she does not reject as such the justice model of liberal democracy, but calls for incorporating care as a necessary ethical principle. This, she argues, should not be perceived as an added component to that of justice. Rather than its being just another civic virtue, Tronto argues that the incorporation of care would transform the liberal democratic citizenship. Moreover, she does not see care as such as a panacea for all evils and, on the contrary, she points out the dangers of paternalism, privilege and parochialism that the rhetoric of care often invokes in contemporary welfare states. In other words, Tronto highlights the fact that one cannot approach ethics of care as a moral and political project without considering the element of power which is inherent in any social relationship. As such, she follows the original feminist insight that 'the personal is political' (as well as feminist analyses of the welfare state, e.g. Fraser and Gordon, 1994; O'Connor et al., 1999), while Held, who no doubt would accept the importance of differential power relations when describing the relationships, including the intimate relationships between women and men, ignores this when discussing the relationships between mothers and their children – both in reality and as an ethical model.

The other important aspect of Tronto's work is that she argues that a principle of care, although universal, cannot be separated from the practices of care in a given situation. For Tronto, a liberal theory of social relations relies on the work of care givers to prop up its version of a just society, but at the same time a liberal discourse provides no way of giving an account of these practices on its terms (other than identifying care as a private choice). Thus liberalism, she claims, is an unrealistic utopia, given the realities of dependency and the need for care unless the ethics of care inform and become an integral part of practices of democratic citizenship.

Tronto defines care as 'a species activity that includes everything that we do to maintain, continue and repair our "world"' (1993: 103). In a sense, then, what Tronto terms as 'care' is what Marxist theorists would call reproductive labour. However, for Tronto, this is an ongoing process of joint action and feeling, both a practice and a disposition, and thus needs to be analyzed primarily in the social and political realms and not just the economic one.

This combination of action and feeling is both the great strength and the great weakness of Tronto's approach. While it enables the analysis of 'care' as a social and political and not just as a moral and ethical question, it also leaves open the possibility of action (performing care) and feeling (emotions of care) being reduced to and/or becoming separate from each other. In fact Tronto herself is implicitly troubled by this problematic when she joins the discussion developed by other feminists of 'ethics of care' who have looked at issues relating to 'care gaps' and 'global chains of care', elaborated on in the next section, which relate to relationships of emotion and action as well as the relationships of emotion to power and have their own implications for contemporary belonging/s and the politics of belonging.

Care and care work

Hochschild (2003), Ehernreich and Hochschild (2003) and others, as well as Tronto (2005), have pointed out the emergence of what they call 'the care gap' and the resulting 'global chains of care'. The 'care gap' has developed as an unintended result of the needs of the economy and technological developments, as well as what can be considered as the limited success of second-wave feminism, which has allowed women fuller and more equal access to the workplace. This removed women, at least partially, from their role as primary carers in nuclear families and created a 'care gap' on both micro and macro levels in society. At the same time, the nature of work itself changed and as Harvey (1990) pointed out, globalized, 'restless capitalism' under conditions of space/time compression, has created demands for a greater physical availability of service-oriented workers (the infamous 24/7). The establishment of the practice of flexitime, especially for women workers, did not mean the reduction of work, but rather more work from different spatial bases. This created, as Tronto points out (2005: 130), 'a huge gap in the care work that they used to do (especially for women but also for men)'. The care work crisis has created a commodification of care work as a 'pink collar ghetto', with less attractive work conditions. There were not enough local women attracted to these jobs, hence 'the care drain' of care workers, skilled and unskilled, from the South (as well as from less developed parts of the South to more developed ones) into 'global chains of care' (B. Anderson, 2000; Lutz, 2008; A. Ahmed, 2009). Thus, although care work seems to be relating to intimate relationships between carers and those cared for, its overall impact has been to break down local boundaries of belonging.

The microchip, communication and transportation revolutions have meant that much of the productive work with unattractive work conditions in the West could be exported to other parts of the world. This is one of the reasons that the previous relative success of labour movements in curtailing the power of capitalists via resistance and organizing, which resulted in the establishment of welfare states in which citizens became entitled to social as well as political and civil rights, could become subverted, and the power of multinational corporations could not be upheld by specific nation-states.

However, not all labour demands can be exported – although certain sectors of the service industry as well as that of the industrial labour could be (e.g. call centres, health tourism, etc.), reproductive and other kinds of care work have much greater spatial constraints. No virtual presence can replace cleaners, nannies, carers for the elderly and the disabled – at home and in institutions – as well as the more skilled labour of nurses, doctors, teachers.

Care work does not only have specific spatial constraints, it usually also demands a specific regime of emotion which is very different from that of other sectors in the labour market (*Soundings*, 2002). To carry out care work, the workers have to care – or, at least, to perform their work as if they care. Often caring – as in the case of migrant nannies who have left their own children to the care of relatives or care workers from an even less privileged parts of their countries or the globe – is the only thing that makes their work bearable (Hochschild, 2003). However, even if this is not the case, and the women have migrated as a way of escaping the bondage of traditional gender relations (Sorensen, 2005), it is the emotional regime of these jobs which is crucial and which also raises the question of the assumed links not only between feeling and acting between 'caring', but also between caring and belonging.

Judith Butler (1990, 1993) talks about the performativity of identities and social action, which are based on a discourse which is not just a given, but also has a history – it 'accumulates the force of authority through the repetition or citation of a prior, authoritative set of practices' (1990: 227). While this is not the place to get into a fuller examination of Butler's approach (see Williams, 2000; and Yuval-Davis, 2010), it is this combination of action and feeling which is assumed by the hegemonic discourse of the regime of emotion in care work. However, such an automatic association, if not conflation, cannot be assumed. Butler herself talks about subversive performances which reject such a conflation and, as Terry Lovell points out (2003), this can be seen as the space where subjects gain agency and can affect social change. Whether or not the ontological construction of the subject in Butler's own theorization is consistent with such a view of social agency and an initiation of change, it is clear that in care work there are many instances where the emotional regime of labour is not being followed. The development of technologies of surveillance for the work of nannies and other care workers[4] is just one symptom of the realization of the extent of the spread of the problem and attempts to suppress it. Another approach, which focuses mainly on types of care work, such as cleaning, where objects rather than people are cared for, is to depersonalize and organize the care work along an industrial model and the creation of cleaning and related work agencies (Ehrenreich & Hochschild, 2003).

Another technology, which is directed mainly towards higher ranks of care workers, can be seen in drives to regulate the labour market and, especially to make it more attractive to local workers, there are attempts to professionalize care work (Dahl & Eriksen, 2005). Such an approach assumes that care work can be separated from care as feeling, and as a specific form of job it can be standardized and bureaucratized. However, as is often reported, in reality such attempts are more often than not doomed to failure. Either it ends up with the informal transfer (usually partial and inefficient) of caring from the professional carers further down the chain (e.g. when the cleaners rather than the nurses in hospitals are the ones on whom patients often depend on for the caring aspects of their stay), or, when such substitutional chains of care are impossible, this ends up with the creation of new kinds of 'care gaps' altogether.

Care of the carers

If until now the discussion has focused on the kind of care work and both performative and counter discourses around them, it is important also to note that feminists writing on the subject often do so in order to call attention to the power relations involved in caring. The association of care work with traditional gendered divisions of labour highlights the fact that women as carers are often not paid for their labour, and are prevented from finding other channels of paid and fulfilling work, which makes them dependent on men (and in many societies also on older women). Even when they are paid, often their work brings with it relatively low payment, especially in relation to local rather than international scales of payments, and they are under-protected in terms of their conditions of labour.

In his sixteenth-century book *Utopia*, Thomas More speaks of one certain kind of inhabitant of that utopian society:

---

[4]See http://www.hiddenpinholecameras.com/

> Another type of slave is the working-class foreigner who, rather than live in wretched poverty at home, volunteers for slavery in Utopia. Such people are treated with respect, and with almost as much kindness as Utopia citizens, except that they're made to work harder, because they're used to it. If they want to leave the country, which doesn't often happen, they're perfectly free to do so, and receive a small gratuity. (More, 1516, quoted in Tronto, 1993: 131)

Joan Tronto is using this quote from More as a description of the social, economic and political situation of contemporary migrant domestic workers. She believes that the solution to their situation is to give them citizenship of the countries in which they work.

Although such a solution is often a necessary step and might help to alleviate some of the most horrendous aspects of the lives of these workers, it is doubtful whether the granting of formal citizenship touches all or even most of the issues involved. The situation highlighted in this quotation from More relates to some of the complex and multi-layered features of contemporary politics of belonging, and changing the legal state of these migrants might be a necessary but definitely not a sufficient condition to resolve their situation.

As discussed earlier in the book, especially in Chapters 2 and 3, there is an automatic assumption that the boundaries of the civil society overlap the boundaries of the nation, which lives in the 'homeland' territory, controlled by the nation-state. This mythical relationship has never been completely true. There were always members of the civil society who were not members of the dominant national collectivity, they were members of 'the nation' who lived outside the state, and often there were disputes and contestations where the 'real' borders passed between one homeland and another. And this relates to the minority of national and ethnic collectivities in the world that were not ruled by other states and empires and in times before the contemporary 'age of migration', to use Castles and Miller's terminology (2003).

Tronto suggests citizenship of the country where the migrant care workers work as a solution to the situation of migrant domestic workers. And indeed, citizenship might give these women some legal rights and a minimum wage (in countries where this exists) that otherwise they would not have. Formal citizenship can bestow not only civil, political and social rights, but also what was called in Chapter 2 spatial security rights. These are the right to enter the territory of a state and once having entered, the right to stay there as long as one wants, to move around it freely and the ability to choose – at least formally – in what and for whom to work; spatial security rights, most basically, provide the right to plan a future and not to be afraid every day of the knock on the door and the order of deportation. Often migrant workers, especially domestic care workers, will depend on their employers for the right to stay legally in the country – an enslavement that has caused a lot of abuse and suffering (Gupta, 2007).

For this reason, Tronto's suggestion to solve the hardships in the lives of the migrant care workers by endowing them with formal citizenship could go some way towards tackling their situation. However, her suggestion does not deal with some of the basic issues involved in the fact that social and cultural citizenship and belonging of most people on the globe today is not a zero-sum game but is actually gradual (Hage, 2002) and multi-layered, including local, ethnic, national, religious, regional, cross-national and supranational collectivities – and this is true of people in hegemonic majorities and not just those in racialized minorities and migrant populations. These multi-layered citizenships and belonging affect and construct each other and dictate people's access to a variety of social, economic and political resources.

This multiplexity has been recognized by Wendy Sarvasy and Patrizia Longo (2004), who embedded the citizenship status, as suggested by Tronto, in a more complex multi-layered citizenship structure in which such citizenship is a necessary facet of an anti-colonial world citizenship. Unfortunately, however, they anchored their suggestion in an uncritical use of the Kantian notion of 'hospitality'. Hospitality, like the notion of tolerance (Wemyss, 2009), assumes pre-given boundaries of belonging that guests, like tolerated minorities, cannot transgress.

Beyond this, care and care work as euphemisms of social and economic exploitation can become part of the discourse of formal citizenship. An illustrative example of this is the notion of 'earned citizenship' mentioned in Chapter 3, which was included in the legislation proposals in the UK[5] in which becoming engaged, without getting paid, with care work, in 'voluntary' and 'charity' organizations, becomes a pre-condition (and given the economic situation of most migrant care workers, a highly exclusionary one) for 'earning' a formal British citizenship.

---

[5]See http://www.workpermit.com/news/2009-09-28/uk/uk-earned-citizenship-transitional-arrangements.htm

Care and power

If, until now, the discussion focused on the deficit of power which involves the relations of care when carrying out care work both in the domestic sphere and in the labour marker, it is important also to focus on the kinds of power that care work does give its bearers.

Traditionally, there have been many persecutions associated with fears of women healers, from 'witches' to nurses (Ehernreich and English, 1993), as there has been a recognition that the other side of giving life and healing injuries and diseases is the ability to cause deterioration and death.

Discussions of this can be found in anthropological literature (Tiffany, 1980). However, much of the discussion of the power of carers can be found in critical discussions of the welfare state. Nancy Fraser and Linda Gordon (1994), for instance, examined the constructed dependency of 'welfare mothers' and other recipients of welfare in welfare states. A whole range of 'caring professions' – the majority of their members are often women – gain entry to and control of people's lives as a result of the latter having to comply with certain expectations of the former in order to gain the care offered. Even when there is no abuse of these powers, the result of the 'caring relationship' means transparency and surveillance of the life of the subject of care which in other types of human relationships are present only in intimate relationships. Beyond that, as has been discussed in the literature on international aid (Collier, 1999), the asymmetrical relationships between the carers and those who receive care and aid often create a long-term dependency and involve normative as well as power hierarchies which undervalue and undermine the attributes of those cared for, whether these are the elderly, the disabled or rural women in the South. Freedom from such dependency relationships has been the focus of much of the disability social movement's focus of campaigning (Oliver, 1990). Moreover, carers do not necessarily care for all their children/dependents in the same way or to the same extent and thus caring itself can become an exercise of manipulative power as well as a subject for an intersectional analysis.

Virginia Held (2005) claims that the care social and political model, developed out of the mother–child relationships model, guarantees mutual equality and respect. In reality, however, although children can wield a lot of emotional power over their parents and others who love them, they do not have the same power as the carer adults and can easily be deprived and abused in many ways. Pointing out, as the feminists who developed the political project of 'the ethics of care' all do, that everyone at certain times of their lives becomes dependent on care, can be the normative basis for the development of 'ethics of care' as a necessary element of social and political solidarity, but cannot guarantee it. It is for this reason that Martha Nussbaum (2001) argues for an approach to compassion in public life that operates at 'both the level of individual psychology and the level of institutional design' (2001: 403). Although she recognizes that some emotions are at least potential allies of, and indeed constituents in, rational deliberation' (2001: 454), she extends her analysis to include the recognition that public institutions play a role in shaping possible emotions (see also Perri 6 et al. (2007)), as well as the role individuals play in creating institutions according to their own values and imagination. Those, in their turn, influence the development of values such as compassion in others.

Nevertheless, in order to be able to influence, let alone construct, public institutions, emotions such as care and compassion are not sufficient, unless there is the power to make them affective. This needs to be recognized, for instance, that while caring for others is the opposite of neo-liberal ethics, which does not recognize notions such as 'public good' or 'public interest', and feminists have developed 'ethics of care' as an ideological and moral alternative to this, it can be argued that the adoption of 'ethics of care' by women, especially those who work in the care sector, facilitates and oils, rather than obstructs and resists, the smooth working of globalized neo-liberalism which depends on local and global chains of care.

As Martin Luther King Jr, stated 'What is needed is a realization that power without love is reckless and abusive. And love without power is at its best power correcting everything that stands against love' (quoted in Gregory, 2008: 195).

Care and political projects of belonging

'Power at its best'. Without power as a resource to, at least, resist if not affect positive change, the normative values of care and love of feminist 'ethics of care' can have very little social and political influence and can, at best, be perceived as utopian. However, as we have seen from reading the excerpt from Thomas More's *Utopia*, situated gazes can delineate boundaries of recognition and care even within Utopias. What is most important to recognize, however, is that not every combination of power and care/love would be compatible with feminist 'ethics of care' political projects of belonging, and neither with those of Martin Luther King, Jr.

While feminists focused on care and love associated with traditional gendered western femininity, as it is constructed in women's roles in family and society, it can be seen clearly from the discussion in the previous chapters that every political project of belonging generates it own intersected constructions of care and that the mere heter-onormative constructions of 'femininity' and 'masculinity' as comple-mentary opposites have detrimental effects on women's powers and autonomy, let alone completely excluding the experiences and values of sexual minorities.

There can be no clearer sign in hegemonic discourses that men care about their community and society than their traditional readiness to perform the ultimate citizenship duty – to sacrifice their lives and to kill others for the sake of the nation. Moreover, as Cynthia Enloe (1990) pointed out, fighting for the nation has been often constructed as fighting for the sake of 'womenandchildren'. More concretely, it has been shown that men care not only for the notions of home and homeland, but also for the other men in their unit with whom they are fighting (Yuval-Davis, 1997a: Chapter 5; Kaplan, 2006). One of the main worries of military commanders about including women in combat military unit has been that their presence will disturb the male bonding which is at the heart of military performance. On their side, women as carers are not only constructed as the biological and cultural reproducers of the nation, but are also the men's 'helpmates' – their role in the formal and informal labour market has been usually defined according to the range of duties demanded by the men, fulfill-ing, in addition to their traditional reproductive duties, all the tasks the men left behind when called to fulfil national duties in times of war and other crises (Yuval-Davis, 1985). Caring, in its different gen-dered forms, therefore, has been at the heart of the performativity, as well as narratives of resistance, of national belonging.

Nowadays, in many states, serving in the military is not any more a male citizenship duty. Just when women started to be allowed to join the military formally in a more equitable manner, the military was transformed from a national duty into a form of professional career, like other agents of national external and internal security. This is also a time in which usually in these states, women bear less children and the national population as a whole starts to age.

This is also the time in which women come to participate in higher and higher percentages in the national labour market, just when, due to neo-liberal globalized economy demands, the nature of service work itself changes and becomes more demanding. This is the time when the 'care gap' appears, not only in the domestic sphere, but in the national sphere as well, and when the growing dependence on migrant and immigrant workers in various sectors of the economy, but especially the care one, raises issues of racialized boundaries of the nation and the various inclusionary and exclusionary political projects of belonging – secular and religious – and the emotions associated with them.

However, maybe even more importantly, this is the time in which in many countries, especially in the West, the percentage of citizens who care enough to vote in the elections falls beyond any previous known rate of the population, especially among younger generations who have grown up under the transformed state institutions as a result of globalized neo-liberalism. A neo-liberal morality of the 'selfish gene' seems to be celebrating, as people cannot see any relationship between engaging in the state and their own interests and concerns. A cynical illustration of this reality has been the demand – from all major political parties in the UK, for instance – to agree to savage cuts in state benefits and services and/or the freezing workers' salaries, when the profitability of banks and most of the incomes of the highest earners are largely not affected or significantly interfered with. Of course, the distance – if not the contradiction – between the care demanded from citizens, driven by feelings of entitlement (Squire, 2007) from states, and the interests of those who rule states can also take very different forms, such as when in ethnocracies, citizens who belong to non-hegemonic minorities are still demanded to show loyalty and care to the state in which the frames of reference are constructed in terms excluding their collectivities.

The probably obvious, and yet groundbreaking at its time, element in Benedict Anderson's theory of nationalism in his book *Imagined Communities* (1991 [1983]) has been a recognition that nationalism, although modern and correlative of the age of enlightenment, is not based on rationality. Like other 'modernist' theorists of nationalism (e.g. Althusser, 1971; Gellner, 1983; Hobsbawm, 1990),

Anderson linked the rise of nationalism to a particular stage in the rise of industrialization and capitalism (print capitalism in his case), and saw it as replacing religion. In this respect, as was discussed in Chapter 3, he was wrong, as we can see that most contemporary nationalist ideologies incorporate, rather than fully replace, religious belonging. However, he was right to emphasize the passion which is at the heart of the nationalist sentiment in which, like religious or familial attachment, there is no actual rational reason and self-interest involved.

As Anderson (1991 [1983]) argues, this care is not based on any notion of self-interest, and this is where it gets its strength from, as it is a substitute construction for 'the sacred'.

'The sacred', constituting the centre of the religious sphere, then, inspires probably the strongest notions of loyalty and sacrifice. The notion of martyrdom is widely spread in various religions, especially the monotheistic ones. The notion of absolute sacrifice is not limited to sacrifice of the self, but also of those the self cares most about, as is illustrated in the stories when a father is prepared to sacrifice his son (Abraham and Isaac) as well as a mother her children – at least in the Jewish tradition in the story of Hannah and her seven children,[6] where she preferred them to be killed rather than to betray the Jewish faith.

One of the factors contributing to the growing strength of religious movements all over the world is that, as was discussed in Chapter 4, religious movements and organizations are often the only ones who will put time, energy and funds in caring for the poor, the home-less, the slum neighbourhood, especially after the growing privatiza-tion of the welfare state and the collapse of socialist and communist movements. What in the Jewish tradition is called '*tzdaka*', charity, in which engaged members of the religious community commit at least 10% of their monies as well as their time to charity and welfare work, has proven to be a sustainable form of care work and caring which constructs and sustains community solidarity and cohesion.

At the same time, it is important to recognize that there are growing secular global social movements concerned with war, poverty and global warming (as discussed in Chapter 5), which transcend borders and boundaries, sharing common human values rather than ethnic, national and religious belongings in cosmopolitan practices and discourses of global and human care.

---

[6]See http://www.jewish-history.com/occident/volume7/jun1849/hannah.html

In discussions of familial, national and religious sentiments, it is sometimes taken for granted that people would not be prepared to sacrifice their lives for any more abstract – or cosmopolitan – cause. And yet we know that strangers and outsiders volunteered to fight for various socialist revolutions – Che Guevara probably embodies this sentiment more than anyone else – and in the Spanish civil war in the 1930s, for example, the international brigade had an important role to play both ideologically and militarily (Richardson, 1982). In recent years the international solidarity movement in support of the Palestinians,[7] for instance, has also been politically important as have other similar organizations in other militarized conflict zones, such as Iraq and Afghanistan.[8] Although some of the volunteers have a religious motivation, for others it is the visceral cosmopolitan sentiment of caring and identification with oppressed strangers and the need to fight in order for their human rights to be recognized.

Feminist 'ethics of care' morality does not ground its ontological base in membership in specific national, ethnic or religious communities but on transcending familial relationships into a universal principle of interpersonal relationships. We need to explore, however, what, if at all, is the relationship between the discourse of 'ethics of care' and collectivity boundaries. Such an exploration should not be carried out only in relation to feminist ethics of care, but also in relation to other similar moral philosophies which put 'love' as the basis of the good society.

'Loving a stranger'

The 'normal' logic of various political projects of belonging is that love and care should primarily, if not exclusively, be directed towards other members of one's own various real and imagined communities. This is true also in cosmopolitan – secular and religious – human rights political projects which justify ethics of care in sharing membership of humankind and of animal rights projects, by sharing membership of living species. When boundaries between 'us' and 'them' are being constructed, then care and love can be bestowed as part of a missionary strategy of persuading 'them' to become part of 'us' or as part of a

---

[7]See http://palsolidarity.org/

[8]See http://en.wikipedia.org/wiki/Human_shield

rational strategy for defending or maximizing collective interests. It is often commented (Beitz, 1999, but of course since the work of Kant in the eighteenth century) how international relations theories – unlike social and political theories – are often devoid of any normative element and will use strategy and simulation games in order to assess which relations to pursue with 'them', which, of course, include the strategy of different kinds of war in which 'them' are to be subjugated or exterminated by force.

The approach of feminist 'ethics of care' projects to issues of individual and collective boundaries is of a different kind – ideally it is not led by interest, indifference or even by shared normative values, but rather by respect and care for all. The difference between such an approach and that which is led by the rights approach is best illustrated by examining the differences that Josephine Donovan and Carol Adams (2007) point out between the attitudes to defending animals promoted by (cosmopolitan) animal rights advocates and those applying a feminist care tradition to animals. They argue that the feminist ethics of care regards animals as individuals who have feelings, who can communicate these feelings and to whom, therefore, humans have moral obligations. (This corresponds to the asymmetrical approach to care that Levinas [1999] calls for, rather than the reciprocal one that is inherent in Buber's approach [1947]). They state that an ethics of care also recognizes the diversity of animals that have a particular history. They argue that as far as possible attention must be paid to these particularities in any ethical determination concerning them.

This is a very different approach to that of animal rights theorists (such as those developed by Tom Regan, 1983, and Peter Singer, 1976) which is characterised by Donovan and Adams (2007) by the assumption of similarity between humans and animals, which, together with the assumption of independence, justifies the animal rights theorists' construction of animals as 'persons with rights' before the law. While animals rights promoters, like ethics of care promoters, pay attention to individual suffering animals, their primary concern is a political analysis of the political and economic systems that are causing the suffering. Abstract animal rights theory requires 'universalable' rules or judgements while erthics of care promoters would argue that many ethical situations require particularistic, situated responses.

Interestingly, and following the 'alternative metaphysical model' of the ethics of care, Donovan and Adams (and the other contributors to their volume) reject the suppression of emotion which is part of the animal rights theoretical perspective, claiming that it is the exclusion of emotional responses of love and care which is a primary cause for animal abuse and exploitation (especially, one can argue, under neo-liberal farming methods).

The political project of belonging of feminist 'ethics of care', as illustrated by Donovan and Adams, therefore, although still assuming common boundaries – of all living beings – rejects in principle the need to find essential similarities and shared belonging as a precondition for emotional and political solidarity.

Nevertheless, there is one basic similarity which is assumed in all ethics of care theories which is, to use Alison Assiter's words (2009: 101) that 'all human beings are needy and all suffer'.

Following Kiekegaard's call to love all human beings, she also argues that 'sometimes, loving another will involve respecting their differences from oneself to the extent that one is able' (Assiter, 2009: 102). The position expressed in the above quote raises two issues which are of fundamental importance to feminist and other emancipatory politics of belonging. First, which criteria should be used to decide when such a difference should or should not be respected, and secondly, how does one determine their ability to respect such differences. I would like to examine these two issues by examining transversal feminist politics (Yuval-Davis, 1994, 1997a, 2006c; Cockburn & Hunter, 1999).

Care, belonging and feminist transversal politics

Transversal feminist political movements were discussed in Chapter 5 as one form of cosmopolitan dialogical politics. It was described how the participants, while being engaged with 'others' belonging to different collectivities, act not as representatives of identity categories or groupings but rather as advocates, how they are reflectively engaged in 'rooting' and 'shifting', and how their strength lies in the construction of common epistemological understandings of particular political situations rather than of common political action. It was also mentioned that transversal politics, unlike 'rainbow coalitions', depend on shared values rather than specific political actions, as differential positioning might dictate prioritizing different political actions and strategies. Most relevant to our discussion here, it was described how transversal politics encompass difference by equality and while continuously crossing collectivity boundaries, the transversal solidarity is bounded by sharing common values.

Shared values as the basis of solidarity and cooperation are generally rejected by ethics of care feminists. The bond between mothers and their children and between carers and their dependents is not that of shared values but that of love and need. The ethics of care feminists and others might share the value of helping the needy, but there is no such demand for the needy to necessarily hold such values. This is an asymmetrical politics of solidarity based on the Levinas principle.

Transversal politics, on the other hand, are based on the symmetrical politics of the Buberian 'I–You' approach. But the symmetry and reciprocity is not based on commercial interest, as Levinas claimed in his critique of Buber, but on the reciprocity of trust. While one might be engaged in defending the rights and/or helping to fulfil the needs of any individual and collective human beings, whatever their values, common political belonging depends on shared values, although these shared values encompass intersectional individual and collective differential positionings. This trust, based on common values, also differentiates transversal politics from the Habermasian (Habermas et al., 1998) deliberative democracy approach.[9]

This is of crucial importance because in this way the transversal perspective helps us to judge which differences matter as well as when and where, and to differentiate between care and compassion towards the oppressed, whoever and wherever they are, and that of accepting them all as potential political allies.[10] Southall Black Sisters (SBS) in London, for instance, are very active in the defence of women of all ethnic and religious communities from domestic violence and abuse, rejecting any cultural and religious justification of such acts. At the

---

[9]In the importance of trust in public political life and the ineffectivity of accountability as its replacement in public culture, please see Onora O'Neil's 2002 BBC Reith Lectures, http://www. bbc.co.uk/radio4/reith2002/

[10]Recently, there have been major debates and political crises in two major human rights organizations, Amnesty International in London and the Centre for Constitutional Rights in the USA, when major feminist activists working in both organizations accused them of crossing the boundary of defending human rights victims and championing them as if they are not only victims but also human rights defenders and thus giving their views political legitimacy. Please see http:// www.human-rights-for-all.org/ and http://www.guardian.co.uk/commentisfree/cifamerica/2010/ nov/15/international-criminal-justice-yemen

same time, they are not political allies and would oppose those who have sought to solve the domestic violence caused by migrant men by deporting them from Britain – after all, men of all classes and ethnic communities commit the crime of domestic violence but are not punished by deportation. Racist solutions should not be the answer to sexist problems and SBS would not establish a transversal political alliance with those who do not share their anti-racist values.

However, while Southall Black Sisters have been an effective campaigning organization in many ways and even managed to overthrow attempts by a politically hostile local authority to stop their funding, they do not have the power to stop such deportations.[11]

Conclusion

Examining feminist ethics of care and feminist transversal dialogical politics brings us back to the question of power and its relations to ethics and to the words of wisdom of Martin Luther King, which were quoted earlier, as

> What is needed is a realization that power without love is reckless and abusive. And love without power is at its best power correcting everything that stands against love. (quoted in Gregory, 2008: 195)

I would argue that a feminist political project of belonging, therefore, should be based on transversal 'rooting', 'shifting', mutual respect and mutual trust. It should be caring, but should also differentiate clearly between care towards transversal allies and care towards the needy. Above all, it should not neglect to reflect upon the relations of power not only among the participants in the political dialogue, but also between these participants and the glocal carriers of power who do not share their values, who need to be confronted, influenced and, when this is not possible, resisted.

---

[11]Although the media were full of stories about the bureaucratic inefficiency of the Home Office which has prevented the deportation of criminals who hold non-British citizenship, as is the official rule.

7

Concluding Remarks

In the introductory chapter of the book we differentiated between belonging and the politics of belonging. Belonging has been described as a mode of relational state of emotion and mind which many psychologists have pointed out as being critical to people's emotional balance and well-being, while sociologists and political theory scholars have focused on the analytical and normative different criteria in which different modes and boundaries of belonging are being constructed in different public, formal and informal, discourses.

However, it was also pointed out that, crucially, people cannot be simply defined, in most situations, as either belonging or not belonging. Emotions – from feeling comfortable, safe or entitled to various rights and resources – are endemic to belonging, but different people who belong to the same collectivity would feel different degrees and kinds of attachment, the same people would feel different in different times, locations and situations and some people would feel that they belong to a particular collectivity while others would construct them as being outside those collectivity boundaries and vice versa. The intersectional analytical perspective, therefore, is crucial for any concrete analysis of belonging/s and political projects of belonging which should involve deconstructing simplistic notions of collectivities' boundaries and their ideological as well as material naturalized constructions, interrogating some of the differential effects that different political projects of belonging have had on different members of these collectivities who are differentially located and/or with different identifications and normative value systems.

It is easiest to carry out such an analysis when one investigates specific case studies. However, as I have argued elsewhere (Yuval-Davis, 2011a), a valid intersectional analysis should combine a broad macro analytical approach with the case study approach in order to be able to gain a proper and valid understanding of any particular social phenomenon. Within the boundaries of one book, however, it is impossible to combine the two, when the phenomenon studied is so global and heterogeneous as contemporary political projects of belonging.

It is for this reason that while in other places I focused on one or a few specific case studies (e.g. in my recent action research project on refugees in East London: Yuval-Davis & Kaptani, 2008, 2009), in this book I could only use some illustrative examples when discussing the field of study as a whole and in this way it should be seen as a necessary but not sufficient step in studying contemporary politics of belonging.

The field of the politics of belonging is indeed very wide and heterogeneous, particularly given the differential effects of the contested hegemony of contemporary neo-liberal globalization on societies, groupings and individuals as well as the state. The introductory chapter of the book outlined its theoretical framework, defined its field of study, and briefly described the global context of the different clusters of political projects of belonging explored within it.

Its various chapters each focused on some of the major clusters of contemporary political projects of belonging, the debates around these in the literature, and some of the most important practices and technologies which are associated with them. As I warn above, however, they should all be read as just introductory generalizations which need to be further investigated (but also reflected upon) within the specific contexts of different, related case studies with their own shifting and intersectional effects.

Chapter 2 focused on the notion of citizenship. I would argue that citizenship should not be seen as limited to state citizenship alone but should be understood as the participatory dimension of membership in all political communities. Indeed, in the subsequent chapters such memberships were discussed. Moreover, I argued that it is impossible to understand state citizenship without analyzing the multi-layered structures of people's citizenships that include, in intersectional ways, citizenships of sub-state, cross-state and suprastate political communities. However, I also argue that in spite of this and in spite of the reconfigurations of states as a result of neo-liberal globalization, different state citizenships (or their absence) and the rights and entitlements associated with them can (still?) be seen as the most important contemporary political projects of belonging, mobilizing people in popular resistance campaigns as well as determining to a great extent a global system of stratification.

Central to my argument here has been the claim that the political project of states and that of nations overlaps only partially and is hegemonic only within specific locations and in specific historical moments. It is for this reason that Chapter 3 discusses nationalism and related ideologies as an autonomous political project of belonging from that of citizenship of states.

Nationalist ideologies usually construct people, states and homelands as being inherently and immutably connected. The fluidity and mobility of the globalized economy, people's migrations and political/religious/social movements, which have all transcended national and ethnic borders and boundaries (in spite of various attempts by states to control or contain them), have also deeply affected nationalist political projects of belonging as well as the ethnocisation of many states. These have contributed to the rise of political movements which embrace the conviviality and richness of multicultural national lives. However, these have also, and in a growing intensity, contributed to the rise and emotional power of autochthonic movements which claim possession of territories and states because 'we were here first'.

This is the other side of the growing legitimacy of the notion of indigeneity, which conversely has proved to be a potent tool for claiming the rights of racialized minorities who survived colonization and the settlement of Europeans in various parts of the world. Their struggles, while different from those of other racialized minorities of people who immigrated to those and other western countries, can be analyzed, on the one hand, as some form of nationalist political projects of belonging. On the other hand, however, they can also be seen as part of the global rise of cosmopolitan political projects of belonging which rely on a human rights discourse to claim their entitlement to individual and collective rights.

The cosmopolitan political projects of belonging are discussed in Chapter 5. Before that, in Chapter 4, there is a discussion on another rising cluster of political projects of belonging which are linked to religion. These can be linked to particular nationalist and ethnic movements or constitute parts of cosmopolitan global movements. However, some of the most important political projects of belonging of our times are religious fundamentalist (or absolutist) movements which have arisen in all major religions and are part – especially some Muslim and Christian fundamentalist movements – of the global 'clash of civilizations' discourse which has come to replace the Cold War as a dichotomizing discourse around the world.

Chapter 5 on cosmopolitanism examines some of the issues relating to the presumption of boundarilessness which are usually assumed in cosmopolitan discourses and political projects of belonging. It examines cosmopolitanism and human rights both as a grass-roots mobilizing tool and as part of the toolkit of militarized international relations.

At the end of each chapter there is also a discussion of some feminist activism which has grown as a particular part of or in resistance to each of the clusters of political projects of belonging which are discussed in them. However, I consider 'ethics of care' to be more specifically a feminist political project of belonging. This relates more to the ways people should relate and belong to each other rather than to what should be the boundaries of belonging. Nevertheless, as I show in Chapter 6, which is focused on this question, in the last instance, the question of boundaries cannot really be avoided once we start questioning who cares for whom and what are both the emotional and the power relations which are involved in this interaction.

It is probably in Chapter 6, especially when I discuss some of the differences between feminist ethics of care and feminist transversal dialogical political projects of belonging, where the boundary between the analytical and the normative in the book is most blurred (or rather, mutually constituted), although, of course, given the situated epistemological perspective of the book as a whole, this can be detected throughout. Analyses of social and political relations which are focused on different constructions of emotions and power need to be valued normatively.

So what is my political project of belonging?

It is multi-layered – recognizing the importance of belonging and the politics of belonging without essentializing this or prioritising any form of naturalized boundaries within the complex glocal realities in which we live; it is transversal, rather than cosmopolitan – transcending borders and boundaries while also recognizing the importance of situated gazes, nevertheless rejecting identity politics and emphasizing the differentiation between social locations, identifications and social values; it is emancipatory, advocating for universal human security, and while recognizing the tremendous importance and value of caring relationships it does not ignore the importance of accounting in these relationships for their contextual power relations.

Politics of belonging are about the intersection of the sociology of power with the sociology of emotions, but it is the normative values lens which filters the meaning of both to individuals and collectivities, differentially situated along intersectional glocal social locations.

Under neo-liberal globalization the ways people are differentially located within the same society and globally have changed, as have their identifications and political values. Of course ideologies, movements and organizations, whether these are socialism, feminism, Islam or the Labour Party, are never homogeneous or fixed. However, the radical changes in the contexts in which they operate, among other things the changes in the technologies of communication as well as the technologies of governance and governmentality, continuously reconstruct them in contested ways which affect in differential ways different people and the same people in different times. *Liquid Modernity* is the name that Zygmunt Bauman (2000) gives to these changes. The contested political projects of belonging described in this book reflect both the continuity as well as the changes within these projects. They all reflect attempts of fixation of inclusionary and exclusionary boundaries via particular performative discourses, as well as using the counter narratives and practices of internal and external resistance and transcendence. However, as has been emphasized throughout the book, even people who adhere to the same political project of belonging affect and are affected by it in differential ways at any moment of time. It is not, or not just, ideological and emotional 'consciousness-raising' which homogenizes discourse, but specific relations of power. However power, in order to be effective in the long term, has to be internalized and naturalized. The problem of feminist, as well as other emancipatory political movements of belonging, is how to gain enough power to change society without internalizing, on the way, at least some of the assumptions about 'what works', which, in the end, would have them co-opted. (The case of 'gender mainstreaming' is but one example, but there also many others.[1])

Some, like Anat Pick (2010) would claim that this is an impossible mission, as granting power to the powerless without a just transfer rather than a transcendence of relations of power is a contradiction in terms except in extraordinary and very short moments of grace (e.g. the 18 days of resistance by the Egyptians masses during February 2011). While I find this warning sobering but valid in many ways, this view also involves a homogeneous construction of power which I take exception to, ignoring the complexities of various systems of power which have different systems of checks and balances that could be mobilized, to a lesser or greater extent, via the containment,

---

[1]See, for example, Walby, 2003; AWID, 2004; Yuval-Davis, 2005b.

contestation and redistribution of power and other social resources. On a more basic level this view of the power of the powerless ignores the Bordieuan insights which sees power as constituted by a constant interaction between the symbolically structured and socially inculcated dispositions of individual agents and the social field structured by symbolically mediated relations of domination.

In the last chapter of her book *The Cultural Politics of Emotions* (2004), Sarah Ahmed talks about the emotion of hope. Hope, as we know, is what was left in Pandora's Box after all the miseries of world were let loose. Ahmed talks about the motivating power of hope for the future in present action, but also warns that on the way hope can become 'sticky' and fixed when no real space for the hoped change is left, and then hope can becomes an obstacle to 'moving on'.[2]

A quote from Gramsci (1994) which is often used in Leftist circles is that in order to act effectively one needs to have a 'pessimism of the mind and optimism of the will'. At the end of *Gender and Nation* (1997a: 132), I stated that 'as we can never accomplish, by definition, what we set out to do, one of the important tasks we have to think about is how to sustain and sometimes even celebrate our lives while struggling'. The trouble is that in the decade+ that has passed since that book was published, the problem has often been not – individually and collectively – one of accomplishing what we set out to do, but in many ways one of watching helplessly while the things we care about are getting worse and when these seem to have been accomplished, they also seem to follow the Chinese curse 'may you get what you wished for'. This can have the effect of making hope taste bitter and allow disillusionment to settle in. The victory, after many years of Tory rule, of New Labour in the UK; the coming to power of a supposedly progressive government in Sri Lanka; the Oslo agreement on Palestine – these are just some examples of when people's hopes were raised only for them to end up even more disillusioned than before. The other side of this, of course, is when things we did not want to happen do happen, like the recent Tory victory in the UK, the results can be even worse…

However – and some of the political projects described in this book can testify to this – there are also some things to celebrate. As

---

[2] AWID's global study on fundamentalist movements notes how 'hope' is mobilized by fundamentalists as a tool of recruitment when rational evaluations become too depressing, when all channels of positive social, political and economic change seem to be blocked (AWID, 2009).

Noam Chomsky in his (2009) SOAS lecture claimed, the resistance movement to the Iraq war developed much earlier than that for the Vietnam war and some major atrocities have been contained because of that; generally many more people are sensitized to issues of human rights and ecological issues and open expressions of racism are much less legitimate now than they used to be. Moreover, we have also seen a growing number of popular resistance movements in various authoritarian and corrupt regimes, using new technologies such as mobile phones and social media on the web in their struggles for freedom and democritisation.

Barak Obama talked about *The Audacity of Hope* (2006). And indeed, personally, for a man of his background to be able to rise to become the President of the USA, is an embodiment of the American Dream. However, as the book tried to show throughout, identity is not the same as social location, and only those blinded by identity politics could see Obama as representative of African Americans. Many of his policies since he has come to power – admittedly with a terrible legacy from Bush and the global economic crisis as well as the major political constraints he is under – reflect a normative value system which is so much less radical than that of many of his supporters, who collapsed locations, identities and values and expected him to transform the USA's global as well as local policies.

However – maybe there is still some hope – a least on some issues …

Going back to the endnote from *Gender and Nation*, I quoted there a Zimbabwean saying that 'as long as you can walk, you can dance, and as long as you can talk, you can sing'.

I do try to remember this. Although I probably don't dance enough these days I still look for occasions to move along with the five rythms dance from flowing to chaos to stillness.[3] And I do – more or less – continue to sing.[4]

---

[3] See http://en.wikipedia.org/wiki/5Rhythms

[4] I would like to dedicate the hope of singing to the lovely Wing-It Singers choir in Hackney.

Bibliography

6, P., S. Radstone, S. Squire and A. Treacher (Eds). (2007). *Public Emotions.* New York, Basingstoke, Palgrave Macmillan.

Abu-Saad, I. and D. Champagne (2001). 'Guest Editorial for the Special Issue on Indigenous Peoples', *Hagar* 2(2): 157–63.

Agamben, G. (1994). 'We Refugees', *Symposium*, 49(2): 114–119, translated by Michael Rocke. http://www.egs.edu/faculty/agamben/agamben-we-refugees.html.

Agamben, G. (2002). 'Security and Terror', *Theory and Event* 5.

Aguirre, M. (2010). 'Brazil–Turkey and Iran: A New Global Balance', *Open Democracy,* http://www.opendemocracy.net. *2 June.*

Ahmad, S. D. (Ed.). (2002). *Gendering the Spirit: Women, Religion and the Post-colonial Response.* London, Zed Books.

Ahmed, A. (2009). 'Locals and Aliens: Maids in Contemporary Egypt'. PhD thesis. School of Social Sciences and Humanities, London, University of East London.

Ahmed, S. (2000). *Strange Encounters: Embodied Others in Post-Coloniality.* London, Routledge.

Ahmed, S. (2004). *The Cultural Politics of Emotions.* Edinburgh, Edinburgh University Press.

Aitamurto, K. (2007). 'Russian Rodnoverie: Negotiating Individual Traditionalism', paper presented at the International Conference on Globalisation, Immigration and Change in Religious Movements, Bordeaux, France.

Al-Ali, N. and N. Pratt (2009). *What Kind of Liberation? Women and the Occupation in Iraq.* Berkeley, CA, University of California Press.

Albrow, M. (1997). Presentation in a panel on 'Nationalism and Diaspora'. ASEN seminar, London School of Economics, June.

Alexander, J. M. (1994). 'Not Just (Any) Body Can Be a Citizen: The Politics of Law, Sexuality and Post-coloniality in Trinidad and Tobago and the Bahamas', *Feminist Review* 98.

Ali, Y. (1992). 'Muslim Women and the Politics of Ethnicity and Culture in Northern England', in G. Sahgal and N. Yuval-Davis (Eds.), *Refusing Holy Orders: Women and the Fundamentalism in Britain.* London, Verso, pp. 101–23.

Al-Khalisi, J. (2005). 'The Gates of Hell are Open in Iraq', *The Guardian*, April 1.

Alkire, S. (2002). 'Conceptual Framework for Human Security', http://humansecurity-chs.org/doc/1.

Allen, S. and M. Macey (1990). 'At the Cutting Edge of Citizenship: Race and Ethnicity in Europe 1992', paper presented at *the Annual Conference of the Centre for Research in Ethnic Relations: New Issues in Black Politics.* University of Warwick, 14th-16th May 1990.

Althusser, L. (1971). *Lenin and Philosophy and Other Essays.* London, New Left Review.

Alund, A. and C.-U. Schierup (1991). *Paradoxes of Multiculturalism: Essays on Swedish Society.* Aldershot, Avebury.

Alvarez, S., E. Dagino, et al. (Eds.). (1997). *Cultures of Politics/Politics of Cultures: Revisioning Latin American Social Movements.* Boulder, CO, Westview Press.

Amin, A. (1994). *Post-Fordism: A Reader.* Cambridge, Blackwell.

Amin, S. (1978). *The Arab Nation.* London, Zed Books.

Amnesty International http://www.amnesty.org/en/economic-social-and-cultural-rights.

Anderson, B. (1991 [1983]). *Imagined Communities: Reflections on the Origins and Spread of Nationalism.* London, Verso.

Anderson, B. (1998). 'Long-Distance Nationalism', in *The Spectre of Comparisons.* London, Verso, pp. 58–74.

Anderson, B. (2000). *Doing the Dirty Work? The Global Politics of Domestic Labour.* London, Zed Books.

Andrews, M. (1999). 'The Politics of Forgiveness', *International Journal of Politics, Culture and Society* 13(1).

Anthias, F. (1998). 'Rethinking Social Divisions: Some Notes Towards a Theoretical Framework', *Sociological Review* 46(3): 557–80.

Anthias, F. (2001). 'The Material and the Symbolic in Theorizing Social Stratification', *British Journal of Sociology* 52(3): 367–90.

Anthias, F. (2002). 'Beyond Feminism and Multiculturalism: Locating Difference and the Politics of Location', *Women's Studies International Forum* 25(3): 275–86.

Anthias, F. (2005). 'Social Stratification and Social Inequality: Models of Intersectionality and Identity', in F. Devine, M. Savage, J. Scott and R. Crompton (Eds.), *Rethinking Class: Culture, Identities and Lifestyles.* New York, Palgrave Macmillan.

Anthias, F. and N. Yuval-Davis (1983). 'Contextualising Feminism: Gender, Ethnic and Class Divisions', *Feminist Review* 15(November): 62–75.

Anthias, F. and N. Yuval-Davis (1992). *Racialized Boundaries: Race, Nation, Gender, Colour and Class and the Anti-Racist Struggle.* London, Routledge.

Antonsich, M. (2009). 'On Territory, the Nation-state and the Crisis of the Hyphen', *Progress in Human Geography* 33(6): 789–806.

Antonsich, M. (2010). 'Searching for Belonging – An Analytical Framework', *Geography Compass* 4(6): 644–59.

Antrobus, P. (2004). *The Global Women's Movement, Origins, Issues and Strategies.* Cambridge, Blackwell.

Anzaldúa, G. (1987). *Borderlands/La Frontera: The New Mestiza* (2nd edition). San Francisco, CA, Aunt Lute Books.

Appadurai, A. (2006). *Fear of Small Numbers: An Essay on the Geography of Anger*. North Carolina: Duke University Press.

Appiah, K. A. (2006). *Cosmopolitanism*. London: Penguin, Allen Lane.

Arendt, H. (1943). 'We Refugees', *The Menorah Journal*, Winter: 77.

Arendt, H. (1958). *The Human Condition*. Chicago, IL, University of Chicago Press.

Arendt, H. (1986 [1951]). *The Origins of Totalitarianism*. London, Secker & Warburg.

Aristotle (2004 [350 BC]). *Politics*. Sioux Falls, SD: NuVision Publications, LLC.

Armstrong, J. (1982). *Nations before Nationalism*. Chapel Hill, NC, University of North Carolina Press.

Armstrong, K. (2007). 'The Idea of the Sacred', the introduction to the catalogue of the exhibition Sacred Texts. London, British Library.

Armstrong, K. (2009). *The Case for God: What Religion Really Means*. London, The Bodley Head.

Asad, T. (1986). *The Idea of an Anthropology of Islam*. Washington, DC, Center for Contemporary Arab Studies.

Asad, T. (2004). 'Reflections on Laicité and the Public Sphere', *Social Science Research Council, Items and Issues* 5(3), http://www.ssrc.org/publications/items/v5n3/index.html.

Asad, T., W. Brown, J. Butler, and S. Mahmood (Eds.). (2009). *Is Critique Secular? Blasphemy, Injury, and Free Speech*. New York, The Regents of the University of California.

Ash, T. G. (2009). 'Europe is Torn between Essential Solidarity and National Egoism', *The Guardian*, February 26.

Ashman, S. (2004). 'Resistance to Neoliberal Globalisation: A Case of "Militant Particularism"?', *Politics* 24(2): 143–53.

Ashman, S. and A. Callinicos (2007). 'Capital Accumulation and the State System: Assessing David Harvey's *The New Imperialism*', *Historical Materialism* 14(4): 117–31.

Assiter, A. (1996). *Enlightened Women, Modernist Feminism in a Postmodern Age*. London, Routledge.

Assiter, A. (2009). *Kierkegaard, Metaphysics and Political Theory: Unfinished Selves*. London, Continuum.

Athukorala, P. C. and C. Manning (2009). *Structural Change and International Migration in East Asia: Adjusting to Labour Scarcity*. Melbourne, Oxford University Press.

Australian Human Rights and Equal Opportunities Commission. (2001). 'HREOC and the World Conference against Racism'. AHREOC: Canberra. http://www.hreoc.gov.au/worldconference/aus_gender.html.

Avineri, S. and A. Shalit (Eds.). (1992). *Communitarianism and Individualism*. Oxford, Oxford University Press.

AWID (Association of Women's Rights in Development) (2004). 'Intersectionality: A Tool for Gender and Economic Justice', *AWID* (special issue), August 9.

AWID (2009). 'Resisting and Challenging Religious Fundamentalisms', http://www.awid.org/eng/About-AWID/AWID-Initiatives/Resisting-and-Challenging-Religious-Fundamentalisms.

Baca Zinn, M. and E. D. Stanley (1986). *The Reshaping of America: Social Consequences of the Changing Economy.* Englewood Cliffs, NJ, Prentice-Hall.

Baird-Windle, P. (2001). *Targets of Hatred: Anti-abortion Terrorism.* New York and Basingstoke, Palgrave for St Martin's Press.

Bakhtin, M. (1981). *The Dialogical Imagination.* Austin, TX, University of Texas Press.

Bakhtin, M. (1984). *Problems of Dostoevsky's Poetics.* Manchester, University of Manchester Press.

Balchin, C. (2003). 'With Her Feet on the Ground: Women, Religion and Development in Muslim Communities', *Development* 46(4): 39–49.

Balchin, C. (2008). *Ten Myths about Religious Fundamentalisms.* Association of Women's Rights in Development, Toronto.

Baliamoune-Lutz, M. (2007). 'Globalisation and Gender Inequality: Is Africa Different?', *Journal of African Economies* 16(2): 301–48.

Balibar, E. (1990). 'Paradoxes of Universality', in D. T. Goldberg (Ed.), *Anatomy of Racism.* Minneapolis, MN, Minnesota University Press.

Balibar, E. (2006). *Strangers as Enemies: Further Reflections on the Aporias of Transnational Citizenship.* California, Institute on Globalization and the Human Condition, McMaster University.

Barber, B. R. (1995). *Jihad vs McWorld: How Globalism and Tribalism are Shaping the World.* New York, Times Books.

Barker, M. (1981). *The New Racism.* London, Junction Books.

Barry, T. (2008). 'Legal Immigrants Next Target of Anti-Immigration Groups', *America's Program,* 16 November.

Barth, F. (1969). *Ethnic Groups and Boundaries.* London, Allen & Unwin.

Barton, L. (2007). 'On with the Show', *The Guardian, February 26.*

Basch, L. (2004). 'Human Security Globalisation and Feminist Visions', *Peace Review* 16(1).

Basch, L., N. Glick Schiller and S. B. Christina (1994). *Nations Unbound.* New York, Routledge.

Bassel, L. (2010). 'Intersectional Politics at the Boundaries of the Nation State', *Ethnicities* 10(2): 155–80.

Bates, C. (2001). *Community, Empire and Migration: South Asians in Diaspora.* Basingstoke and New York, Palgrave.

Bauer, O. (2001 [1924]). *The National Question and Social Democracy.* Minneapolis, MN, University of Minnesota Press.

Bauman, G. (1994). 'Dominant and Demotic Discourses of Culture', paper presented at the conference Culture, Communication and Discourse: Negotiating Difference in Multi-Ethnic Alliances, University of Manchester, December.

Bauman, Z. (1995). *Life in Fragments: Essays On Post-Modern Morality*. Oxford, Blackwell.

Bauman, Z. (1998). *Globalization: The Human Consequences*. Cambridge, Polity Press.

Bauman, Z. (2000). *Liquid Modernity*. Cambridge, Polity Press.

Bauman, Z. (2004). *Wasted Lives*. Cambridge, Polity Press.

Bauman, Z. (2005). 'Identity for Identity's Sake is a Bit Dodgy', *Soundings* 29: 12–20.

Beasley, C. and C. Bacchi (2007). 'Envisaging a New Politics for an Ethical Future: Beyond Trust, Care and Generosity – Towards an Ethic of Social Flesh', *Feminist Theory* 8(3): 279–98.

Beck, U. (1992). *Risk Society: Towards a New Modernity*. London, Sage.

Beck, U. (1998). 'The Cosmopolitan Manifesto', *New Statesman* 127(4377).

Beck, U. (2003). 'The Analysis of Global Inequality: From National to Cosmopolitan Perspective', in M. Kaldor, H. Anheier and M. Glasius (Eds.), *Global Civil Society*. Oxford, Oxford University Press.

Beck, U. (2009). 'This Crisis Cries Out to be Transformed into the Founding of a New Europe', *The Guardian*, April 13.

Beck, L., P. Cohen, et al. (1999). 'Between Home and Belonging: Critical Ethnographies of Race, Place and Identity'. *Finding the Way Home Working Papers* (Working Paper 2). London Centre for New Ethnicities Research, University of East London.

Beebee, S.D.A & M. Kaldor (2010). *The Ultimate Enemy is No Enemy*. New York: Perseus Books.

Beitz, C. R. (1999). *Political Theory and International Relations*. Princeton, NJ, Princeton University Press.

Bell, P. M. H. (2007). *The Origins of the Second World War in Europe*. Harlow, Pearson Education.

Bell, V. (1999). 'Performativity and Belonging: An Introduction', *Theory, Culture and Society* (special issue on Performativity and Belonging), 16(2): 1–10.

Bell, V. (2005). 'On the Critique of Secular Ethics: An Essay with Flannery O'Connor and Hanna Arendt', *Theory, Culture and Society* 22(1).

Benhabib, S. (1992). *Situating the Self*. New York, Routledge.

Benhabib, S. (1999). 'Citizens, Residents, and Aliens in a Changing World: Political Membership in the Global Era', *Social Research* 66.

Benhabib, S. (2002). *The Claims of Culture*. Princeton, NJ, Princeton University Press.

Benhabib, S. (2007). 'Twilight of Sovereignty or the Emergence of Cosmopolitan Norms? Rethinking Citizenship in Volatile Times', *Citizenship Studies* 11(1): 19–36.

Benjamin, J. (1998). *Shadow of the Other: Intersubjectivity and Gender in Psychoanalysis*. New York, Routledge.

Bennoune, K., D. Buss, P. Danchin, G. Sahgal and S. Yildirim (2006). 'Human Rights and Fundamentalism', *ASIL (American Society of International Law. Proceedings of the Annual Meeting) Proceedings*, 1st January.

Benvenisti, M. (2001). 'The Privatization of Love', *Haaretz Op-Ed*, February 2, hyyp://3.haaretz.co.il/eng/htnls/kat9_2.htm.

Berdahl, D. (1999). *Where the World Ended: Re-unification and Identity in the German Borderland*. Berkeley, CA, University of California Press.

Berlin, I. (1958). *Two Concepts of Liberty*. Oxford, Clarendon Press.

Bertossi, C. (2003). 'Transforming the Boundaries of Citizenship in Europe: from Nationality to Anti-Discrimination?', paper presented at the conference Whither Europe? Borders, Boundaries, Frontiers in a Changing World, Gutenberg University, Gutenberg, January 16–17.

Beth-Halakhmi, B. (1996). 'Interview with Nira Yuval-Davis', *WAF (Women Against Fundamentalism) Journal* 8: 32–4.

Bettio, F., A. Simonazzi, et al. (2006). 'Change in Care Regimes and Female Migration: The "Care Drain" in the Mediterranean', *Journal of European Social Policy* 16(3): 271–85.

Beyer, J. (2007). 'Imagining the State in Rural Kyrgyztan: How Perceptions of the State Create Customary Law in the Kyrgyz Aksakal Courts', *Working Papers No. 95*. Halle/Saale, Max Planck Institute.

Beyer, P. (1994). *Religion and Globalization*. London, Sage.

Bezlova, A. (2008). 'Asia–EU Summit to Address "Financial Tsunami"', *Other News*, http://www.other-net.info/index.php.

Bhabha, H. (Ed.). (1990a). *Nation and Narration*. London, Routledge.

Bhabha, H. (1990b). 'The Third Space', in J. Rutherford (Ed.), *Identity: Community, Culture, Difference*. London, Lawrence and Wishart.

Bhabha, H. (1994). 'Dissemination: Time, Narrative and the Margins of the Modern Nation', in H. Bhabha, *The Location of Culture*. London, Routledge, pp. 139–70.

Bhabha, H. (1996). 'Unsatisfied: Notes on Vernacular Cosmopolitanism', in L. Garcia-Morena and P. C. Pfeifer (Eds.), *Text and Nation*. London, Camden House.

Bhabha, J. and S. Shutter (1994). *Women's Movement: Women under Immigration, Nationality and Refugee Law*. Stoke-on-Trent, Trentham Books.

Bhatt, C. (2004). 'Democracy and Hindu Nationalism', *Democratization* 11(4): 133–54.

Bhatt, C. (2006). 'The Fetish of the Margin: Religious Absolutism, Anti-racism and Post-colonial Silence', *New Formations* (special issue on Post Colonial Studies after Iraq) 59: 98–115.

Bhatt, C. (2007). 'Frontlines and Interstices in the Global War on Terror', *Development and Change* 38(6): 1073–93.

Bhatt, C. (2008). 'The Times of Movements: a Response', *The British Journal of Sociology* 59: 25–33.

Bhatt, C. (2009). 'The "British Jihad" and the Curves of Religious Violence', *Ethnic and Racial Studies* 33(1): 39–59.

Bhavnani, K.-K. (2008). 'Dancing around Difference: The Power of Film', paper presented at the conference *Imagining the Other: Narrative and Culture*, Centre for Narrative Research, University of East London, November 19.

Bhavnani, K.-K., J. Foran and P. Kurian (Eds.). (2003). *Feminist Futures: Re-imagining Women, Culture and Development*. London, Zed Books.

Bichler, S. and J. Nitzan (2004). 'Dominant Capital and the New Wars, http://www.bnarchives.net', *Journal of World-Systems Research (JWSR)* 10(2): 255–327.

Bichler, S. and J. Nitzan (2009). 'Contours of Crisis III: Systemic Fear and Forward-Looking Finance, Dollars and Sense: Real World Economics', http://www.dollarsandsense.org/archive/2009/0609bichlernitzan.html.

Bichler, S. and J. Nitzan (2010). 'Capital as Power: Toward a New Cosmology of Capitalism', *Dissident Voice*, http://dissidentvoice.org/2010/05/capital-as-power/ (Retrieved May 6).

Bigo, D. (2002). 'Security and Immigration: Toward a Critique of the Governmentality of Unease', *Alternatives: Global, Local, Political* 27.

Billig, M. (1976). *Social Psychology and Intergroup Relations*. New York, Academic Press.

Billig, M. (1995). *Banal Nationalism*. London, Sage.

Binnie, J. and D. Bell (2004). 'Authenticating Queer Space: Citizenship, Urbanism and Governance', *Urban Studies* 41(9): 1807–20.

Bisley, N. (2007). *Rethinking Globalization*. Basingstoke, Palgrave Macmillan.

Blackburn, S. (2009). 'All Quiet on the God Front', *The Guardian* (Saturday), July 4.

Blair, T. (2006). 'Speech on Multiculturalism and Integration' http://www.number10.gov.uk/Page10563.

Blanchard, E. (2003). 'Gender, International Relations, and the Development of Feminist Security Theory', *Signs: Journal of Women in Culture and Society* 28(4).

Blaser, M., H. A. Feit and G. McRae (Eds.). (2004). *In the Way of Development*. London, Zed Books. See http://www.idrc.ca/en/ev-64521-201-1-DO_TOPIC.html

Block, D. (2004). 'Globalization, Transnational Communication and the Internet', *International Journal on Multicultural Societies (IJMS)* 6(1): 13–28.

Blumental, M. (2009). *Republican Gomorrah: Inside the Movement that Shattered the Party*. New York, Nation Books.

Blunkett, D. (2002). *Secure Borders, Safe Haven* (White Paper). London, Home Office.

Boal, A. (1979). *Theatre of the Oppressed*. London, Pluto Press.

Boden, D. and D. Zimmerman (Eds.). (1991). *Talk and Social Structure: Studies in Ethnomethodology and Conversational Analysis*. Cambridge, Polity Press.

Bond, M. (2004). 'Top Down or Bottom Up? A Reply to David Held', *Open Democracy*, http://opendemocracy.net. *September 24*.

Bond, M. (2008). 'Human Rights You Can Enforce', *Open Democracy*, http:// opendemocracy.net. *December 12*.

Bottomley, G. (1992). *From Another Place: Migration and the Politics of Culture*. Cambridge, Cambridge University Press.

Bourdieu, P. (1984). *Distinction: A Social Critique of the Judgement of Taste*. Trans. Richard Nice. London, Routledge & Kegan Paul.

Bourdieu, P. (1990). *The Logic of Practice*. Cambridge, Polity Press.

Bourdieu, P. and R. Nice (1977). *Outline of a Theory of Practice*. Cambridge, Cambridge University Press.

Bourne, J. and A. Sivanandan (1980). 'Cheerleaders and Ombudsmen: The Sociology of Race Relations in Britain', *Race and Class* 21(4): 331–52.

Bowlby, J. (1969). *Attachment. Vol. 1 of Attachment and Loss*. London, Hogarth Press, and New York, Basic Books.

Bowlby, J. (1973). *Separation: Anxiety and Anger. Vol. 2 of Attachment and Loss*. London and New York, Basic Books.

Boyarin, J. (1994). 'The Other Within and the Other Without', in L. J. Silberstein and L. C. Robert (Eds.), *The Other in Jewish Thought and History: Constructions of Jewish Thought and Identity*. New York, New York University Press.

Boyle, M. (2001). 'Towards a (Re)theorisation of the Historical Geography of Nationalism in Diasporas: The Irish Diaspora as an Exemplar', *International Journal of Population Geography* 7: 429–46.

Bradley, H. (1996). *Fractured Identities: The Changing Patterns of Inequality*. Cambridge, Polity Press.

Brah, A. (1996). *Cartographies of Diaspora*. London, Routledge.

Brah, A. and A. Phoenix (2004). 'Ain't I a Woman? Revisiting Intersectionality', *Journal of International Women's Studies* 5(3): 75–86.

Braidotti, R. (1991). *Patterns of Dissonance*. Cambridge, Polity Press.

Braidotti, R. (1994). *Nomadic Subjects*. New York, Columbia University Press.

Brecher, J., T. Costello and B. Smith (2000). 'Globalization from Below: International Solidarity is the Key to Consolidate the Legacy of Seattle', *The Nation*, December 4.

Brecht, B. (1962). *Mother Courage and Her Children; a Chronicle of the Thirty Years War*. Translated by Eric Bentley. London, Methuen.

Brenner, N., B. Jessop, M. Jones and G. MacLeod (2003). *State/Space: A Reader*. Maldern, MA, and Oxford, Blackwell.

Bricmont, J. (2009). 'The Problem with the "Responsibility to Protect": Bombing for a Juster World?' *Counter Punch*, July 28.

Britwum, A. O. and P. Martens (2008). 'The Challenge of Globalisation, Labour Market Restructuring and Union Democracy in Ghana', *African Studies Quarterly* 10(2 & 3).

Brown, G. (2004). 'At the British Museum', *Daily Mail*, September 14.

Brown, G. (2005a). *Newsnight*, BBC2, March 14.

Brown, G. (2005b). It's Time to Celebrate the Empire, says Brown', *Daily Mail*, January 15, see: http://www.dailymail.co.uk/news/article-334208/ Its-time-celebrate-Empire-says-Brown.html#ixzz18aZdl7cx.

Brown, K. (2007). 'China Goes Global', *Open Democracy*, http://www.open democracy.net. *2 August*.

Brown, W. (2006). *Regulating Aversion: Tolerance in the Age of Identity and Empire*. Princeton, NJ, Princeton University Press.

Brubaker, R. (1992). *Citizenship and Nationhood in France and Germany*. Cambridge, MA, Harvard University Press.

Brubaker, R. and F. Cooper (2000). 'Beyond Identity', *Theory and Society* 29(1): 34–67.

Bruce, S. and D. Voas (2004). 'The Resilience of the Nation-state: Religion and Polities in the modern era', *Sociology* 38(5): 1025–34.

Bryan, B., S. Dadzie and S. Scafe (1985). *The Heart of the Race: Black Women's Lives in Britain*. London, Virago.

Buber, M. (1947). *Between Man and Man*, London, Routledge and Kegan Paul.

Bunch, C. (2001). 'Women's Human Rights: The Challenges of Global Feminism and Diversity', in M. DeKoven (Ed.), *Feminist Locations: Global and Local, Theory and Practice*. New Brunswick, NJ, Rutgers University Press, pp. 129–46.

Bunting, M. (2009). 'In Control? Think Again. Our Ideas of Brain and Human Nature are Myths', *The Guardian*, August 24.

Bunting, M. (2010). 'My Stuffed Bookcase Shows that God is Attracting More Debate than Ever', *The Guardian*, April 5.

Burkitt, I. (2005). 'Powerful Emotions: Power, Government and Opposition in the "War on Terror"', *Sociology* 39(4): 679–95.

Buss, D. and D. Herman (2003). *Globalizing Family Values: The Christian Right in International Politics*. Minneapolis, MN, Minnesota University Press.

Butler, J. (1990). *Gender Trouble: Feminism and the Subversion of Identity*. New York, Routledge.

Butler, J. (1993). *Bodies That Matter*. New York, Routledge.

Butler, J. (1997). *The Psychic Life of Power*. Stanford, CA, Stanford University Press.

Butler, J. (2008). 'Sexual Politics, Torture and Secular Time', *The British Journal of Sociology* 59(1): 1–23.

Byrne, S., G. Mirescu and S. Muller (2007). *Decentralisation and Access to Justice*. Fribourg, International Research and Consulting Centre (IRCC), Institute of Federalism.

Cain, H. and N. Yuval-Davis (1990). 'The Equal Opportunities Community and the Anti-racist Struggle', *Critical Social Policy* 29: 5–26.

Caldwell, K. L. (2002). 'Claiming Citizenship from the Margins: Black Women and the Struggle for Belonging in Brazil', in *Gender, Cultural*

Citizenship, and the Nation: Notions of Belonging, the Claiming of Rights. University of California, Santa Cruz.

Calhoun, C. (1997). *Nationalism.* Buckingham, Open University Press.

Calhoun, C. (2003a). 'Belonging in the Cosmopolitan Imaginary', *Ethnicities* 3: 531–53.

Calhoun, C. (2003b). 'The Variability of Belonging: A Reply to Rogers Brubaker', *Ethnicities* 3(4).

Calhoun, C. (2006). *Cosmopolitanism and Belonging.* London, Routledge.

Calhoun, C. (2007). *Nations Matter: Culture, History, and the Cosmopolitan Dream.* London, Routledge.

Cantle, T. (2001). *Community Cohesion: A Report of the Independent Review Team.* London, Home Office.

Carter, E., J. Donald and J. Squire (Eds.). (1993). *Space and Place: Theories of Identity and Location.* London, Lawrence & Wishart.

Castells, M. (1996–98). *The Information Age: Economy, Society, Culture.* Oxford, Blackwell.

Castells, M. (1997). *The Power of Identity.* Oxford, Blackwell.

Castells, M. (2000 [1998]). *End of Millennium.* Oxford, Blackwell.

Castles, S. (2003). 'Immigration and Asylum', paper presented at the Muslims in Europe, post 9/11: Understanding and Responding to the Islamic World Conference, St Antony's College and Princeton University, Princeton, NJ, April 25–26.

Castles, S. (2009 February). 'Migration and the Global Financial Crisis: A Virtual Symposium', http://www.age-of-migration.com/na/index.asp.

Castles, S. and M. J. Miller (2003). *The Age of Migration.* London, Macmillan.

Castoriadis, C. (1987). *The Imaginary Institution of Society.* Cambridge, Polity Press.

Cavarero, A. (1997). *Relating Narratives: Storytelling and Selfhood.* Trans. P. Kottman. London, Routledge.

Cavarero, A. (2000). *Relating Narratives: Storytelling and Selfhood.* London, Routledge.

Center for Women's Global Leadership (2001). 'A Women's Human Rights Approach to the World Conference against Racism', www.cwgl.rutgers. edu/globalcenter/policy/gcpospaper.html, Durban, South Africa, August 31 - September 7.

Champagne, D. and I. Abu-Saad (Eds.). (2003). *The Future of Indigenous Peoples: Strategies for Survival and Development.* Los Angeles, CA, UCLA American Indian Studies Center.

Chandler, D. (2002). *From Kosovo to Kabul: Human Rights and International Intervention.* London, Pluto Press.

Chandler, D. (2004). *Constructing Global Civil Society: Morality and Power in International Relations.* London, Palgrave Macmillan.

Chatterjee, P. (1990). 'The Nationalist Resolution of The Women's Question', in K. Sangari and S. Vaid (Eds.), *Recasting Women: Essays in Colonial History.* New Brunswick, NJ, Rutgers University Press.

Chatterjee, P. (1993 [1986]). *Nationalist Thought and the Colonial World: A Derivative Discourse*. London, Zed Books.

Cheah, P. (1997). 'Posit(ion)ing Human Rights in the Current Global Conjuncture', *Public Culture* 9: 233–66.

Chen, L. C. (1995). 'Human Security: Concepts and Approaches', in T. Matsumae and L. C. Chen (Eds.), *Common Security in Asia: New Concepts of Human Security*. Tokyo, Tokyo University Press.

Chesterman, S. (2005). *You, the People: The United Nations, Transitional Administration, and State-building*. Oxford, Oxford University Press.

Chhachhi, A. (1991). 'Forced Identities: the State, Communalism, Fundamentalism and Women in India', in D. Kandiyoti (Ed.), *Women, Islam and the State*. London, Macmillan, pp. 144–75.

Chomsky, N. (2009). 'Crises and the Unipolar Moment', *The Globalisation Lectures*. School of Oriental and African Studies, London, October 27, http://www.soas.ac.uk/events/event52739.html.

Clifford, J. (1992). 'Travelling Culture', in L. Grossberg, C. Nelson and P. Treichler (Eds.), *Cultural Studies*. New York, Routledge.

Cockburn, C. (2003). *The Space between Us: Negotiation, Gender and National Identities in Conflict*. London, Zed Books.

Cockburn, C. (2004). *The Line: Women, Partition and the Gender Order in Cyprus*. London, Zed Books.

Cockburn, C. (2007). *From Where We Stand: War, Women's Activism and Feminist Analysis*. London, Zed Books.

Cockburn, C. and L. Hunter (1999). 'Transversal Politics and Translating Practices', *Soundings* (special issue on Transversal Politics) 12(Summer).

Cohen, J.L. (1999). 'Changing Paradigms of Citizenship and the Exclusiveness of the Demos', *International Sociology* 14(3): 245–68.

Cohen, M. (1992). 'Rooted Cosmopolitanism', *Dissent* Fall: 478–83.

Cohen, P. and H. S. Bains (1988). *Multi-racist Britain*. London, Macmillan.

Cohen, R. (1997). *Global Diasporas*. London, UCL Press.

Cohen, R. (2006). *Migration and it Enemies: Global Capital, Migrant Labour and the Nation-state*. Aldershot, Ashgate.

Collier, P. (1999). 'Aid "Dependency": A Critique', *Journal of African Economics* 8: 528–46.

Commission on Human Security (2003). *Commission on Human Security Outline Report*, New York: Human Security Unit, Commission on Human Security, http://humansecurity-chs.org/finalreport/index.html.

Commission on Legal Empowerment of the Poor (2008). *Commission on Legal Empowerment of the Poor Report*, New York: UNDP. http://www.undp.org/legalempowerment/reports/concept2action.html.

Community Cohesion Review Team (2001). *A Report of the Independent Review Team, Chaired by Ted Cantle*. London, Home Office.

Condor, S. (2006). 'Temporality and Collectivity: Diversity, History and the Rhetorical Construction of National Entitativity', *British Journal of Psychology* 45: 657– 82.

Connell, D. (1998). 'Strategies for Change: Women and Politics in Eritrea and South Africa', *Review of African Political Economy* 76: 189–206.

Contention (1995). *Comparative Fundamentalism* 2 (winter) (special issue).

Cooley, C. H. (1912). *Human Nature and the Social Order*. New York, Charles Scribner's Sons.

Cooper, D. (2004). *Challenging Diversity: Rethinking Equality and the Value of Difference*. Cambridge, Cambridge University Press.

Copelon, R. (2003). 'Rape and Gender Violence: From Impunity to Accountability in International Law', *Human Rights Dialogue* 2(10).

Crenshaw, K. (1989). *Demarginalizing the Intersection of Race and Sex*. Chicago, IL, University of Chicago.

Crenshaw, K. (1993). 'Beyond Racism and Misogyny: Black Feminism and 2 Live Crew', in M. Matsuda, C. Lawrence and K. Crenshaw (Eds.), *Words that Wound: Critical Race Theory, Assaultive Speech and the First Amendment*. Boulder, CO, Westview Press, pp. 111–32.

Crenshaw, K. (2001). 'Mapping the Margins: Intersectionality, Identity Politics and Violence against Women of Color', paper presented at the *World Conference Against Racism*, Durban South Africa, September 2–5 www.hsph.harvard.edu/grhf/WoC/feminisms/crenshaw.html.

Crick, B. (and Advisory Group on Citizenship) (1998). *Education for Citizenship and the Teaching of Democracy in Schools*. (The Crick Report.) London, Qualification and Curriculum Authority.

Crone, P. (2009). 'No Pressure, Then: Religious Freedom in Islam', *Open Democracy*, http://opendemocracy.net. 7 November.

Cronin, C. (1996). 'Bourdieu and Foucault on Power and Modernity', *Philosophy and Social Criticism* 22(6): 55–85.

Crowley, J. (1999). 'The Politics of Belonging: Some Theoretical Consideration', in A. Geddes and A. Favell (Eds.), *The Politics of Belonging: Migrants and Minorities in Contemporary Europe*. Aldershot, Ashgate, pp. 15–41.

Curtis, A. (2007). *The Trap*, BBC2 (3-part documentary series).

Curtis, K. (1999). *Our Sense of the Real: Aesthetic Experience and Arendtian Politics*. Ithaca, NY, and London, Cornell University Press.

Cusack, I. (2003). 'Pots, Pens and "Eating Out the Body": Cuisine and the Gendering of African Nations', *Nations and Nationalism* 9(2): 277–96.

Dahl, H. M. (2000). 'A Perspective and Reflective State?', *The European Journal of Women's Studies* 7: 475–94.

Dahl, H. M. (2004). 'A View from the Inside', *Acta Sociologica* 47(4): 325–37.

Dahl, H. M. and T. R. Eriksen (2005). *Dilemmas of Care in the Nordic Welfare State: Continuity and Change*. Aldershot, Ashgate.

Daly, M. (1993). *Communitarianism: Belonging and Commitment in a Pluralist Democracy*. Belmont, CA: Wadsworth.

*Davalos, P. (2009). 'Reflections on Sumak Kawsay (Good Living) and Theories of Development', *Other News*. http://www.other-net.info/index.php.

Davis, A. Y. (1981). *Women, Race and Class*. London, Women's Press.

Dawkins, R. (1976). *The Selfish Gene*. Oxford, Oxford University Press.

De Angelis, M. (2008). 'Globalization No Questions! Labour Commanded and Foreign Direct Investment', *Review of Radical Political Economics* 40(4): 429–44.

De Greiff, P. and C. Cronin (2002). *Global Justice and Transnational Politics: Essays on the Moral and Political Challenges of Globalization*. Cambridge, MA, MIT Press.

De Haas, H. (2005). 'International Migration, Remittances and Development: Myths and Facts', *Third World Quarterly* 26(8): 1269–84.

Delanty, G. (1995). *Inventing Europe: Idea, Identity, Reality*. Basingstoke, Macmillan.

Delanty, G. (2006). 'The Cosmopolitan Imagination: Critical Cosmopolitanism and Social Theory', *The British Journal of Sociology* 57(1).

Delanty, G. and K. Kumar (Eds.). (2006). *The Sage Handbook of Nations and Nationalism*. London, Sage.

Delanty, G. and P. O'Mahony (2002). *Nationalism and Social Theory*. London, Sage.

deLepervanche, M. (1980). 'From Race to Ethnicity', *Australian and New Zealand Journal of Sociology* 16(1).

Deleuze, G. (1990). 'Post Scripts on the Societies of Control', *L'Autre Journal* 1.

Deutch, K. W. (1966 [1953]). *Nationalism and Social Communication: An Enquiry into the Foundations of Nationality* (2nd edition). Cambridge, MA, MIT Press.

Dhumma, N. (2008). '"Common Values" Campaign'. Press release, October 23. The Institute of Race Relations. http://www.irr.org.uk/

Dicken, P. (2003). *Global Shift: Reshaping the Global Economic Map in the 21st Century*. Thousand Oaks, CA, Sage.

Dill, T. B. (1983). 'Race, Class, and Gender: Prospects for an All-Inclusive Sisterhood', *Feminist Studies* 9(1): 131–50.

Dixon, A. C. (1910–1915) *The Fundamentals: A Testimony to the Truth*. Los Angeles: Bible Institute of Los Angeles.

Donovan, J. and C. J. Adams (Eds.). (2007). *The Feminist Care Tradition on Animal Ethics*. New York, Colombia University Press.

Douzinas, C. (2000). *The End of Human Rights*. Oxford and Portland, OR, Hart Publishing.

Duncan, H. (2009). 'Non-governmental Organisations and Immigrant Integration', *Studies in Ethnicity and Nationalism* 9(2): 304–9.

Durkheim, E. (1965 [1893]). *The Divisions of Labour in Society*. Trans. G. Simpson. New York, Free Press.

Durkheim, E. (1968 [1912]). *The Elementary Forms of Religious Life*. New York, Free Press.

Durkheim, E. (1968 [1952]). *Suicide: A Study in Sociology*. London, Routledge and Kegan Paul.

Economist (2008). 'Capitalism at Bay', *The Economist*, October 16.

Edensor, T. (2002). 'Performing National Identity', *International Social Science* 3(2): 249–69.

Ehrenreich, B. and D. English (1993). *Witches, Midwives and Nurses: A History of Women Healers*. New York, The Feminist Press.

Ehrenreich, B. and A. R. Hochschild (2003). *Global Woman: Nannies, Maids and Sex Workers in the New Economy*. London, Granta.

Eisentein, Z. (2004). *Against Empire*. London, Zed Books.

Eley, G. and R. G. Suny (Eds.). (1996). *Becoming National: A Reader*. Oxford, Oxford University Press.

Enloe, C. (1990). 'Women and Children: Making Feminist Sense of the Persian Gulf Crisis', *The Village Voice*, September 25.

Enloe, C. (2000). *Manoevres: The International Politics of Militarizing Women's Lives*. Berkeley, CA, University of California Press.

Enloe, C. (2007). *Globalization and Militarism: Feminists Make the Link*. Lanham, MD, Rowman & Littlefield.

Esping-Andersen, G. (1990). *The Three Worlds of Welfare Capitalism*. Cambridge, Polity Press.

Essed, P. (1991). *Understanding Everyday Racism: An Interdisciplinary Theory*. Newbury Park, CA, Sage.

Essed, P. (2001). 'Towards a Methodology to Identify Continuing Forms of Everyday Discrimination', www.un.org/womenwatch/daw/csw/essed45.htm.

*Estrada, D. (2009). 'Indigenous Rights Appeals Increasingly Reach Inter-American System', *Other News*. http://www.other-net.info/index.php.

Etzioni, A. (1993). *The Spirit of Community*. New York, Crown Publishers.

Evans, D. (1993). *Sexual Citizenship: The Material Construction of Sexualities*. London, Routledge.

Ewans, T. (2000). 'Citizenship and Human Rights in the Age of Globalization', *Alternatives: Social Transformations & Humane Governance* 25(4): 415–38.

EWCO (2007). '(European Migrant Workers Observatory) Employment and Working Conditions of Migrant Workers', http://www.eurofound. europa.eu/ewco/studies/tn0701038s/tn0701038s.htm.

Fahybrycesa, D. and U. Vuorerla (1984). 'Outside the Domestic Labour Debate', *Review of Radical Political Economics* 16(2–3): 137–66.

Fanon, F. (1967). *Black Skin, White Masks*. New York, Grove Press.

Farr, D. (2002). *Crime and Punishment in Dalston*. London, Arcola Theatre.

Favell, A. (1999). 'To Belong or Not to Belong: The Postnational Question', in A. Geddes and A. Favell (Eds.), *The Politics of Belonging: Migrants and Minorities in Contemporary Europe*. Aldershot, Ashgate, pp. 209–27.

Fawcett, E. (2004). 'Drop the Pilot', *The Guardian*, July 17.

Fekete, L. (2005). 'New Danish Government Will Link Development Aid to Asylum, Independent Race and Refugee News Networks', *IRR News Service*, February 17.

Fekete, L. (2009). *A Suitable Enemy: Racism, Migration and Islamophobia in Europe*. London, Pluto.

Feldman, A. (2001). 'Transforming People and Subverting States: A Pedagogical Approach to the International Indigenous Peoples Movement', *Ethnicities* 1(2): 147–78.

Fenster, T. (2004a), *The Global City and the Holy City: Narratives of Planning, Knowledge and Diversity*, New Jersey: Pearson/Prentice Hall.

Fenster, T. (2004b). 'Belonging, memory and the politics of planning in Israel', *Social & Cultural Geography*, 5: 403–417.

Fenton, S. (2004). 'Beyond Ethnicity: The Global Comparative Analysis of Ethnic Conflict', International Journal of Comparative Sociology 45(3–4): 179–94.

Fichte, J. G. (1806). *Die Grundzuge des gegenwartigen Zeitalters.* Berlin.

Fine, R. (2003). 'Taking the "Ism" out of Cosmopolitanism: An Essay in Reconstruction', *European Journal of Social Theory* 45.

Fine, R. (2008). *Cosmopolitanism.* London, Routledge, Taylor & Francis.

Fisk, R. (2002). 'A strange kind of freedom', *Independent*, July 9.

Fortier, A.-M. (2000). *Migrant Belongings: Memory, Space, Identities.* Oxford, Berg.

Foster, E. (1992). 'Women and the Inverted Pyramid of the Black Churches in Britain', in G. Sahgal and N. Yuval-Davis (Eds.), *Refusing Holy Orders: Women and Fundamentalism in Britain.* London, Verso, pp. 45–68.

Foucault, M. (1979). *Discipline and Punish: The Birth of the Prison.* Harmondsworth, Penguin.

Foucault, M. (1980). *Power/Knowledge: Selected Interviews and Other Writings 1972–1977.* Trans. C. Gordon. Brighton, Harvester.

Foucault, M. (1986 [1969]). 'What is an Author?', in P. Rabinow (Ed.), *The Foucault Reader.* Harmondsworth, Penguin.

Foucault, M. (1991a). *The History of Sexuality, Vols 1–3: The Use of Pleasure.* Trans. Robert Hurly. London, Penguin.

Foucault, M. (1991b). 'Governmentality', in G. Burchell, C. Gordon and P. Miller (Eds.), *The Foucault Effect: Studies in Governmentality.* Hemel Hempstead, Harvester Wheatsheaf, pp. 87–104.

Fox, J. (1994). *Acts of Service: Spontaneity, Commitment, Tradition in the Non-scripted Theatre.* New Paltz, NY, Tusitala Publishing.

Fraser, N. (1995). 'From Redistribution to Recognition? Dilemmas of Justice in a "Post-socialist" Age', *New Left Review* 212: 68–93.

Fraser, N. (1997). *Justice Interruptus.* New York, Routledge.

Fraser, N. and L. Gordon (1994). 'A Genealogy of a Dependency: Tracing a Keyword in the American Welfare State', *Signs: Journal of Women in Culture and Society* 19(2): 309–36.

Fraser, N. and A. Honneth (1998). *Redistribution or Recognition? A Philosophical Exchange.* London, Verso.

Freedland, J. (2007). 'The Internet Will Revolutionise the Very Meaning of Politics', *The Guardian*, May 30.

Freeman, J. (1970). The Tyranny of Structurelessness. USA, Women's Liberation Movement. http://flag.blackened.net/revolt/hist_texts/structurelessness.html.

Freire, P. (1970). *Pedagogy of the Oppressed.* Trans. M. Bergman Ramos. New York, Continuum.

Friedman, J. (1994). *Cultural Identity and Global Process.* London, Sage.

Friedman, M. (Ed.). (2005). *Women and Citizenship.* Oxford, Oxford University Press.

Frosh, S. and L. Baraitser (2003). 'Thinking, Recognition and Otherness', *Psychoanalytic Review* 90(6): 771–89.

Fukuyama, F. (1992). *The End of History and the Last Man.* New York, Free Press.

Fukuyama, F. (2004). *State-Building: Governance and World Order in the 21st Century.* Ithaca, NY, Cornell University Press.

Fukuyama, F. (2006). 'Neoconservatism Has Evolved into Something I Can No Longer Support', *The Guardian*, February 22.

Galanter, M. and J. K. Krishnan (2004). 'Bread for the Poor: Access to Justice and the Rights of the Needy in India', *Hastings Law Review* 55(4): 789–834.

Galbraith, J. K. (2010). 'The Wolf Pack Stalks Europe', *Le Monde diplomatique* (English Edition), June.

Gans, H. J. (1996 [1979]). Symbolic ethnicity: The future of ethnic groups and cultures in America. In W. Sollars (ed.), *Theories of ethnicity: A classical reader* (pp. 425-459). New York: New York University Press.

Geertz, C. (1966). 'Religion as a Cultural System', in M. Bainton (Ed.), *Anthropological Approaches to the Study of Religion.* London, Tavistock.

Geertz, C. (1993 [1973]). *The Interpretation of Cultures: Selected Essays.* London, Fontana.

Gellner, E. (1983). *Nations and Nationalism.* Oxford, Blackwell.

Geschiere, P. (2009). *The Perils of Belonging: Autochthony, Citizenship, and Exclusion in Africa and Europe.* Chicago, IL, and London, University of Chicago Press.

Geschiere, P. and S. Jackson (2006). 'Autochthony and the Crisis of Citizenship: Democratization, Decentralization, and the Politics of Belonging', *African Studies Review* 49(2): 1–7.

Geschiere, P. and F. Nyamnjoh (2000). 'Capitalism and Autochthony: The Seesaw of Mobility and Belonging', *Public Culture* 12(2): 432–53.

Giddens, A. (1985). *A Contemporary Critique of Historical Materialism, Vol. 2: The Nation-State and Violence.* Cambridge, Polity Press.

Giddens, A. (1991). *Modernity and Self Identity.* Cambridge, Polity Press.

Giddens, A. (1999). 'Risk', *Reith Lectures*, BBC, http://news.bbc.co.uk/hi/english/static/events/reith_99/week2/week2. htm.

Gilligan, C. (1982). *In a Different Voice: Psychological Theory and Women's Development.* Cambridge, MA, Harvard University Press.

Gilroy, P. (1987). *There Ain't No Black in the Union Jack: The Cultural Politics of Race and Nation.* London, Hutchinson.

Gilroy, P. (1997). 'Diaspora and the Detours of Identity', in K. Woodward (Ed.), *Identity and Difference.* London, Sage.

Gilroy, P. (2004). *After Empire: Melancholia or Convivial Culture?* London, Routledge.

Gilroy, P. (2005). 'Melancholia or Conviviality: The Politics of Belonging in Britain', *Soundings* 29: 35–46.

Glazer, N. and P. Moynihan (1970 [1963]). *Beyond the Melting Pot.* Cambridge, MA, MIT Press.

Goffman, E. (1968). *Asylums: Essays on the Social Situation of Mental Patients and Other Inmates.* Harmondsworth, Penguin.

Goffman, E. (1969). *The Presentation of Self in Everyday Life.* London, Allen Lane.

Gomez-de-Agreda, A. (2010). 'The Meeting of the Shanghai Cooperation Organisation Could Hail a Realignment of Power Politics in Asia', *Open Democracy*, June 4, http://www.opendemocracy.net.

Goodhart, D. (2004). 'Too Diverse', *Prospect Magazine*, February.

Graham, D. T. and N. K. Poku (Eds.). (2000). *Migration, Globalisation and Human Security.* Routledge Research in Population and Migration. London, Routledge.

Gramsci, A. (1994). *Letters from Prison.* Trans. Raymond Rosenthal. New York, Columbia University Press.

Green, J. (2001). 'Canaries in the Mines of Citizenship: Indian Women in Canada', *Canadian Journal of Political Science* XXXIV(4): 715–38.

Greenfeld, L. (1992). *Nationalism: Five Roads to Modernity.* Cambridge, MA, Harvard University Press.

Gregory, E. (2008). *Politics and the Order of Love: The Augustinian Ethic and Democratic Citizenship.* Chicago, IL, University of Chicago Press.

Guibernau, M. (1996). *Nationalisms: The Nation-State and Nationalism in the Twentieth Century.* Cambridge, Polity Press.

Guibernau, M. (1999). *Nations without States: Political Communities in the Global Age.* Cambridge, Polity Press.

Guibernau, M. (2001). 'Globalization and the Nation-state', in M. Guibernau and J. Hutchinson (Eds.), *Understanding Nationalism.* Cambridge, Polity Press.

Gülalp, H. (2006). *Citizenship and Ethnic Conflict: Challenging the Nation-state.* London, Routledge.

Gunkel, H. (2010). *The Cultural Politics of Female Sexuality in South Africa.* London, Routledge.

Gupta, R. (2007). *Enslaved: The New British Slavery.* London, Portobello Books.

Habermas, J. and C. Cronin (2006). *The Divided West.* Cambridge, Polity Press.

Habermas, J., C. Cronin and P. De Greiff (1998). *The Inclusion of the Other: Studies in Political Theory.* Cambridge, MA, MIT Press.

Habermas, J., C. Cronin and M. Pensky (2006). *Time of Transitions.* Oxford, Polity Press.

Hage, G. (1997). 'At Home in the Entrails of the West: Multiculturalism, "Ethnic Food" and Migrant Home Building', in H. Grace, G. Hage, L. Johnson, J. Langsworth and M. Symonds (Eds.), *Home/World Space, Community and Marginality in Sydney's West.* Western Sydney, Pluto Press.

Hage, G. (2000). *White Nation: The Fantasies of White Supremacy in a Multicultural Society.* New York, Routledge.

Hage, G. (2002). *Arab-Australians Today: Citizenship and Belonging*. Melbourne, Melbourne University Press.

Hajjaj, N. (2007). *The Shadow of Absence*. Film.

Hall, S. (1990). 'Cultural Identity and Diaspora', in J. Rutherford (Ed.), *Identity, Community, Culture, Difference*. London, Lawrence & Wishart.

Hall, S. (1992). 'New Ethnicities', in J. Donald and A. Rattansi (Eds.), *'Race', Culture and Difference*. London, Sage.

Hall, S. (1996). 'Who Needs Identity?', in S. Hall and P. du Gay (Eds.), *Questions of Cultural Identity*. London, Sage, pp. 1–17.

Hall, S. (2006). ESRC Ethnicities Workshop. London School of Economics and Political Science, 6 June.

Hall, S. and D. Held (1989). 'Citizens and Citizenship', in S. Hall and M. Jacques (Eds.), *New Times*. London, Lawrence and Wishart.

Hall, S., with N. Yuval-Davis (2004). 'Rethinking the Multicultural Question', a video conversation with Nira Yuval-Davis at the ISA RC05 and RC32 interim conference on Racisms, Sexisms and Contemporary Politics of Belonging, London, August.

Halliday, F. (2008). 'Tibet, Palestine and the Politics of Failure', *Open Democracy*, http://opendemocracy.net. *13 May*.

Halper, J. (2005). 'Israel as an Extension of American Empire', *Counter Punch*, 7 November. http://www.counterpunch.org/halper11072005.html.

Hannerz, U. (2002). 'Where Are We and Who We Want To Be', in U. Hedetoft and M. e. Hjort (Eds.), *The Post National Self: Belonging and Identity*. Minneapolis, MN, and London, University of Minnesota Press.

Haraway, D. (1988). 'Situated Knowledge: The Science Question in Feminism and the Privilege of Partial Perspective', *Feminist Review* 14: 575–99.

Haraway, D. (1991). *Simians, Cyborgs and Women: The Reinvention of Women*. London, Free Association Press.

Harding, S. (1986). *The Science Question in Feminism*. Ithaca, NY, Cornell University Press.

Harding, S. (1991). *Whose Science? Whose Knowledge?* Ithaca, NY, Cornell University Press.

Harding, S. (1997). 'Comment on Hekman's "Truth and Method: Feminism Standpoint Theory Revisited": Whose Standpoint Needs Regimes of Truth and Reality?', *Signs: Journal of Women in Culture and Society* 22(2): 382–91.

Hari, J. (2009). 'You Are Being Lied to about Pirates', *The Independent*, January 5.

Harris, P. (2009). 'Native Americans Find Their Voice', *The Observer*, March 22.

Harvey, D. (1990). *The Condition of Postmodernity*. New York, Blackwell.

Hechter, M. (2000). *Containing Nationalism*. Oxford, Oxford University Press.

Hedetoft, U. and M. e. Hjort (2002). *The Postnational Self: Belonging and Identity*. Minneapolis, MN, and London, University of Minnesota Press.

Held, D. (1995). *Democracy and the Global Order*. Cambridge, Polity Press.

Held, V. (1993). *Feminist Morality: Transforming Culture, Society and Politics*. Chicago, IL, University of Chicago Press.

Held, V. (2005). *The Ethics of Care: Personal, Political and Global*. Oxford, Oxford University Press.

Helie-Lucas, M. (2006). 'The Veil vs Citizenship', *Peace News*, November, http://www.peacenews.info/issues/2479/2479091.html.

Helmreich, S. (1992). 'Kinship, Nation and Paul Gilroy's Concept of Diaspora', *Diaspora* 2(2): 243–50.

Herman, E. C. (2002). 'Foreword', in D. Chandler (Ed.), *From Kosovo to Kabul: Human Rights and International Intervention*. London, Pluto Press.

Hernes, H. M. (1987). *Welfare State and Woman Power: Essays in State Feminism*. Oslo, Norwegian University Press.

Hesse, B. (Ed.). (2000). *Un/Settled Multiculturalism: Diasporas, Entanglement and Transruptions*. London, Zed books.

Hill-Collins, P. (1990). *Black Feminist Thought, Consciousness and the Politics of Empowerment*. London, Harper & Row.

Hill-Collins, P. (2009). 'The New Politics of Community', paper presented at the American Sociological Association conference, San Francisco, August.

Hitchens, C. (2007). *God Is Not Great: How Religion Poisons Everything*. London, Atlantic Books.

Ho, E. (2009). 'Constituting Citizenship through the Emotions: Singaporean Transmigrants in London', *Annals of the Association of American Geographers* 99(4): 788–804.

Hobsbawm, E. J. (1990). *Nations and Nationalism since 1780: Programme, Myth, Reality*. Cambridge, Cambridge University Press.

Hobsbawm, E. and T. Ranger (Eds.). (1983). *The Invention of Traditions*. Cambridge, Cambridge University Press.

Hochschild, A. R. (2003). *The Commercialization of Intimate Life: Notes from Home and Work*. Berkeley, CA, University of California Press.

Hollway, W. (2009). 'Relational to the Core: Unconscious Intersubjectivity and Conflict in Becoming a Mother', in M. Wetherell and C. Mohanty (Eds.), *Sage Handbook of Identities*. London, Sage.

Holmwood, J. (2000). 'Three Pillars of Welfare State Theory: T. H. Marshall, Karl Polanyi and Alva Myrdal in Defence of the National Welfare State', *European Journal of Social Theory* 3(1): 23–50.

Home Office (2001). *Secure Borders, Safe Haven* (CM 5387). London, HMSO.

hooks, b. (1981). *Ain't I a Woman*. Cambridge, MA, Sound End Press.

hooks, b. (1989). *Talking Back: Thinking Feminist, Thinking Black*. Toronto: Between the Lines.

Hugill, P. J. (1992). *World Trade since 1431*. Baltimore, MD, Johns Hopkins University Press.

Humphry, D. and M. Ward (1974). *Passports and Politics*. Harmondsworth, Penguin.

Huntington, S. (1993). 'The Clash of Civilizations', *Foreign Affairs* 72(3): 22–50.

Hussain, A. and Miller, W. L. (2006) *Multicultural Nationalism, Islamophobia, Anglophobia and Devolution*. Oxford, Oxford University Press.

Huysmans, J. (2002). 'Defining Social Constructivism in Security Studies: The Normative Dilemma of Writing Security', *Alternatives: Global, Local, Political* 27(1): 41–62.

Huysmans, J. (2006). *The Politics of Insecurity: Fear, Migration and Asylum in the EU*. Oxford and New York, Routledge.

Hyman, A. (1985). *Muslim Fundamentalism*, Institute for the Study of Culture, *Conflict Studies*, No. 174: 3–27.

ICHRP (2009). 'When Legal Worlds Overlap: Human Rights, State and Non-State Law', The International Council on Human Rights Policy, http://www.ichrp.org/en/zoom-in/when_legal_worlds_overlap.

Ifekwunigwe, J (1999). *Scattered Belongings: cultural paradoxes of "race", nation and gender*, London, Routledge

Ignatieff, M. (1993). *Blood and Belonging: Journeys into the New Nationalism*. London, Chatto & Windus.

Ignatieff, M. (2001). *Human Rights as Politics and Idolatry*. Princeton, NJ, Princeton University Press.

IIJ (International Initiative for Justice) (2003 December). *Threatened Existence: A Feminist Analysis of the Genocide in Gujarat*. Mumbai, IIJ.

Imam, A., A. Morgan and N. Yuval-Davis (Eds.). (2004). *Warning Signs of Fundamentalisms*. London, Women Living Under Muslim Laws.

IMF (International Monitary Fund). http://www.mees.com/postedarticles/finance/iran/a45n33b02.htm.

Internet World Statistics (2009). *Internet World Statistics*, http://www.internet worldstats.com/stats.htm.

Isin, E. F. (2008). *Recasting the Social in Citizenship*. Toronto, Buffalo, NY, and London, University of Toronto Press

Isin, E. F. (2009). 'Citizenship in Flux: The Figure of the Activist Citizen', *Subjectivity* 29: 367–88.

Jack, I. (2009). 'The Unstoppable Rise of the Citizen Cameraman', *The Guardian*, April 11.

Jackson, S. (2008). 'Materialist Feminism, Pragmatism and the Sexual Self in Global Late Modernity' (unpublished paper).

James, P. (1996). *Nation Formation: Towards a Theory of Abstract Community*. London, Sage.

James, S. (1986). *Sex, Race and Class*. London, Housewives in Dialogue.

Jameson, F. (1986). 'Third World Literature in the Era of Multinational Capitalism', *Social Text* Fall.

Jansen, S. (2008) 'Cosmopolitan Opening and Closures in Post-Yugoslav Antinationalism', in M. Novicka and M. Rovisco (eds.) *Cosmopolitanism in Practice*. Aldershot: Ashgate.

Jaura, R. (2010). 'Remembering the Three Rio Conventions', *Other News*, http://www.other-net.info/index.php.

Jayasuriya, L. (1990). 'Citizenship, Democratic Pluralism and Ethnic Minorities in Australia', in R. Nile (Ed.), *Immigration and the Politics of Ethnicity and Race in Australia and Britain*. London, Bureau of Immigration Research Australia, Sir Robert Menzies Centre for Australian Studies, University of London, pp. 27–43.

Jayasuriya, L. (1991). 'Multiculturalism, Citizenship and Welfare: New Directions in the 1990s', in R. Niles (Ed.), *Immigration and the Politics of Ethnicity and Race in Australia and Britain*. London, Institute of Commonwealth Studies.

Jayawardena, K. (1986). *Feminism and Nationalism in the Third World*. London, Zed Books.

Jayawardena, K. (1995). *The White Woman's Other Burden: Western Women and South Asia During British Rule*. New York and London, Routledge.

Jessop, B. (2002). 'Liberalism, Neo-liberalism, Urban Governance and the State: A Theoretical Perspective'. *Antipode*, 34, 452–472.

Jiryis, S. (1973). 'The Legal Structure for the Expropriation and Absorption of Arab Lands in Israel', *Journal of Palestine Studies* 2(4): 82–104.

Jones, R. (2006). 'The Salience of Citizenship and Nationality' *AWID*, *(Association for Women's Rights in Development)* http://www.awid.org/eng/Issues-and-Analysis/Library/The-salience-of-citizenship-and-nationality.

Jones, R. (2008). '"Purity Balls" and Fundamentalisms in the United States', *AWID (Association for Women's Rights in Development)* http://www.awid.org/eng/Issues-and-Analysis/Library/Purity-balls-and-fundamentalisms-in-the-United-States.

Jutila, M. (2006). 'Desecuritizing Minority Rights: Against Determinism', *Security Dialogue* 37(2): 167–85.

Jutila, M. (2009). 'Societal Securization: Constructing Ethno-national Identities and Their (In)Security', paper presented at the Summer School From Cold War to the Bronze Soldier, Vilnius, June 7–13.

Kabir, N. (Ed.). (2005). *Inclusive Citizenship*. London, Zed Books.

Kaldor, M. (2003). *Global Civil Society: An Answer to War*. Cambridge, Polity Press.

Kaldor, M. (2004). 'Nationalism and Globalisation', *Nations and Nationalism* 10(1/2): 161–77.

Kaldor, M. (2007). *Human Security: Reflections on Globalization and Intervention*. Cambridge, Polity Press.

Kaldor, M. (2008). '"New Thinking" Needs New Direction', *Open Democracy*, http://www.opendemocracy.net. *25 September*.

Kalmus, J. (2010). 'Liverpool School Forced to Reject 10-year-old Girl under New Admission Rules', *The Jewish Chronicle Online*, June 11.

Kandiyoti, D. (1991). *Women, Islam and the State*. London, Macmillan.

Kant, I. (1998). *Critique of Pure Reason*. Cambridge, Cambridge University Press.

Kant, I. (1999 [1795]). '*Perpetual Peace*' in *Practical Philosophy* (Cambridge edition of the works of Immanuel Kant). Cambridge, Cambridge University Press.

Kaplan, D. (2006). *The Men We Loved: Male Friendship and Nationalism in Israeli Culure*. Oxford, Berghahan Books.

Kaptani, E. and N. Yuval-Davis (2008a). 'Participatory Theatre as a Research Methodology', *Sociological Research Online* 13(5), http://www.socresonline.org.uk/13/5/2.

Kaptani, E. and N. Yuval-Davis (2008b). 'Doing Embodied Research: Participatory Theatre as a Sociological Research Tool', *Qualitative Researcher* 9: 8–10.

Karner, C. and A. E. Aldrige (2004). 'Theorizing Religion in a Globalizing World', *International Journal of Politics, Culture and Society* 18(1–2): 5–32.

Keenan, T. and E. Weizman (2010). 'Israel: The Third Strategic Threat', *Open Democracy*, http://opendemocracy.net. *7 June*.

Keith, M. (2005). *After the Cosmopolitan: Multicultural Cities and the Future of Racism*. Oxford and New York, Routledge.

Kennedy, P. (2007). 'Global Transformations but Local, "Bubble" Lives: Taking a Reality Check on Some Globalisation Concepts', *Globalizations* 4(2): 267–82.

Kerwin, J. and M. Donald (2009). 'The Role of Government–NGO Partnerships in Immigrant Integration: A Response to Howard Duncan from the Perspective of US Civil Society', *Studies in Ethnicity and Nationalism* 9(2): 310–15.

Kienle, E. (2010). 'Global Competitiveness, the Erosion of Checks and Balances, and the Demise of Liberal Democracy', *Open Democracy*, http://opendemocracy.net. May 10.

Kitching, G. (1985). 'Nationalism: The Instrumental Passion', *Capital and Class* 25: 98–116.

Kitzinger, C. (1987). *The Social Construction of Lesbianism*. London, Sage.

Klare, M. T. (2007). 'Behold the Rise of Energy-based Fascism', *Information Clearing House*, http://www.informationclearinghouse.info.

Klein, N. (2007). *The Shock Doctrine*. New York, Metropolitan Books.

Knapp, A. (1999). 'Fragile Foundations, Strong Traditions, Situated Questioning: Critical Theory in German-Speaking Feminism', in M. O'Neill (Ed.), *Adorno, Culture and Feminism*. London, Sage.

Knoweles, C. (2006). 'Seeing Race through the Lens', *Ethnic and Racial Studies* 29(3): 512–29.

Knoweles, C. and D. Harper (2010). *Hong Kong: Migrant Lives: Landscapes and Journeys*. Chicago, IL, University of Chicago Press.

Kofman, E. (2004). 'Figures of the Cosmopolitan: Privileged Nationals and National Outsiders', paper presented at the Cosmopolitanism and Europe conference, Royal Holloway College, Egham, Surrey, April.

Kohlberg, L. (1973). *Collected Papers on Moral Development and Moral Education*. Cambridge, MA, Moral Education Research Foundation, Harvard University.

Kramarae, C. and D. Spender (Eds.). (2000). *Routledge International Encyclopaedia of Women*. New York and London, Routledge.

Kwinjeh, G. (2008). 'Rwandan Women's Liberation: Nationalism Versus Social Liberation', *Pambazuka News*, 23 November, http://www.awid.org/Library/Rwandan-women-s-liberation-Nationalism-versus-social-liberation.

Kymlicka, W. (1995). *Multicultural Citizenship*. Oxford, Clarendon Press.

Lacan, J. (1977). *The Four Fundamental Concepts of Psychoanalysis*. London, Hogarth Press.

Lacan, J. (1966 [1936]). 'Le stade du miroir comme formateur de la fonction du Je', *Ecrits*. Paris, Seuil, pp. 93–100.

Larana, E., H. Johnson, J. R. Gusfield (1994). *New Social Movements: From Ideologies to Identities*. Philadelphia, PA, Temple University Press.

Lavie, S. and T. Swedenburg (1996). *Displacement, Diaspora and Geographies of Identity*. Durham, NC, and London, Duke University Press.

Lawler, S. (2008). *Identity: Sociological Perspectives*. Cambridge, Polity Press.

Leaning, J. and S. Arie (2000). 'Human Security: A Framework for Assessment in Conflict and Transition', Working Paper Series Harvard Center for Population and Development Studies. Prepared for USAID (Africa Bureau)/Tulane CERTI.

Leira, A. (1994). 'Concepts of Care', *Social Service Review* 68(2): 185–201.

Leira, A. and C. Saraceno (2002). 'Care: Actors, Relationships and Contexts', in B. Hobson, J. Lewis and B. Siim (Eds.), *Contested Concepts in Gender and Social Politics*. Cheltenham, Edward Elgar, pp. 55–83.

Lemke, T. (2000). 'Foucault, Governmentality and Critique', paper presented at the Rethinking Marxism Conference, University of Amherst, MA, September 21–24.

Lentin, R. (1999). 'Constitutionally Excluded: Citizenship and (Some) Irish Women', in N. Yuval-Davis and P. Werbner (Eds.), *Women, Citizenship and Difference*. London, Zed Books.

Levinas, E. (1985). *Ethics and Infinity*. Pittsburgh, PA, Duquesne University Press.

Levinas, E. (1999). *Alterity and Transcendence*. London, Athlone Press.

Lewin, K. (1948). *Resolving Social Conflicts: Selected Papers on Group Dynamics*. New York, Harper & Row.

Lewis, G. and S. Neale (2005). 'Introduction', *Ethnic and Racial Studies* (special issue on Migration and Citizenship) 28(3).

Lichtenberg, J. (1999). 'How Liberal Can Nationalism Be?', in R. Beiner (Ed.), *Theorizing Nationalism*. Albany, NY, State University of New York Press.

Lijphart, A. (1997). 'Unequal Participation: Democracy's Unresolved Dilemma', *American Political Science Review* 91(March): 1–14.

Lippet, R. K. (2005). *Sanctuary, Sovereignty, Sacrifice: Canadian Sanctuary Incidents, Power and the Law*. Vancouver: University of British Columbia Press.

Lipschutz, R. D. (2002). 'The Clash of Governmentalities: The Fall of the UN Republic and America's Reach for Imperium', *Exploring Imperium*, see: www.theglobalsite.ac.uk/press/212lipschutz.htm.

Lister, R. (1990) *The Exclusive Society: Citizenship and the Poor*. London: Child Poverty Action Group.

Lister, R. (1997). *Citizenship: Feminist Perspectives*. Basingstoke, Macmillan.

Lloyd, T. (1971). *Suffragettes International: The Worldwide Campaign for Women's Rights*. New York, American Heritage Press.

Lovell, N. (1998). 'Introduction', in N. Lovell, *Locality and Belonging*. London, Routledge, pp. 1–24.

Lovell, T. (2003). 'Resisting with Authority: Historical Specificity, Agency and the Performative Self', *Theory, Culture and Society* 20(1): 1–17.

Lowell, R. (2004). 'Afflicted Powers: The State, The Spectacle and September 11th', *New Left Review*, May–June 27, http://newleftreview.org/A2506.

Luckman, T. (1967). *The Invisible Religion*. London, Macmillan.

Lutz, H. (1991). *Migrant Women of 'Islamic Background'*. Amsterdam, Middle East Research Associates.

Lutz, H. (2002). 'Intersectional Analysis: A Way Out of Multiple Dilemmas?', paper presented at the International Sociological Association conference, Brisbane, July.

Lutz, H. (2006). 'Can Intersectionality Help?', paper presented at a joint session on Intersectionality, International Sociological Association Research Committee 05 (on Racism, Nationalism and Ethnic Relations) and RC32 (Women in Society). Durban, South Africa.

Lutz, H. (2008). *Migration and Domestic Work: A European Perspective on a Global Theme*. Aldershot, Ashgate.

Machover, M. (2006). 'Neoliberaism and Iran's President Ahmadinejad', *Iran News Link*, September 9.

MacIntyre, A. (1981). *After Virtue: A Study in Moral Theory*. Notre Dame, IN, University of Notre Dame Press.

Macklin, A. (2007). 'The Securitisation of Dual Citizenship', in *Dual Citizenship in Global Perspective: From Unitary to Multiple Citizenship*, http://ssrn.com/abstract=1077489.

Macklin, A. (2009). 'Particularized Citizenship: Encultured Women and the Public Sphere', in S. Benhabib and J. Resnik (Eds.), *Migration and Mobilities: Citizenship, Borders and Gender*. New York and London, New York University Press.

Macpherson, W. (1999), *The Stephen Lawrence Inquiry Report*, The Stationary Office   http://www.archive.official-documents.co.uk/document/cm42/4262/4262.htm

Magelssen, S. (2002). 'Remapping American-ness: Heritage Production and the Staging of the Native American and the African American as Other in "Historyland"', *National Identities* 4(2).

Mahmoud, S. (2005). *Politics of Piety: The Islamic Revival and the Feminist Subject*. Princeton, NJ, Princeton University Press.

Mahmoud, S. (2009). 'Religious Reason and Secular Affect: An Incomm ensurable Divide?', in T. Asad, W. Brown, J. Butler and S. Mahmoud

(Eds.), *Is Critiquw Secular? Blasphemy, Injury, and Free Speech*. Berkeley, CA, University of California Press.

Maitland, S. (1992). 'Biblicism: A Radical Rhetoric?', in G. S. Yuval-Davis and N. Yuval-Davis (Eds.), *Refusing Holy Orders: Women and Fundamentalism in Britain*. London, Verso, pp. 26–44.

Mani, L. (1989). 'Contentious Traditions: The Debate on Sati in Colonial India', in K. Sangari and S. Vaid (Eds.), *Recasting Women: Essays in Colonial History*. New Delhi, Kali for Women.

Mann, M. (2005). *The Dark Side of Democracy: Explaining Ethnic Cleansing*. Cambridge, Cambridge University Press.

Marfleet, P. (2011). 'Understanding "Sanctuary": Faith and Traditions of Asylum', *Journal of Refugee Studies*. Special Issue on Faith-Based Humanitarianism in Contexts of Forced Displacement

Marsden, G. (1980). *Fundamentalism and American Culture*. Oxford, Oxford University Press.

Marshall, T. H. (1950). *Citizenship and Social Class*. Cambridge, Cambridge University Press.

Marshall, T. H. (1975 [1965]). *Social Policy in the Twentieth Century*. London, Hutchinson.

Marshall, T. H. (1981). *The Right to Welfare and Other Essays*. London, Heinemann Educational Books.

Martin, D. (1979). *A General Theory of Secularization*. New York, Harper & Row.

Martin, D. C. (1995). 'The Choices of Identity', *Social Identities* 1(1): 5–16.

Marx, K. (1977[1843]). *Critique of Hegel's Philosophy of Right*. Cambridge: Cambridge University Press.

Marx, K. (1975 [1844]). *Early Writings*. Harmmondsworth, Penguin.

Massey, D. (2005). *For Space*. London, Sage.

Maxwell, S. and D. Messner (2008). 'A New Global Order: Bretton Woods II …and San Fransisco II', *Open Democracy*, http://www.opendemocracy.net.

May, S. (1999). *Critical Multiculturalism*. London, Routledge.

Maynard, M. (1994). '"Race", Gender and the Concept of "Difference" in Feminist Thought'. in H. Afshar and M. Maynard (Eds.), *The Dynamics of 'Race' and Gender*. London, Taylor & Francis.

McAfee, N. (2004). 'The Ends of Arendtian Politics', *Hyptia* 19(4): 221–9.

McBride, S. (2005). *Paradigm Shift: Globalization and the Canadian State*. Halifax, NS, Fernwood.

McCall, L. (2005). 'The Complexity of Intersectionality', *Signs: Journal of Women in Culture and Society* 30(3).

McDonald, H. (2009). 'Belfast Has Three Times as Many "Peace Walls" since the Ceasefire', *The Guardian*, July 29.

McGirr, L. (2001). *Suburban Warriors: The Origins of the New American Right*. Princeton, NJ, Princeton University Press.

McLennan, G. (2001). 'Problematic Multiculturalism', *Sociology* 35(4): 985–89.

Mead, G. H. (1934). *Mind, Self and Society*. Chicago, IL, University of Chicago Press.

Mead, G. H. (2001). *Essays in Social Psychology*. New Brunswick, NJ, Transaction.

Meekosha, H. and L. Dowse (1997). 'Enabling Citizenship: Gender, Disability and Citizenship in Australia', *Feminist Review* 57: 49–72.

Meisels, T. (2009). 'Global Justice and Territorial Rights', *Studies in Ethnicity and Nationalism* 9(2): 231–51.

Melucci, A. (1996). *Challenging Codes: Collective Action in the Information Age*. Cambridge: Cambridge University Press.

Menzies, G. (2002). *1421: The Year China Discovered the World*. London, Bantam.

Merton, R. K. (1957). 'Patterns of Influence: Local and Cosmopolitan Influentials', in R. K. Merton, *Social Theory and Social Structure*. New York: Free Press, pp. 387–420.

Meyer, J. W. (1980). 'The World Polity and the Authority of the Nation-state', in A. J. Bergesen (Ed.), *Studies of the the Modern World-System*. New York, Academic Press.

Michaels, A. (1996). *Fugitive Pieces*. London, Bloomsbury.

Mihelj, S. (2007). '"Faith in Nation Comes in Different Guises": Modernist Versions of Religious Nationalism', *Nations and Nationalism* 13(2): 265–84.

Milne, S. (2005). 'Britain: Imperial Nostalgia', *Le Monde diplomatique*, May.

Mitter, S. (1994). 'Organizing Women in Casualised Work: A Global Overview', in S. Rowbottham and S. Mitter (Eds.), *Dignity and Daily Bread: New Forms of Economic Organizing among Poor Women*. London, Routledge, pp. 14–53.

Moallem, M. and I. A. Boal (1999). 'Multicultural Nationalism and the Poetics of Inauguration', in N. Alarcón and M. Moallem (Eds.), *Between Woman and Nation: Nationalisms, Transnational Feminisms, and the State*. Durham, NC, Duke University Press, pp. 243–263.

Modood, T. (2003). 'Muslims and the Politics of Difference', *Political Quarterly* 74: 100–15.

Modood, T. and P. Werbner (Eds.). (1997). *The Politics of Multiculturalism in the New Europe*. London, Zed Books.

Mohanty, C. T. (1986). 'Under Western Eyes: Feminist Scholarship and Colonial Discourses', in A. R. C. T. Mohanty and L. Torres (Eds.), *Third World Women and the Politics of Feminism*. Bloomington, IN, Indiana University Press.

Molineus, M. (1979). 'Beyond the Domestic Labour Debate', *New Left Review* 1(116).

Monbiot, G. (2005). 'The New Chauvinism', *The Guardian*, August 9.

Mongia, R. V. (1999). 'Race, Nationality, Mobility: A History of the Passport', *Public Culture* 11(3): 527–56.

Moran, M. (2010). 'Nicolas Sarkozy: A One-trick Pony?', *Open Democracy*, September 17, http://opendemocracy.net.

Moruzzi, C. N. (2000). *Speaking through the Mask: Hannah Arendt and the Politics of Social Identity*. Ithaca, NY, and London, Cornell University Press.

Mouffe, C. (2000). *The Democratic Paradox*. London, Verso.

Mulholland, H. (2009). 'Gordon Brown Unveils Tougher Immigration Rules', *The Guardian*, Novermber 12, http://www.guardian.co.uk/politics/2009/nov/12/gordon-brown-announces-new-immigration-rules.

Mullard, C. (1984). *Anti-racist Education: The Three O's*. Bath: National Association for Multiracial Education.

Najmabadi, A. (1995). *Feminisms in an Islamic Republic: Years of Hardship, Years of Growth*. London, School of Oriental and African Studies, University of London.

Nandy, A. (1983). *The Intimate Enemy: The Loss and Recovery of Self under Colonialism*. Oxford, Oxford University Press.

Nash, J. C. (2008). 'Re-thinking Intersectionality', *Feminist Review* 89(1): 1–15.

Nash, J. F. (1951). 'Non Cooperative Games', *The Annals of Mathematics* 54(2): 286–95.

Nash, K. (2009). 'Between Citizenship and Human Rights', *Sociology* 43(6): 1067–83.

Nava, M. (2007). *Visceral Cosmopolitanism: Gender, Culture and the Normalisation of Difference*. Oxford and New York, Berg.

Nenadich, R.A. (Ed.). (2001). *In Persuit of Self Determination*. Clarity Press.

Newell, P. and J. Wheeler (Eds). (2006). *Rights, Resources and the Politics of Accountability*. London, Zed Books.

Nimni, E. (2009). 'Nationalism, Ethnicity and Self-determination: A Paradigm Shift?', *Studies in Ethnicity and Nationalism* 9(2): 319–32.

Nugent, A. and P. Asiwaju (Eds). (1996). *African Boundaries: Barriers, Conduits and Opportunities*. London, Pinter.

Nussbaum, M. (2000). *Sex and Social Justice*. Oxford, Oxford University Press.

Nussbaum, M. (2001). *Upheavels of Thought: The Intelligence of Emotions*. Cambridge, Cambridge University Press.

Nussbaum, M. (2002 [1996]). 'Patriotism and Cosmopolitanism', in M. C. Nissbaum (Ed.), *For Love of Country*. Boston, MA, Beacon, pp. 1–17.

Nussbaum, M. C. (1995). 'Human Capabilities: Capable Human Beings', in M. Nussbaum and J. Glover (Eds.), *Women, Culture and Development: A Study of Human Capabilities*. Oxford, Clarendon Press, pp. 61–104.

Nussbaum, M. C. and A. Sen (1993). *The Quality of Life*. Oxford, Oxford University Press.

Nyamnjoh, F. B. (2005). *Africa's Media: Democracy and the Politics of Belonging*. London, Zed Books.

O'Brien, R. (2005). *Bodies in Revolt: Gender, Disability and a Workplace Ethic of Care*. New York, Routledge.

O'Connor, J. S., A. S. Orloff and S. Shaver (1999). *States, Markets, Families: Gender, Liberalism, and Social Policy in Australia, Canada, Great Britain, and the United States*. Cambridge, Cambridge University Press.

O'Neill, B. (2008). 'The Myth of Trafficking', *New Statesman*, March 27, http://www.newstatesman.com.

O'Reilly, K. (2000). *The British on the Costa del Sol: Transnational Identities and Local Communities*. New York Routledge.

Oaks, L. (2003). 'Antiabortion Positions and Young Women's Life Plans in Contemporary Ireland', *Social Science and Medicine* 56(9): 1973–86.

Obama, B. (2006). *The Audacity of Hope*. New York, Crown/Three Rivers Press.

Offe, C. (1996). *Modernity and the State: East West*. Cambridge, Polity Press.

Ogata, S. (1999). 'Human Security: A Refugee Perspective', Keynote Speech at the Ministerial Meeting on Human Security Issues of the Lysoen Process Bergen, Norway, May 19.

Oldfield, A. (1990). *Citizenship and Community: Civic Republicanism and the Modern World*. London, Routledge.

Oliver, M. (1990). *The Politics of Disablement*. London, Macmillan.

Oliver, M. (1996). *Understanding Disability: From Theory to Practice*. London, Macmillan.

Ong, A. (1996). 'Cultural Citizenship as Subject-Making: Immigrants Negotiate Racial and Cultural Boundaries in the United States', *Current Anthropology* 37(5): 737–62.

Orenstein, K. (2010). 'Developing Countries Resist World Bank Power Play', *Other News*, http://www.other-net.info/index.php.

Østergaard-Nielsen, E. (2001). 'Turkish and Kurdish Transnational Political Mobilisation in Germany and the Netherlands', *Global Networks* 1(3).

Ostrower, G. B. (1996). *The League of Nations: From 1919 to 1929.*, Garden City Park, New York, Avery Publishing.

Our Kingdom (2008). 'Networking Democracy: Can the Internet Help Democracy Work Better?', *Open Democracy*, March 24, http://opendemocracy.net.

Ozkirimli, U. (2000). *Theories of Nationalism: A Critical Introduction*. Basingstoke, Macmillan.

Ozkirimli, U. (2005). *Contemporary Debates on Nationalism: A Critical Engagement*. Basingstoke, Palgrave Macmillan.

Pallas, C. (2005). 'Canterbury to Cameroon: A New Partnership between Faiths and the World Bank', *Development in Practice* 15(5): 677–84.

Pallister, D. (2007). 'A Multibillion Dollar Industry Built on the Most Dangerous Jobs in the World', *The Guardian*, May 30.

Panitch, L. (1994). 'Globalisation and the State', *Socialist Register* 30: 60–93.

Parekh, B. (2000a). *The Future of Multi-Ethnic Britain?* London, Runnymede Trust/Profile Books.

Parekh, B. (2000b). *Rethinking Multiculturalism: Cultural Diversity and Political Theory*. Basingstoke, Macmillan.

Parsons, T. (1952). *The Social System*. London and New York, Tavistock Publications.

Pateman, C. (1988). *The Sexual Contract*. Cambridge, Polity Press.

Peck, J. (2001). *Workfare States*. New York, Guilford Press.

Pecora, V. P. (Ed.). (2001). *Nations and Identities*. Malden, MA, Blackwell Publishers.

Peled, Y. (1992). 'Ethnic Democracy and the Legal Construction of Citizenship: Arab Citizens of the Jewish State', *American Political Science Review* 86(2): 432–42.

Perera, S. (2008). 'The Gender of Borderpanic: Women in Circuits of Security, State, Globalisation and New (and Old) Empire', in M. Cain and A. Howe (Eds.), *Women, Crime and Social Harm: Towards a Criminology for the Global Age*. Oxford, Hart Publishing.

Petchesky, R. (2005). *Rights of the Body and Perversion of War: Sexual Rights and Wrongs Ten Years Past Beijing*. Beijing and Malden, MA, Blackwell Publishing.

Peterson, V. S. (2010), 'A Long View of Globalization and Crisis', *Globalizations* 7(1–2): 187–202.

Pettifor, A. (2007). 'Debtonation: How Globalisation Dies', *Open Democracy*, http://www.opendemocracy.net. *15 August*.

Phillips, A. (Ed.). (1998). *Feminism and Politics*. Oxford, Oxford University Press.

Peterse, H. (1998), *Love and Law in Europe*, Aldershot: Ashgate Publishing Company.

Pieterse, J. N. (1995). 'Global System, Globalization and the Parameters of Modernity', in M. Featherstone, S. Lash and R. Robertson (Eds.), *Global Modernities*. London, Sage.

Plaskow, J. (1990). *Standing Again in Sinai: Judaism from a Feminist Perspective*. San Francisco, CA, Harper & Row.

Plummer, K. (2003). *Intimate Citizenship: Private Decision and Public Dialogues*. Seattle, WA, University of Washington Press.

Plummer, K. (2005). 'Intimate Citizenship in an Unjust World', in M. Romero and E. Margolis (Eds.), *The Blackwell Companion to Social Inequalities*. Oxford, Blackwell, pp. 75–99.

Pollini, G. (2005). 'Elements of a Theory of Place Attachment and Socio-territorial Belonging', *International Review of Sociology* 15(3): 497–515.

Pollock, S., H. K. Bhabha, C. A. Breckenridge and D. Chakrabaty (Eds.). (2002) *Cosmopolitanism*. Durham, NC, Duke University Press, pp. 1–14.

Poole, R. (1999). *Nation and Identity*. London, Routledge.

Potamianou, A. (1997). *Hope: A Shield in the Economy of Borderline States*. London, Routledge.

Powell, E. (1968). Speech to London Rotary Club (Subject: immigration), Eastbourne, November 16, http://www.enochpowell.net/fr-83.html.

Probyn, E. (1996). *Outside Belongings*. London, Routledge.

Raban, J. (2006). 'We Have Mutated into a Surveillance Society – and Must Share the Blame', *The Guardian*, May 20.

Ramirez, R. K. (2010). 'Gender, Belonging and Native American Women: The Activism of Cecelia Fire Thunder and Sarah Deer', in K. L. Caldwell, R. Ramirez, K. Coll, L. Siu and T. Fisher (Eds.), *Gendered Citizenship: Transnational Perspectives on Knowledge Production, Political Activism and Culture*. Basingstoke, Palgrave Macmillan.

Rampton, R. (1981). *The West Indian Children in our Schools*. London: Her Majesty's Stationary Office.http://www.dg.dial.pipex.com/documents/docs1/rampton.shtml.

Rank, O. (1973 [1929]). *The Trauma of Birth*. London, Routledge & Kegan Paul.

Rattansi, A. (1992). 'Changing the Subject? Racism, Culture and Education', in J. Donald and A. Rattansi (Eds.), *Race, Culture and Difference*. London, Sage.

Rattansi, A. (1994). 'Western Racisms, Ethnicities and Identities in "Postmodern" Frame', in A. Rattansi and S. Westwood (Eds), *Racism, Modernity and Identity*. Cambridge, Polity Press.

Rattansi, A. (2007). *Racism: A Very Short Introduction*. Oxford, Oxford University Press.

Raz-Krakotzkin, A. (1994). 'Diaspora within Sovereignty: A Critic of the Negation of Diasporism in the Israeli Culture, Parts I and II', *Teoria Vebikoret* (*Theory and Critique*) 4 & 5.

Regan, T. (1983). *The Case for Animal Rights*. Berkeley, CA, University of California Press.

Reicher, S. and N. Hopkins (2001). *Self and Nation*. London, Sage.

Reilly, N. (2009). *Women's Human Rights: Seeking Gender Justice in a Globalizing Age*. Cambridge, Polity Press.

Rex, J. (1995) Ethnic identity and the nation state: The political sociology of multi-cultural societies. *Social Identities: Journal for the Study of Race, Nation and Culture*, 1, 21–34.

Reynolds, H. (1996). *Aboriginal Sovereignty: Three Nations, One Australia?* Sydney, Allen & Unwin.

Richardson, R. D. (1982). *Comintern Army: The International Brigades and the Spanish Civil War*. Lexington, KY: University Press of Kentuky.

Ricoeur, P. (1992). *Oneself as Another*. Chicago, IL, University of Chicago Press.

Robbins, J. (2010). 'Indigenous Peoples, Representation and Sovereignty in Australia', *Ethnicities* 10(2): 155–80.

Robertson, R. (1992). *Globalization: Social Theory and Global Culture*. London, Sage.

Robertson, R. (1995). 'Glocalization: Time–Space and Homogeneity–Heterogeneity', in M. Featherstone, S. Lash and R. Robertson (Eds.), *Global Modernities*. London, Sage.

Robins, W. (2000). *Making Identity Matter: Identity, Society and Social Interaction*. Durham, Sociology Press.

Robinson, F. (1999). *Globalizing Care: Ethics, Feminist Theory and International Relations*. Boulder, CO, Westview Press.

Rodrigue, J.-P. (2006). 'Transporation and the Geographical and Functional Integration of Global Production Networks', *Growth and Change* 37(4): 510–25.

Rogers, P. (2008). 'A Crisis-Opportunity Moment', *Open Democracy*, 27 October. http://opendemocracy.net.

Rogers, P. (2009). 'Drone Wars', *Open Democracy*, 19 August, http://www.opendemocracy.net.

Rosaldo, R. (1997). 'Cultural Citizenship, Inequality and Multi-culturalism', in W. V. Flores and R. Benmayor (Eds.), *Latino Cultural Citizenship: Claiming Identity, Space and Rights*. Boston, MA, Beacon Press, pp. 27–38.

Rose, J. (1982). 'Introduction II', in J. Mitchell and J. Rose (Eds.), *Feminine Sexuality: Jacques Lacan and the Ecole Freudienne*. London, Macmillan, pp. 27–58.

Roseneil, S., I. Crowhurst, T. Hellesund, A. C. Santos and M. Stoilova (2011). 'Intimate Citizenship and Gendered Well-being: The Claims and Interventions of Women's Movements in Europe', in A. Woodward et al. (Eds.), *Social Movements: Gendering Well-being*. Aldershot, Ashgate.

Rousseau, J. J. (1953 [1772]). 'Considerations in the Government of Poland', in *Rousseau: Political Writings*. Trans. F. Watkins. Edinburgh, Nelson & Sons.

Rowbotham, S. (1973). *Hidden from History: 300 Years of Women's Oppression and the Fight against It*. London, Pluto Press.

Rowe, A. C. (2005). 'Be Longing: Towards a Feminist Politics of Relation', *NWSA Journal* 17(2): 15–46.

Ruddick, S. (1983). *Maternal Thinking: Towards a Politics of Peace*. London, The Women's Press.

Rundell, J. (2004). 'Strangers, Citizens and Outsiders: Otherness, Multiculturalism and the Cosmopolitan Imaginary in Mobile Societies', *Thesis Eleven* 28(1): 85–101.

Runnymede, T. (2009). *The Future of Multi-ethnic Britain: Report of the Commission on the Future of Multi-Ethnic Britain*. (Parekh Report.). London: Profile Books.

Saad-Ghorayb, A. (2009). 'The Hizbollah Project: Last War, Next War', *Open Democracy*, http://opendemocracy.net. *13 August*.

Sacks, H. (1992). *Lectures on Conversation* (Vols 1 & 2). Oxford, Blackwell.

Safran, W. (1999). 'Comparing Diasporas: A Review Essay', *Diaspora* 8(3): 255–91.

Sahgal, G. and N. Yuval-Davis (2001 [1992]). *Refusing Holy Orders: Women and Fundamentalism in Britain*. London, Virago Press (reprinted by Women Living Under Muslim Law).

Sahlins, P. (1989). *Boundaries: The Making of France and Spain in the Pyrenees*. Berkeley, CA, University of California Press.

Sandel, M. J. (1982). *Liberalism and the Limits of Justice*. Cambridge, Cambridge University Press.

Santos, B. D. S. (2006). *The Rise of the Global Left: The World Social Forum and Beyond*. London: Zed Books.

Saraceno, C. (1997). *Family, Market and Community*. Paris, OECD.

Sartre, J.-P. (1989 [1944]). *No Exit and Three Other Plays*. New York, Vintage International.

Sarvasy, W. and P. Longo (2004). 'The Globalization of Care: Kant's World Citizenship and Filipina Migrant Domestic Workers', *International Feminist Journal of Politics* 6(3): 392–415.

Sassen, S. (2006). *Territory, Authority, Rights: From Medieval to Global Assemblages*. Princeton, NJ, Princeton University Press.

Sassen, S. (2007). 'Globalisation, the State and the Democratic Deficit', *Open Democracy*, July 20, http://opendemocracy.net.

Savage, M., G. Bagnall and L. Brian (2004). *Globalization and Belonging*. London, Sage.

SBS (Southhall Black Sisters) (1990). *Against the Grain: A Celebration of Survival and Struggle*. London, SBS.

Schierup, C.-U. (1995). 'Multiculturalism and Universalism in the USA and EU Europe', paper presented at the workshop Nationalism and Ethnicity, Berne, March.

Schierup, C.-U., P. Hansen and S. Castles. (2006). *Migration, Citizenship, and the European Welfare State: A European Dilemma*. Oxford, Oxford University Press.

Schlesinger, S. C. (2003). *Act of Creation: The Founding of the United Nations*. Boulder, CO, Westview Press.

Scholte, J. A. (2005). *Globalization: A Critical Introduction* (2nd edition). New York, Macmillan.

Schutz, A. (1994 [1976]). 'The Stranger: An Essay in Social Psychology', in A. Brodersen (Ed.), *Alfred Schutz: Studies in Social Theory. Collected Papers II*. The Hague, Martinus Nijhoff, pp. 91–106.

Scott, A. (1990). *Ideology and the New Social Movements*. London: Alan & Unwin.

Sen, A. (1981). *Poverty and Famines: An Essay on Entitlement and Deprivation*. Oxford, Clarendon Press.

Sen, A. (1992a). *Inequality Re-examined*. Oxford, Clarendon Press, and Cambridge, MA, Harvard University Press.

Sen, A. (1992b). 'Missing Women', *British Medical Journal* 304(March).

Sen, A. (2000a). 'Why Human Security?', text of a paper presented at the International Symposium on Human Security, Tokyo, July 28, http://humansecurity-chs.org/activities/outreach/Sen2000.pdf.

Sen, A. (2000b). 'Social Exclusion: Concept, Application and Scrutiny', *Social Development Papers No. 1*, Office of Environment and Social Development, Asian Development Bank.

Sennett, R. (1977). *The Fall of Public Man*. Cambridge, Cambridge University Press.

Sennett, R. (2005). 'Fragmented Politics, Fragmented Lives', *Spiked Politics*, September 26.

Shakspeare, T. (2006). *Disability, Rights and Wrongs*. London, Routledge.

Shanin, T. (1986). 'Soviet Concepts of Ethnicity: The Case of the "Missing Term"', *New Left Review* 158.

Shapiro, H. (2002). 'Convicted Terrorist's Citizenship Revoked', *Just Peace UK*. http://groups.yahoo.com/group/JustPeaceUK/

Sharma, A. (2006). *Are Human Rights Western? A Contribution to the Dialogue of Civilizations*. Oxford, Oxford University Press.

Shaver, S. (1994). 'Body Rights, Social Rights and the Liberal Welfare State', *Critical Social Policy* 13(39): 66–93.

Short, D. (2003). 'Australian "Aboriginal" Reconciliation: The Latest Phase in the Colonial Project', *Citizenship Studies* 7(3): 291–312.

Sidaway, J. D., T. Bunnell, et al. (2004). 'Translating Political Geographies', *Political Geography* 2(8): 1037–49.

Silva, G. M. D. and L. F. Schwartzman (2006). 'Discourses of Difference and Equality in an Affirmative Action Context in Brazil: the Local, the National, the Global', paper presented at the XIV International Sociological Association World Congress in Sociology. Durban, South Africa, July.

Silverman, D. (1998). *Discourse of Counselling: HIV Counselling as Social Interaction*. London, Sage.

Simmel, G. (1950). 'The Stranger', in H. K. Wolff (Ed.), *The Sociology of George Simmel*. Glencoe, IL, and New York, Free Press, pp. 402–9.

Singer, P. (1976). *Animal Liberation: A New Ethics for Our Treatment of Animals*. London, Cape.

Sivanandan, A. (2008). 'Catching History on the Wing', speech by the Institute of Race Relations' director at the IRR's 50th celebration, London, November 1, http://www.irr.org.uk/2008/november/ha000016.html.

Skjeie, H. and J. Squires (2011). *Institutionalizing Intersectionality*. London, Palgrave.

Skrbiš, Z. (1997). 'Homeland – Diaspora Relations: From Passive to Active Interactions', *Asian and Pacific Migration Journal* 6(3–4): 439–55.

Skrbiš, Z. (2005). 'The Apparitions of the Virgin Mary of Medjugorje: The Convergence of Croatian Nationalism and Her Apparitions', *Nations and Nationalism* 11(3): 442–61.

Skrbiš, Z., L. Baldassar, et al. (2007). 'Introduction – Negotiating Belonging: Migration and Generations', *Journal of Intercultural Studies* 28(3): 261–9.

Smith, A. (2008 [1776]). *An Inquiry into the Nature and Causes of the Wealth of Nations*. Oxford, Oxford University Press.

Smith, A. D. (1995). *Nations and Nationalism in a Global Era*. Cambridge, Polity Press.

Smith, A. D. (1971). *Theories of Nationalism*. London, Duckworth.

Smith, A. D. (1986). *The Ethnic Origins of Nations*. Oxford, Basil Blackwell.

Smith, D. (1990). *The Conceptual Practices of Power: A Feminist Sociology of Knowledge*. Boston, MA, Northeastern University Press.

Smith, J. (2001). 'Globalizing Resistance: The Battle for Seattle and the Future of Social Movements', *International Quarterly* 6(1): 1–19.

Smith, N. (1995). 'Remaking Scale: Competition and Cooperation in Prenational and Postnational Europe', in H. Eskelinen and F. Snickars (Eds.), *Competitive European Peripheries*. Berlin, Springer Verlag.

Snyder, L. L. (1968). *The Meaning of Nationalism*. Santa Barbara, CA, Greenwood Press.

Sorensen, N. N. (2005). 'Narratives of Longing, Belonging and Caring in the Dominican Diaspora', in J. Besson and K. F. Olwig (Eds.), *Caribbean Narratives of Belonging: Fields of Relations, Sites of Identity*. London, Macmillan.

Soros, G. (2008). 'The Crisis and What To Do about It', *The New York Review of Books*, December 4, http://www.nybooks.com/articles/archives/2008/dec/04/the-crisis-what-to-do-about-it/.

Soros, G. (2010). 'Soros on the Future of the Euro', speech delivered at Humboldt University, Germany, June 23.

Soundings (2002). Special issue on Regimes of Emotion, 20 (Spring).

Soysal, Y. (1994). *Limits of Citizenship: Migrants and Postnational Membership in Europe*. Chicago, IL, University of Chicago Press.

Spivak, G. C. (1993). *Outside in the Teaching Machine*. New York and London, Routledge.

Spivak, G. C. (1994). 'Can the Subaltern Speak?', in P. Williams and L. Chrisman (Eds.), *Colonial Discourses and Post Colonial Theory: A Reader*. New York, Columbia University Press.

Spurlock, M. (2004). *Super Size Me*. Samuel Goldwyn Films.

Squire, C. (2001). 'The Public Life of Emotions', *International Journal of Critical Psychology* (launch issue): 16–27.

Squire, C. (2007). *HIV in South Africa: Talking about the Big Thing*. London, Routledge.

Squire, V. J. (2009). *The Exclusionary Politics of Asylum: Migration, Minorities, Citizenship*. Basingstoke, Palgrave.

Stalin, J. (1941 [1917]). *Marxism and the National and Colonial Question*. London, Lawrence and Wishart.

Stalin, J. (1976 [1929]). *The National Question and Leninism*. Calcutta, Mass Publications.

Stasiulis, D. (2006). 'Globalisation and Multiple Citizenships', paper presented at the XIV International Sociological Association World Congress in Sociology. Durban, South Africa, July.

Stasiulis, D. and N. Yuval-Davis (1995). *Unsettling Settler Societies*. London, Sage.

Stewart, H. (2006). 'Is This the End of Globalisation?', *The Observer*, March 5.

Stoetzler, M. and N. Yuval-Davis (2002). 'Standpoint Theory, Situated Knowledge and the Situated Imagination', *Feminist Theory* 3(3): 315–34.

Stolcke, V. (1995). 'Talking Culture: New Boundaries, New Rhetorics of Exclusion in Europe', *Current Anthropology* 16(1): 1–23.

Sullivan, J. P. and A. Elkus (2009). 'Security in the Network-state', *Open Democracy*, http://opendemocracy.net. *6 October*

Svenhuijsen, S. (1998). *Citizenship and the Ethics of Care: Feminist Considerations on Justice, Morality and Politics*. London, Routledge.

Swann Report (1985) Report of the Committee of Inquiry into the Education of Children from Ethnic Minority Groups. London, HMSO. http://www.dg.dial.pipex.com/documents/docs3/swann.shtml.

Swyngedouw, E. (1997). 'Neither Global nor Local: "Glocalization" and the Politics of Scale', in K. Cox (Ed.), *Spaces of Globalization*. New York, Guilford Press, pp. 137–66.

Swyngedouw, E. (2005). 'Governance Innovation and the Citizen: The Janus Face of Governance – Beyond-the-state', *Urban Studies* 41(11): 1991–2006.

Szerszynski, B. and J. Urry (2006). 'Visuality, Mobility and the Cosmopolitan: Inhabiting the World from Afar', *The British Journal of Sociology* 57(1): 113–31.

Tajfel, H. (1982). 'Social Psychology of Intergroup Relations', *Annual Review of Psychology* 33: 1–39.

Tamir, Y. (1993). *Liberal Nationalism*. Princeton, NJ, Princeton University Press.

Tarrow, S. (2003). 'Rooted Cosmopolitanism: Transnational Activists in a World of States', http://sociology.berkeley.edu/faculty/evans/evans_pdf/Tarrow%20RootedCosmops%204-03%2. (A more complete version of this article also appeared as Chapter Three of the author's *The New Transnational Activism*, Cambridge University Press, 2005).

Taylor, C. (1992). *Multiculturalism and the Politics of Recognition: An Essay with Commentary by Amy Gutmann et al.* Princeton, NJ, Princeton University Press.

Taylor, H. (2009). 'Landscapes of Belonging: The Meaning of Home for Cypriot Refugees in London', PhD thesis, School of Humanities and Social Sciences, University of East London.

Taylor, P. J. (2003). 'The State as Container: Territoriality in the Modern World System', in N. Brenner, B. Jessop, M. Jones and G. MacLeod (Eds.) *State/Space: A Reader*. Malden, MA, and Oxford, Blackwell.

Teivaiunen, T. (2002). 'The Global Social Forum and Global Democratisation: Learning from Porto Allegro', *Third World Quarterly* 23(4): 621–32.

Therborn, G. (2009). 'The Killing-fields of Inequality', *Open Democracy*, http://opendemocracy.net. *6 April*.

Thompson, G. (2007). 'Responsibility and Neo-libralism', *Open Dempcracy*, http://www.opendemocracy.net. *3 July*.

Tiffany, S. W. (1980). 'Anthropology and the Study of Women: A Review Article', *American Anthropologist* 82(2): 374–80.

Tillich, P. (1957). *The Dynamics of Faith*. New York, Harper & Row.

Timmins, N. (2001). *The Five Giants: A Biography of the Welfare State*. London, HarperCollins.

Timothy, K. (2004). 'Human Security Discourse at the United Nations', *Peace Review* 16(1): 19–24.

Tisdall, S. and E. MacAskill (2006). 'America's Long War', *The Guardian*, February 15.

Titmuss, R. M. (2002). *Commitment to Welfare*. Basingstoke, Palgrave Macmillan.

Tokhtakhodjaeva, M. (1995). *Between the Slogans of Communism and the Laws of Islam: The Women of Uzbekistan*. Lahore, Shirkat Gah Women's Resource Center.

Tönnies, F. (1940 [1935]). *Fundamental Concepts of Sociology (Gemeinschaft und Gesellschaft)*. New York, American Book Company [English translation of the 1935 German edition].

Torpey, J. C. (2000). *The Invention of Passports: Surveillance, Citizenship and the State*. Cambridge, Cambridge University Press.

Tronto, J. (1993). *Moral Boundaries: A Political Argument for the Ethics of Care*. New York, Routledge.

Tronto, J. (2005). 'Care as the Work of Citizens: A Modest Proposal', in M. Friedman (Ed.), *Women and Citizenship*. Oxford, Oxford University Press, pp. 130–48.

Tronvoll, K. (1999). 'Borders of Violence – Boundaries of Identity: Demarcating the Eritrean Nation-state', *Ethnic and Racial Studies* 22(6): 1037–60.

Trudeau, D. (2006). 'Politics of Belonging in the Construction of Landscape: Place-making, Boundary-drawing and Exclusion', *Cultural Geographies* 13: 421–43.

Tsosie, R. (2001). 'Land, Culture and Community: Envisioning Native American Sovereignty and National Identity in the 21st Century', *Hagar* 2(2): 183–200.

Tully, J. (2002). 'Reimagining Belonging in Circumstances of Cultural Diversity: A Citizen Approach', in U. Hedetoft and M. Hjort (Eds.), *The Postnational Self: Belonging and Identity*. Minneapolis, MN, and London, University of Minnesota Press.

Turner, B. (1990). 'Outline of a Theory on Citizenship', *Sociology* 24(2): 189–218.

Turner, V. (1979). *Process, Performance and Pilgrimage*. New Delhi, Concept Publishing.

Tyler, K. (2007). '"Street Forever": Ethnicity, Collective Action, and the State', *Identities: Global Studies in Culture and Power* 14: 579–602.

Ugba, A. (2009). *Shades of Belonging: African Pentecostals in Twenty-first Century Ireland*. Trenton, NJ, Africa World Press.

UN (2008) International Migrant Stock: The 2008 Revision, http://esa.un.org/migration/

UNDP (1999). *Human Development Report*. New York, United Nations Development Programme.

United Nations Commission on the Elimination of Racial Discrimination (CERD). (2000). 'General Comment 25, adopted on 25th of March'.

New York, CERD. http://sim.law.uu.nl/SIM/CaseLaw/Gen_Com.nsf/0/4696490f7608080ac12568bf00509b83?OpenDocument.

United Nations' Fourth World Conference on Women. (1995). *Platform for Social Action*. Beijing.

United Nations Millenium Report (2000) *We The People: The Role of the UN in the 21st Century*. New York: United Nations Department of Public Information.

Urry, J. (1995). *Consuming Places*. London, Sage.

Urry, J. (2002). *The Tourist Gaze*. London, Sage.

Van den Bergh, P. (1979). *The Ethnic Phenomenon*. New York, Elsevier.

Vargas, G. and N. Yuval-Davis (1999). 'Latin American Feminism in the 90's – A Conversation with Gina Vargas in October 1998', *International Feminist Journal of Politics* 1(2): 299–322.

Vidmar Horvat, K. (2010), 'Multiculturalism in time of terrorism', *Cultural Studies* vol. 24(5): 747–766.

Vidmar Horvat, K. (2011), 'Patriotic Cosmopolitanism? Rethinking Cosmopolitanism From A Western Balkans' Perspective' unpublished paper.

Vieten, U. (2007). 'Situated Cosmopolitanisms', PhD thesis, School of Social Sciences, Media and Cultural Studies, London, University of East London.

Vogel, U. (1989). 'Is Citizenship Gender Specific?', paper presented at the PSA (Political Studies Association) Annual Conference, April.

Vymtal, P. (2007). 'Networked Governance', PhD thesis, Department of Political Science, University of Economics, Prague (http://vz.fmv.vse.cz/english/wp-content/uploads/Sbornik_Wroclaw.pdf#page=129).

Walby, S. (1994). 'Is Citizenship Gendered?', *Sociology* 28(2): 379–95.

Walby, S. (2003). 'The Myth of Nation-State: Theorizing Society and Politics in a Global Era', *Sociology* 37(3): 529–46.

Wallerstein, I. (1976). *The Modern World-System: 1. Capitalist Agriculture and the Origins of the European World-Economy in the Sixteenth Century*. New York and London, Academic Press.

Wallerstein, I. (1980). *The Modern World-System: 2. Mercantilism and the consolidation of the European world-economy, 1600–1750*. New York and London, Academic Press.

Wallerstein, I. (1989). *The Modern World-System: 3. The second era of great expansion of the capitalist world-economy, 1730–1840s*. San Diego, CA, and London, Academic Press.

Walters, F. P. (1952). *A History of the League of Nations*. Oxford, Oxford University Press.

Walzer, M. (2004). *On Toleration*. New Haven, CT, Yale University Press.

Waterman, P. and J. Sen (Eds.). (2003). *World Social Forum: Challenging Empires*. New Delhi, Viveka.

Weber, M. (1905). *The Protestant Ethic and the Spirit of Capitalism*. London and New York, Penguin.

Weber, M. (1968). *Economy and Society*. New York, Bedminister Press.

Weber, M. (1948 [1947]). *Essays in Sociology*. Trans H. H. Gerth. London, Kegan Paul, Trench, Trubner & Co.

Wemyss, G. (2006). 'The Power to Tolerate: Contests over Britishness and Belonging in East London', *Patterns of Prejudice* 40(3): 215–36.

Wemyss, G. (2009). *The Invisible Empire*. Farnham, Ashgate.

Werbner, P. (1999a). 'Global Pathways: Working Class Cosmopolitans and the Creation of Transnational Ethnic Worlds', *Social Anthropology* 7: 17–35.

Werbner, P. (1999b). 'Political Motherhood and the Feminisation of Citizenship: Women's Activisms and the Transformation of the Public Sphere', in N. Yuval-Davis and P. Werbner (Eds.), *Women, Citizenship and Difference*. London, Zed Books, pp. 221–45.

Werbner, P. (2002). 'The Place which is Diaspora: Citizenship, Religion and Gender in the Making of Chaordic Transnationalism', *Journal of Ethnic and Migration Studies* 28(1): 119–33.

Werbner, P. (2006). 'Vernacular Cosmopolitanism', *Theory, Culture and Society* (special issue on Problematizing Global Knowledge, 23(1–2).

Werbner, P. and T. Modood (Eds.). (1996). *The Politics of Multiculturalism in New Europe: Racism, Identity and Community*. London, Zed Books.

Wernick, A. (2001). *Auguste Comte and the Religion of Humanity: The Post-Theistic Program of French Social Theory*. Cambridge, Cambridge University Press.

Westen, D. (2007). 'Voting with Their Hearts', *The Guardian*, August 8.

Wetherell, M. (2006). 'Introduction of the Day: Identity and Social Action', residential conference, ESRC programme, University of Aston, Birmingham, July.

Wieviorke, M. (1997). 'Is It So Difficult To Be Anti-Racist?', in P. Werbner and T. Modood (Eds.), *Debating Cultural Hybridity*. London, Zed Books.

Williams, R. (2000). *Making Identity Matter: Identity, Society and Social Interaction*. Durham, Sociology Press.

Williams, Z. (2007). 'Faith Schools Should Not Be Tax-funded, and Here's Why', *The Guardian*, September 19.

Wilson, T. M. and H. Donnan (Eds). (1998). *Border Identities, Nation and State at International Frontiers*. Cambridge, Cambridge University Press

WING (Women, Immigration and Nationality Group) (1985). *Worlds Apart: Women under Immigration and and Nationality Laws.*. London, Pluto.

Winnicott, D. W. (1967). 'Mirror-role of Mother and Family in Child Development', in *Playing and Reality*. London, Tavistock, pp. 11–18.

WLUML (Women Living Under Muslim Laws) (2006). *Occasional Paper 15, Iraq Women's Right under Attack, Occupation, Constitution and Fundamentalism*. London, WLUML.

WLUML (Women Living Under Muslim Laws) (2009). http://www.wluml.org/zh-hant/node/5768.

Wollstonecraft, M. (1792) The Vindication of the Rights of Woman: with Strictures on Political and Moral Subjects, London.

Woodward, A. (2005). 'Translating Diversity: The Diffusion of the Concept of Diversity to European Union Equality Policy and the Potential for an

Intersectional Approach', paper presented at the conference Theorizing Intersectionality, Keele, University of Keele, May 21.

Working Group on Forced Mariage for the Foreign and Commonwealth Office (2000), *A Choice By Right*, www.fco.gov.uk/resources/en/pdf/a-choice-by-right/.

Yeatman, A. (1992). 'Minorities and the Politics of Difference', *Political Theory Newsletter* 4(1): 1–11.

Yiftachel, O. (2003). 'Homelands and Territories', in A. J. Motyl (Ed.) *Encyclopaedia of Nationalism*. New York, Academic Press.

Yuval-Davis, N. (1980) The Bearers of the Collective: Women and Religious Legislation in Israel. *Feminist Review*, 4, 15-27.

Yuval-Davis, N. (1985). 'Front and Rear: Sexual Divisions of Labour in the Israeli Military', *Feminist Studies* 11(3): 649–76.

Yuval-Davis, N. (1991). 'The Citizenship Debate: Women, Ethnic Processes and the State', *Feminist Review* 39: 58–68.

Yuval-Davis, N. (1992a). 'Fundamentalism, Multiculturalism and Women', in J. Donald and A. Rattansi (Eds.), *'Race', Culture and Difference*. London, Sage, pp. 278–92.

Yuval-Davis, N. (1992b). 'Jewish Fundamentalism and Women's Empowerment', in G. Sahgal and N. Yuval-Davis (Eds.), *Refusing Holy Orders: Women and Fundamentalism in Britain*. London, Virago.

Yuval-Davis, N. (1994). 'Women, Ethnicity and Empowerment', *Feminism and Psychology* (special Issue on Shifting Identities, Shifting Racisms) 4(1): 179–98.

Yuval-Davis, N. (1997a). *Gender and Nation*. London, Sage.

Yuval-Davis, N. (1997b). 'Women, Citizenship and Difference', *Feminist Review* (special issue on Citizenship: Pushing the Boundaries) 57(Autumn): 4–27.

Yuval-Davis, N. (1999). 'Multi-layered Citizenship in the Age of "Glocalization"', *International Feminist Journal of Politics* 1(1): 119–37.

Yuval-Davis, N. (2000). 'Citizenship, Territoriality and the Gendered Construction of Difference', in E. Inis (Ed.), *Democracy, Citizenship and the Global City*. Oxford, Routledge.

Yuval-Davis, N. (2003). 'Belonging: From the Indigene to the Diasporic', in U. Ozkirimli (Ed.), *Nationalism and its Futures*. Basingstoke, Macmillan, pp. 127–44.

Yuval-Davis, N. (2004a). 'Citizenship, Identity and Belonging', in S. May, T. Modood and J. Squires (Eds.), *Nationalism, Ethnicity and Minority Rights*. Cambridge, Cambridge University Press.

Yuval-Davis, N. (2005a). 'Human Security and Asylum-seeking', *Mediactive* 4: 38–55.

Yuval-Davis, N. (2005b). 'Gender Mainstreaming and Intersectionality: A Complex Relationship', *Swedish Journal of Gender Studies* (in Swedish *Kvinno-vetenskaplig tidskrift*) 2–3(5): 19–30.

Yuval-Davis, N. (2005c). 'Racism, Cosmopolitanism and Contemporary Politics of Belonging', *Soundings* no.30, Summer.

Yuval-Davis, N. (2006a). 'Belonging and the Politics of Belonging', *Patterns of Prejudice* 40(3): 197–214.

Yuval-Davis, N. (2006b). 'Intersectionality and Feminist Politics', *European Journal of Women's Studies* (special Issue on Intersectionality) 13(3): 193–209.

Yuval-Davis, N. (2006c). 'Human/Women's Rights and Feminist Transversal Politics', in M. M. Ferree and A. M. Tripp (Eds.), *Transnational Feminisms: Women's Global Activism and Human Rights*. New York, New York University Press.

Yuval-Davis, N. (2007). 'Neoliberalism and Fundamentalism: The Breakdown of the Secularisation Thesis', paper presented at the meeting of the socialist group, School of Oriental and African Studies, London, November 29.

Yuval-Davis, N. (2009a). 'Intersectionality, Citizenship and Contemporary Politics of Belonging', *CRISPP (Contemporary Review of International Social and Political Philosophy)* (special issue on Contesting Citizenship), 10(4): 561–574.

Yuval-Davis, N. (2010). 'Theorizing Identity: Beyond the "Self" and "Other" Dichotomy', *Patterns of Prejudice*, 44, 261–280.

Yuval-Davis, N. (2011a). 'Beyond the Recognition and Re-distribution Dichotomy: Intersectionality and Stratification', in H. Lutz, M. T. H. Vivar and L. Supik (Eds) *Framing Intersectionality: Debates on a Multi-faceted Concept in Gender Studies*. Aldershot, Ashgate.

Yuval-Davis, N. (2011b). 'Citizenship, Autochthony and the Question of Forced Migration', paper presented at the seminar series 'Conceptual Issues in Forced Migration', organized by the CMRB (Centre for Research on Migration, Refugees and Belonging) and Oxford Refugee Studies Centre, Oxford, February.

Yuval-Davis, N. and F. Anthias (1989). *Woman – Nation – State*. Basingstoke, Macmillan.

Yuval-Davis, N., F. Anthias and E. Koffman (2005). 'Secure Borders and Safe Havens and the Gendered Politics of Belonging: Beyond Social Cohesion', *Ethnic and Racial Studies* (special issue on Migration and Citizenship) 28(3): 513–35.

Yuval-Davis, N. and E. Kaptani (2008). *Identity, Performance and Social Action: Participatory Theatre among Refugees*. ESRC end of the project report (RES-148-25-0006). Swindon, ESRC.

Yuval-Davis, N. and E. Kaptani (2009). 'Identity, Performance and Social Action: Participatory Theatre among Refugees', in M. Whetherell (Ed.), *Theorizing Identity and Social Action*. Basingstoke, Palgrave Macmillan.

Yuval-Davis, N. and M. Stoetzler (2002). 'Imagined Border and Boundaries: A Gendered Gaze', *European Journal of Women's Studies* August.

Yuval-Davis, N. and P. Werbner (Eds). (1999). *Women, Citizenship and Difference*. London, Zed Books.

Zakaria, F. (2009). *The Post-American World*. London, Allen Lane.

Zimmern, A. (1936). *The League of Nations and the Rule of Law, 1918–1935*. London, Macmillan.

Zubaida, S. (1978). 'Theories of Nationalism', in G. Littlejohn, B. Smart, J. Wakefield and N. Yuval-Davis (Eds.), *Power and the State*. London, Croom Helm, pp. 52–71.

Zubaida, S. (1989). 'Nations: Old and New. Comments on Anthony D. Smith's "The Myth of Modern Nation and the Myths of Nations"', *Ethnic and Racial Studies* 12(3): 329–39.

Zubaida, S. (2003). 'Multiculturalism in Europe', paper presented at the conference on *Muslims in Europe, Post 9/11: Understanding and Responding to the Islamic World*, St Antony's College and Princeton University, Princeton, NJ, April 25–26.

Zubaida, S. (2008). 'Sharia: Practice of Faith, Politics of Modernity', *Open Democracy*, http://www.opendemocracy.net/. *22 February*

Zubrzycki, G. (2006). *The Crosses of Auschwitz: Nationalism and Religion in Post-Communist Poland*. Chicago, IL, Chicago University Press.

Index

Modood, Tariq, 138
mojahidin forces, 132
morality, *male* and *female*, 180–3
More, Thomas, 187–8, 191–2
mother–child relationship, 182–4,
    190, 198
multiculturalism, 22–6, 43, 64–7, 79,
    137–9; critical, 66; *see also*
    citizenship: multi-cultural;
    nationalism: multicultural
multi-faithism, 67, 137–9
Murray Ki, Tania, 149
Muslim communities, 46–7, 136, 139

Nandy, Ashish, 71, 118
nation-states, 31, 44, 48–9, 81, 86–9
nationalism, 1, 44, 86, 193–4, 202; 'banal',
    92–3; and belonging, 81–2; *civic* and
    ethnic, 86–7; definition of, 81–5, 93;
    discourse of, 98; and feminism, 109–
    10; and globalization, 111; historical
    models of, 87–8; multicultural, 98–9;
    and nation-states, 86–9; and national
    borders, 89–97; and religion, 119,
    122–6
Nava, Mica, 146, 148, 150
Nenadich, Ramon, 112
neo-liberalism, 22, 26–32, 54–7, 66,
    170–1, 204
Nitzan, J., 34, 41
non-governmental organizations (NGOs),
    133, 155–6, 163, 174
Nussbaum, Martha, 147, 165, 191
Nyamnjoh, Francis B., 2

Obama, Barak, 42, 67, 206
Ogata, Sadako, 166
Oliver, Mike, 58
Opus Dei, 127
Ozkirimli, Umut, 83

Pakistan, 120, 125
Pallas, Christopher, 133
parliamentary democracy, 49–52
passports, 74–6
Pateman, Carol, 77
Peace and Conflict Studies, 163–4
Peter the Great, 75
Peterse, Hannah, 178
Phillipines, the, 69
Phillips, Trevor, 67
Phoenix, A., 4
Pick, Anat, 204
Pieterse, Jan, 30
Plaskow, Judith, 140
Plummer, Ken, 60–1

political rights, 49–52
Pollock, S., 146–7, 175
Poole, R., 90–1
Powell, Enoch, 21–2, 25, 90
power, theory of, 19–20, 32, 204–5
privatization, 32–3, 40–1, 52–7, 62–3
Probyn, E., 15

racism, 99–101
Rashtriya Swayamsewak Sangh, 127
Rattansi, Ali, 79
Reagan, Ronald, 26
refugee status, 37–9, 70–1, 156–7
regulation, 34
Reicher, S., 93
religion, 44; and civil society, 132–3; and
    culture, 115–17, 123; definition
    of, 114–19; and feminism, 140–3;
    and fundamentalism, 126–41, 144,
    202; and nationalism, 119, 122–6;
    revitalization of, 113–14, 194;
    separation from the state, 120–2
remittances, 69
Rex, John, 64
rights *see* babies, rights of; civil rights;
    collective rights; cultural rights;
    human rights; political rights;
    security rights; social and economic
    rights; women's rights
Robertson, R., 30
Robinson, Mary, 71
Roma people, 81–2, 138
Roosevelt, Eleanor, 158
Roseneil, Sasha, 60
Rousseau, Jean Jacques, 94
Rowe, Carrillo, 10
Ruddick, Sarah, 182–3
Rwanda, 161–2, 183

Sahgal, Gita, 119
Sahlins, P., 95
sanctuary movement, 134
Sarkozy, Nicolas, 139
Sartre, Jean-Paul, 99
Sarvasy, Wendy, 189
Sassen, Saskia, 27, 29, 33
Saudi Arabia, 69
Savage, Mike, 152
Schierup, Carl-Ulrik, 64–7
Scholte, J.A., 26–7
Schwartzman, L.F., 30
Seattle protests (1999), 169–70
secularism and secularization, 114, 119–24
securitization of borders, 40–3
security rights, 57
self-determination, national, 85, 111–12